To Emma —
Remembering the moonlight
night, any
other ___.

Louisa Ward Arps

HIGH COUNTRY NAMES

❖

ROCKY MOUNTAIN NATIONAL PARK

Elinor Eppich Kingery

HIGH COUNTRY NAMES

❖

Rocky Mountain National Park

by

Louisa Ward Arps
and
Elinor Eppich Kingery

assisted by
Hugh E. Kingery

Denver
The Colorado Mountain Club
1966

Published by: The Colorado Mountain Club

1400 Josephine Street

Denver, Colorado 80206

Printed by: Johnson Publishing Company

Boulder, Colorado

Dedicated to the memory of
Ellen Glasier Morris
by her friends in
The Colorado Mountain Club

OUR THANKS

To Hugh Kingery, administrator of The Colorado Mountain Club, who gave generously of his time, of his ability, and of his enthusiasm.

To our fellow members of The Colorado Mountain Club, who have spent days—even weekends when they could have been in the hills—correcting our creative spelling, untangling our syntax, reading proof, and locating pictures.

To government agencies, like the U.S. Board on Geographic Names, the Geological Survey, the Forest Service, and the Bureau of Land Management; to state agencies, such as the office of the Colorado State Engineer, and the Game and Fish Department; to county and city officials in many towns; and, of course, to the staff, both past and present, of Rocky Mountain National Park.

To libraries where we have camped as we followed the old Trappers Trail from Pikes to the Poudre, stopping at each piedmont town, especially the library of the State Historical Society of Colorado; to every department of the Denver Public Library, including the Western History Department and the Conservation Library; and to libraries and museums across the Middle West which have answered our myriad inquiries.

To friends we have made as, like the beaver trappers, we ventured up the Boulder Creeks, up Lefthand, up the St. Vrains, up the Thompsons Big and Little, up the Poudre, and across the Continental Divide to Grand Lake and Middle Park. All along the way we have made new friends and seen old friends who happily talked to us and wrote to us about names — names — names.

To, finally, our critics. When a woman demanded that Samuel Johnson account for an error in his dictionary, he replied, "Ignorance, madam; pure ignorance." May others interested in names please instruct our ignorance!

SOURCES

In the summer of 1965, The Colorado Mountain Club wished to celebrate the 50th anniversary of Rocky Mountain National Park. The Club devoted an issue of its monthly publication *Trail & Timberline* to the Park's history. One of the articles was to be a history of the names of the geographic features in the Park. Now, a year later, this overgrown article is as ready as it will ever be for the printer.

This project was a busman's holiday for a librarian and a researcher. We—who have always gone to the mountains for our recreation—found recreation, along with hard work, in looking up the names of mountains. We are aware that this is not a scholarly opus; it lacks footnotes, "op. cits.," and an exhaustive bibliography. We hope the fun we had in compiling this dictionary will balance its shortcomings.

If, however, anyone wishes to follow our trail through the world of print, here are some of the blazes we followed.

We made a card for each name on the Rocky Mountain National Park map published in 1961 by the U.S. Geological Survey, except names of campgrounds, trails, and modern resorts. The campgrounds and trails bear names already listed as geographic features, like Timber Creek Campground and Ypsilon Lake Trail. We regretfully omitted the names of modern ranches, resorts, and camps, like McGraw Ranch, Camp Chief Ouray, or the Y.M.C.A. Camp.

We also made cards for names of features south of the Park, as far south as Mt. Neva in the Indian Peak area of the Front Range. These names we took from four U.S. Geological Survey quadrangle maps (commonly called quad maps, or just plain quads): Allens Park (1957), Isolation Peak (1958), Monarch Lake (1958), and Ward (1957). Then we listed a few names outside of the reaches of the maps we used, names that demanded to be included because of historical interest, such as Muggins Gulch and Mt. Olympus. We ended with 428 distinctive names—counting all the features named Columbine as one, named Beaver as one, named Arapaho as one, etc.

Then we started reading the history of the area, jotting down any nomenclature information on the appropriate cards. The best history of Estes Park is a thesis at the University of Denver written by June Carothers. It is interesting, with a scholarly bibliography.

We scanned or read books by authors named Bird, Cairns, Carothers, Chapin, Crossen, Dunning, Dunraven, Fry, Hayden, Hewes,

Hondius, King, Kingsley, Lamb, LeMassena, McQueary, Mills (Joe and Enos), Moomaw, Nesbit, Toll (Oliver and Roger), Watrous, Wolle, ad infinitum.

We bought every pamphlet for sale at the Rocky Mountain National Park visitor's center. These—attractive, numerous, and recent—are on the history, natural history, and trails in the area.

The most helpful periodicals, all of which have indexes, are *The Trail,* published by the Sons of Colorado; the *Colorado Magazine,* published by the Colorado State Historical Society; the monthly *Roundup* and the yearly *Brand Book* of the Denver Posse of The Westerners; and, most important for mountain information, *Trail & Timberline,* published by The Colorado Mountain Club. Abner Sprague's reminiscences appeared in the *Estes Park Trail,* and are in manuscript form at the State Historical Society of Colorado Library.

The library of The Colorado Mountain Club contains scrapbooks, pictures, trip records, correspondence, and registers from the tops of peaks. The records of the Rocky Mountain Club are there.

James Grafton Rogers, president of The Colorado Mountain Club and chairman of the Colorado Geographic Board, deposited his papers at the Colorado State Archives and at the Colorado State Historical Society Library. These include much correspondence concerning the formation of Rocky Mountain National Park.

The Colorado Geographic Board minutes and other papers collected by its secretary, Harriet Vaille Bouck, were given to the Colorado State Historical Society Library. These records are disappointing in that they give very little information about why the mountains were given certain names. Until the time that Ellsworth Bethel's papers are found, which probably have the complete history of the names, the historian must do the best he can to surmise the reason for undocumented names in the area.

Louisa Ward Arps
Elinor Eppich Kingery

June 1966

CONTENTS

	Page
The Namers	1
How to Name a Mountain	12
Key to Dictionary	16
Dictionary of Names	17-202
Pictures—Group 1	61-76

Copeland Mountain
Grand Lake in 1868
Fishing in the Outlet of Grand Lake
Indian Peaks, 1894 (Toll, Paiute, and Audubon)
Indian Peaks, 1965 (Navajo, Apache, and Shoshoni)
Longs Peak from the air, 1921
Shelter House on the Boulder Field
The Keyhole
Longs Peak from Trail Ridge Road (color)
Mt. Baker and the Grand Ditch
Mt. Richthofen
Arrowhead Lake
Forest Canyon Overlook
Horseshoe Park
Spectacle Lakes
Hallett Peak and Tyndall Glacier
Andrews Glacier, 1913
Arapaho Glacier, 1965
North Face of Lone Eagle Peak, 1940
The Sharkstooth

Pictures—Group 2   157-164

Joseph Wescott
Anna Dickinson
William L. Hallett
Stanley Steamers at Longs Peak Inn, 1913
Dedication of Rocky Mountain National Park, 1915
Arapaho Indians in Estes Park, 1914
Map of Estes Park cabins prior to 1878
James Grafton Rogers
Harriet Vaille
Ellsworth Bethel
George Barnard
Trail to Odessa Lake
Lulu City, 1889
Squeaky Bob Wheeler

| Index | 203-212 |

Maps   Last 12 pages of book
    Section Maps:
        Estes Park
        Forest Canyon
        Glacier Gorge
        Grand Lake
        Indian Peaks
        Lake Granby
        Mummy Range
        Never Summers
        Wild Basin
    Key to section maps   Last page of book

Cover design by Brian Novak
Sketch on page 202 by Gwen Meux
Sketches by Dean Babcock, courtesy of Harold Dunning

HIGH COUNTRY NAMES

❖

ROCKY MOUNTAIN NATIONAL PARK

The Namers

This book attempts to trace the origins of the place names in Rocky Mountain National Park and the high country south of it. Some of the names just happened, as names do; but when the Park was proposed, various people set out systematically to name features in the area. The story of these givers of names—these namers—may well start with the beginnings of the Park.

Camp cooking in a mountain storm is chancy. The fire under the pot which held the idea of a national park for the northern Front Range of the Colorado Rockies had to weather six years of storms before Rocky Mountain National Park was established—from about 1909 when Enos Mills kindled the fire until January 25, 1915, the day President Woodrow Wilson signed the bill.

The flame was alternately fanned by women's clubs, Chambers of Commerce, conservationists, editors, and organizations like The Colorado Mountain Club; and doused by opposition groups such as other Chambers of Commerce, the Front Range Settlers League of Estes Park, cattlemen, hunters, lumbermen, and mining men who refused to believe that the rich mineral belt of Colorado did not extend north of Boulder County.

By 1912 the heat from this fire was felt in Washington. That summer the U.S. Geological Survey sent their chief topographer, R. B. Marshall, to look over the scenery. He borrowed two men already in the field working on the Geological Survey of the Longs Peak area, and made a circle tour on horseback from Longs Peak Inn, over the Grand River Trail to Squeaky Bob's, to Grand Lake, Monarch Lake, and back to the Eastern Slope by "the wild Arapaho Pass."

With the scenery of this trip shining in his eyes, Marshall came to Denver to consult with Governor John Shafroth, Governor-elect Elias Ammons, Mayor Arnold of Denver, and other citizens. One of these was a young man he had met seven years before on top of a mountain. In 1905, when Marshall was surveying for the special Georgetown quad map, the young man, James Grafton Rogers, and two companions were spending five months at Jack Truesdell's cabin on upper Bear Creek, an idyllic interlude between their graduation from Yale and the business of making a living. The day they happened to meet Marshall on a mountain was a propitious day for nomenclature in Colorado. They sat and talked of many things, including Marshall's difficulties in determining the right names for mountains on the Bear Creek watershed. Rogers helped solve the problems, one of which was Mt. Evans. After years of jumping from summit to summit Governor John Evans' name at this time came to rest on the

1

highest peak, the highest of the three sentinels of the Front Range—
Pikes, Evans, and Longs.

Seven years later when Marshall returned to Colorado with the
problems of a national park on his mind, he looked up Jim Rogers.
He found the young lawyer not only more interested in mountains
than he had been in 1905, but the president of an organization of like-
minded men and women. The Colorado Mountain Club had been
organized in April of 1912.

Suggesting to Rogers that a map with many named peaks might
interest the U.S. Congress in authorizing a national park more than a
map full of unnamed mountains, Marshall returned to Washington.
His report, published in January 1913, stated that turning the northern
Front Range into a national park was both feasible and desirable. Two
things he suggested changing from the original proposal. He com-
mended the name Rocky Mountain National Park instead of Estes
National Park, and reduced the acreage of the original dream which
embraced all the country from the Poudre on the north to Rollins
Pass on the south, from Grand Lake to the eastern plains, and a non-
contiguous section around Mt. Evans.

THE COLORADO MOUNTAIN CLUB

After Marshall's report, The Colorado Mountain Club decided
to turn all its considerable energy into forwarding the formation of
Rocky Mountain National Park. It decided it should learn first hand
the area it was sponsoring. In 1913 it held an outing at Bear Lake and
the next year essayed a movable outing, camping at Grand Lake in the
rain, at Shipler Park in the rain, at Fall River Ranger Station in the
rain, and at Horseshoe Park in the rain. Despite this unusual weather,
the Club descended to the flatland determined to help create the
national park. As president, James Grafton Rogers led the campaign,
drawing up each bill presented to Congress. Anyone interested in the
birth pangs of Rocky Mountain National Park should study his papers
from 1912 to 1914 on file in the Colorado state archives.

The Colorado Mountain Club took to heart Marshall's suggestion
that the mountains needed names. The rosters of the early outings of
the Club include persons prominent in the history of nomenclature of
the Park such as James and Edmund Rogers, Roger and Oliver Toll,
Morrison Shafroth, George Barnard, and Harriet Vaille. The Club
organized a nomenclature committee with Harriet Vaille as chairman.
She formed the Colorado Reading Party, consisting of a few people
who promised to research and make notes of names connected with
early Colorado history—Spanish, French, explorers, mountain men.
Miss Vaille's task was Indian names. She systematically undertook this
study, even going to the Newberry Library in Chicago, then the closest
center of Indian information.

2

She soon felt that books were inadequate. Why not go to the Indians themselves? But what Indians? The Utes had lived in the mountains and the Arapahos on the plains of early Colorado, but both tribes had hunted around Estes Park and Grand Lake, fighting every time they met. Miss Vaille, educated at Bryn Mawr and other eastern schools, knew the value of consulting authorities. She talked to Dr. Livingstone Farrand, president of the University of Colorado and an authority on Indians. He advised her to seek out the northern Arapahos. After much correspondence to secure official permission and letters of introduction, Miss Vaille and Miss Edna Hendrie, also of Denver—two young women venturing alone—went by train and wagon to the Wind River Reservation in Wyoming. Indian police rounded up the oldest men of the nation. At headquarters the young ladies selected the two old men they thought would best remember their youth in the Estes Park area. The young women then returned to Denver to raise money to bring the two old men and an interpreter to Estes Park. They secured $50 from The Colorado Mountain Club, $50 from the Colonial Dames, and Frederick O. Vaille, president of the telephone company and father of Miss Harriet, agreed to pay the remaining bills which amounted to almost as much as the two clubs had provided.

In July 1914 three Arapahos stepped off the train at Longmont and were driven to Longs Peak Inn in the automobiles of Mr. Vaille and Mr. Hendrie. A chauffeur drove for Mr. Hendrie, president of the Hendrie & Bolthoff Machinery Company of Denver, but Mr. Vaille drove his own touring car with the oldest Indian sitting contentedly beside him. Shep Husted of Estes Park furnished horses and a pack outfit and escorted the Indians on the regular circle tour—Grand River Trail to Squeaky Bob's—Grand Lake—Flattop—back to Bear Lake. A cousin of Harriet Vaille, Oliver Toll, fresh from college, took down every word said by the two older Indians as interpreted by the younger. Toll's report, with glossary of Arapaho words and the Indian names for innumerable points in northern Colorado, told the tale of the trip with youthful charm. In manuscript form this report was available in a few local libraries. In 1962 Oliver Toll revised and printed most of it with the title *Arapaho Names and Trails*.

ELLSWORTH BETHEL

In the spring of 1914 another person beside Harriet Vaille was studying Indian names in relation to Colorado mountain nomenclature. Ellsworth Bethel (1863-1925) taught botany at East Denver High School at 19th and Stout. For 25 years from the window of his classroom he had watched the northern Rockies, noting their daily moods. This spring of 1914 was to be his last as a teacher, so with a certain nostalgia he saw the snow melt from the long line of peaks "imprinted in bold indentures upon the luminous margin of the sky," a phrase, he remembered, that Dr. Edwin James, Colorado's first botanist, had written in 1820. It worried Bethel that the mountains of the Snowy Range from the Arapahos on the south to Longs and Meeker on the north had no generally accepted names. There was Mt. Alice, but who was Alice? And Audubon, named for the ornithologist by C. C. Parry, botanist. Perhaps he should suggest naming other peaks for naturalists. But that was riding his personal hobbyhorse. The Arapaho Peaks were well named. What about using the names of other Indian tribes which had looked on these snowy peaks before the white men had seen them?

Bethel made a sketch map of the range; on each peak he wrote the name of an Indian tribe important in the history of the Great Plains. On May 14, 1914 he sent the map and a letter to the U.S. Board on Geographic Names in Washington. Though the map has not been located, the letter lists the names as Apache, Arapaho (already named), Arikaree, Cheyenne, Comanche, Kiowa, Navajo, Ogalalla, Pawnee, Shoshone, Sioux and Ute. The Board rejected five of the names—Cheyenne, Comanche, Shoshone, Sioux and Ute. That Ute was refused must have pained Bethel because the Ute nation was the most important in western Colorado. The Board pointed out that other mountains were already named Ute, and Bethel comforted himself by naming over the mountains in the Sawatch Range and the San Juans that bore the name of Ute leaders, like Shavano, Antero and Ouray. On the Front Range Bethel compromised and substituted the name Paiute, a related tribe dwelling west of Colorado.

Perhaps Bethel did not grieve over the Board's rejection of Sioux since the Ogalallas were a branch of that nation. He gave up trying to rename Chiefs Head for the Comanches. A mountain north of the Mummy Range had been named Comanche since 1876. (As the names stand in 1966, the Comanches are well represented by two mountains at the head of North St. Vrain Creek; both Tanima and Mahana are Comanche names.) The Board's refusal to change the name of Alice to Shoshone made Bethel boil. In a red-hot letter he said the Board had "spoiled the whole scheme of representing the ten tribes connected with Colorado history by peaks visible from Denver and the other Plains towns."

COLORADO GEOGRAPHIC BOARD

Thus the year 1914 was important for mountain names in Colorado. Mr. Bethel's Indian tribal names in the spring, The Colorado Mountain Club's outing from Grand Lake to Estes Park in the summer, and Harriet Vaille's Arapaho project in July. Then in the fall

4

Governor Ammons was approached by J. G. Rogers, president of The Colorado Mountain Club, and others on the subject of forming an official Colorado nomenclature committee. The approach was easy enough, since the Vailles were often guests at the governor's ranch in Middle Park, and the families of Rogers, Toll, and Shafroth were all influential in Colorado politics.

Governor Ammons sent out a letter to people all over the state bidding them come to a meeting "to consider the jumble of geographic names in Colorado." On October 28, 1914 in the Senate Chamber of the State Capitol, at 10:00 a.m., 62 people signed the roster. From this initial meeting came the Colorado Geographic Society, constitution dated November 6, 1914, open to any reputable citizen, dues $1.00. An advisory committee was selected, including Enos Mills of Estes Park, Irving Howbert of Colorado Springs, J. M. Crawford of Steamboat Springs, Mrs. Gordon Kimball of Ouray, Otto Mears of Silverton, Alva Adams of Pueblo, Ansil Watrous of Fort Collins, and Max Clark of Greeley. Their duty was to advise a four-man executive committee called the Colorado Geographic Board, appointed by the Colorado State Assembly.

The four men were J. G. Rogers, chairman, Ellsworth Bethel, Jerome Smiley, and Hugh Steele. Ex-officio, R. D. George, state geologist, was a member, though he seldom could attend meetings since he lived in Boulder which was farther away in 1914 than it is today.

Rogers and Bethel were obvious choices, with Jerome C. Smiley almost as obligatory. Historian of the State Historical and Natural History Society, he had authored the classic *History of Denver* published in 1901. The fourth man on the Board, a director of the same society, was white-haired, blue-eyed, ruddy-skinned Hugh R. Steele (1849-1923). His father had been governor of Jefferson Territory for a few months in 1859 before Colorado Territory was formed, so the son knew everybody of importance in early Colorado. After living in mining camps all over the state, Hugh Steele had come to Denver. In 1914 he was secretary of the Society of Colorado Pioneers with an office in the Charles Building where he could hold his own as a story-teller with any old-timer who dropped in.

The secretary of the Colorado Geographic Board was not a member of the Board but, being the attractive Harriet Vaille, she did not need a vote to make her influence felt.

The letterhead of the Colorado Geographic Board stated that they were "engaged in the task of recording, systematizing, and clarifying the geographical place names of the state so as to fix an appropriate and historical nomenclature." The meetings of the Board were faithfully attended by all official members and recorded by the secretary. At the first meeting, November 27, 1914, they decided their mission was not to make a general revision of place names in the state,

5

but to collect information and deal with specific problems as they arose. The urgent problem at the first meeting was the nomenclature of the proposed Rocky Mountain National Park. The U.S. Geological Survey, in the process of preparing the Longs Peak quad, would gladly accept help, especially from an official state board.

The Board voted to turn this problem over to the chairman, James Grafton Rogers, and to George Barnard of The Colorado Mountain Club, leader of the two trips the Club had taken into the proposed Park area in 1913 and 1914. These two men already had ideas. Within two weeks, on December 9, 1914, they submitted revisions for the advance sheet of the Longs Peak quad. Then they continued to work. On February 21, 1915 they petitioned the U.S. Geological Survey to defer the printing of the Longs Peak quad until they could submit further suggestions.

NAMERS FROM 1820 TO 1914

Rogers and Barnard, aided especially by Miss Vaille, were thorough. They interviewed local residents and summer cottagers, read books, even lugged transits to the mountains to determine altitudes, but above all studied maps. A quick review of the many maps available to them starts with the first map showing the northern Colorado Front Range—the 1820 map of Long's expedition. On it they found two names in the area: Highest Peak and Bull Pen (present North Park). The very next maps used Longs Peak for Highest Peak. The first map of Colorado alone was that by Francis Case, surveyor general of Colorado Territory, published in 1862. On its northern Colorado Rockies two names appear—Longs Peak, and Mt. Edmunds for the peak that stands at the head of the Boulder Creeks. Some succeeding maps accepted Mt. Edmunds, but Thayer's map of 1873 switched to Arapaho Peak. Mt. Audubon appeared on detailed maps soon after 1864 when Dr. Edwin James and Professor J. W. Velie climbed and named it.

Then came the government surveyors, the prolific mountain namers. They were the first men to make it their business to identify mountains—what is a map without names? The face of the mountainous West is full of their christenings. To the Estes Park country first came Clarence King's surveyors who had ridden from California following, more or less, the 40th Parallel, which is today the Baseline Road that runs through Boulder. The top of Longs Peak was as far south as these surveyors got. They named Hagues Peak, Comanche Peak, and Mt. Richthofen, all printed on King's atlas published in 1876. The next year Hayden's Atlas of Colorado displayed names now familiar, names like Estes Park, Estes Cone, Muggins Gulch, Lillie's Mountain, Black Canyon, Fall River, and Grand Lake, a name in common use since the 1860's.

6

Rogers and Barnard supplemented their study of maps of the 1870's by reading the classic of Estes Park, *A Lady's Life in the Rocky Mountains,* written by a British gentlewoman named Isabella Bird who spent the autumn of 1873 at Griff Evans' cottage camp on Fish Creek. The name of Jims Grove dates from her book. Rogers and Barnard also read reminiscences of sportsmen like the Irish Earl of Dunraven and Dr. George Kingsley, and found the reason for the name of Bierstadt Lake.

For the late 1880's they read Chapin's *Mountaineering in Colorado.* Here was the book that gave the reason for names like Chapin, Hallett, and Otis, mountaineers all.

For the 1890's Rogers and Barnard thought they had found a gold mine when they saw the map Abner Sprague had made when he was official surveyor for Larimer County, but were disappointed to find few names on it. However, Sprague and Stevens published a map in Loveland, later and non-officially, with more names. To find the history of these names for the Colorado Geographic Board, Harriet Vaille interviewed Abner Sprague at his hotel in Glacier Basin in August 1915. A friendly hotel keeper since 1875, Sprague had named many features for his neighbors and guests, like Andrews, McHenry and the Hayden brothers, as well as Alberta Falls for his wife.

Two other hotel men of the area who named places in the Park were Enos Mills and Dr. W. J. Workman. Their names reflect their hobbies. Enos Mills, with his love of nature, named Ouzel Lake, Marten Peak, and Storm Peak. On Mills' 1905 map he wrote Silent Place as a name for an area near present Tahosa Creek, but this name appears on no other map. Dr. Workman, the dedicated angler, amused himself by naming the many lakes in which he fished for the numerous girls of his family or lady guests at his Fern Lake Lodge, such as Grace Workman Hansen, Helene Stidger, Marguerite Turck, and Odessa Workman. Fortunately their last names are in various records, but the identities of other feminine names in the Park have not been found, names such as Mt. Alice, Lake Dorothy, Eugenia Mine, Irene Lake and Lake Irene, Olive Lake, and Lake Verna—the mystery women of the northern Front Range!

The Board discarded most of the personal names from the first map of Wild Basin, "and rightly, too," says Dr. W. S. Cooper today. He made this first map in his youth, but now deplores his attempt to fasten family names on the great Rocky Mountains. (Dr. Cooper, an ecologist of note, is pleased that the Colorado Geographic Board retained the bird and flower names he gave to creeks and falls in Wild Basin.) Enos Mills had planned to publish Cooper's map in 1908, but Mills disliked two persons after whom Cooper had named lakes. When the young man refused to change the names, Mills refused to publish the map. In June 1911, Cooper and Dean Babcock, artist of

Estes Park, published the map themselves. The cover reads: "The only authentic map from original survey. Price 15 cents."

The two maps that doubtless were most useful to the Colorado Geographic Board were the 1910 map published by the Burlington Railroad and a 1913 map published by J. P. Clatworthy, owner of Estes Park's first photographic studio. For the information of its prospective customers, the Burlington map located almost every resort and hotel in the area. The great puzzle on this map is Mt. Barrett where Chiefs Head is today. On Clatworthy's map in large letters is printed Elkanah Valley, showing on which side he fought in the battle of Elkanah vs. Tahosa Valley.

The Colorado Geographic Board painstakingly collected names from each small community, from Glen Haven south to Allenspark, from Estes Park across the range to Grand Lake. They balanced them with the names on maps—names that seemed right against names that meant nothing except to one family, names that conflicted with other names, duplicate names, hackneyed names, and a few "great, proud, glittering names fit for the immense and lonely land they inhabit," as Thomas Wolfe wrote about names on the western landscape.

1915 DECISIONS

To find most of the names the Colorado Geographic Board left on the northern Front Range compare the maps of the Burlington Railroad and Clatworthy's map, both studied by Rogers and Barnard, with the U.S. Geological Survey map of the Rocky Mountain National Park, edition of 1919. On the earlier maps not one Indian name appears: the later map has a rash of Indian names. This dictionary of names in the Rocky Mountain National Park area includes 36 Indian names, not counting names in translation like Gianttrack and Lumpy Ridge and Never Summer. This is one of the greatest concentrations of Indian names in one small area on the face of the U.S.A.

The comparison of the maps shows some of the trouble spots smoothed over by the Colorado Geographic Board. The Grand River Trail, sometimes called Squeaky Bob's Trail, or Poudre Lakes Trail, or North Fork Trail, over Tombstone Ridge becomes the Ute Trail over Trail Ridge. Lily Mountain has not only simplified its spelling but securely rests on the hill near Lily Lake, disassociated from Twin Sisters. Rogers and Barnard probably settled the argument as to which hill the Indians called Gianttrack Mountain by climbing, on a nice winter weekend, all the adjacent hills until they found the giant's tracks. In the vicinity of the Mummy Range the Colorado Geographic Board added Tileston for the author of a book named *Chiquita,* already on the map; Dunraven for the absentee landlord of Estes Park; and Dickinson for the first woman to climb Longs Peak.

8

Over the valley of the North Fork of the Grand River the Board peppered the map with new names. The valley became the Kawuneeche Valley, the mountains became the Never Summer Mountains, and in that range Rogers named the Cloud Peaks—Cirrus, Cumulus, and Nimbus. The Board added Mt. Neota, Nokhu Crags, and Seven Utes Mountain. Near Grand Lake the Board accepted Craig and Cairns from earlier maps, but eradicated Bald Mountain by naming it Mt. Senator. (This became Mt. Patterson.) It added Wescott and Irving Hale.

MOUNTAIN INDEX AT CHEESMAN PARK

When the May 1915 edition, the first, of the Longs Peak quad went to press in March of that year, the work of the team of Rogers and Barnard was over for the area of Rocky Mountain National Park. But the Board and The Colorado Mountain Club had another commitment to complete. When the Board was first organized *The Denver Post* pointed out that their "first duty was to fix definitely and for all time the nomenclature of the peaks in sight of Denver." The team of Bethel and Rogers worked on this. They studied the view from Cheesman Park and sketched the mountains in outline in a semi-circle from south to north—from Pikes to the Poudre. After on-the-spot investigations of certain localities, they added refinements as the work progressed, such as a flat map indicating altitudes, distances from Denver as the crow flies, and even the position of some unseen but important peaks. The final draft they turned over to Paul Weiss, Denver optician, who cast it in bronze and added a sighting device. In the spring of 1916 The Colorado Mountain Club erected a pedestal in front of Cheesman Memorial for the mountain indicator. Today the indicator is still there, and the mountains still stand, but the view from one to the other has been curtailed by high trees and higher buildings.

THE COLORADO GEOGRAPHIC BOARD DISSOLVES

The Colorado Geographic Board worked on names for mountains in other parts of the state until its last official minutes, dated November 23, 1916. James Grafton Rogers had already resigned from the Board. The secretary wrote that his resignation was "an unmitigated calamity," but Rogers pleaded that he had no time left over from being president of The Colorado Mountain Club and the Civic League of Denver, which he organized. He did not mention his private law practice nor his growing family. Presently Rogers taught at the University of Denver Law School, became president of the Colorado Bar Association and the University Club of Denver. He wrote poetic dramas for the Cactus Club to perform in the open air on Lookout

Mountain and two of his songs—"The Santa Fe Trail" and "Old Dolores"— have become folk songs. After serving as dean of the Law School of the University of Colorado, Rogers continued his distinguished career in the East, as professor of law at Yale, assistant to the U.S. Secretary of State, in the office of Strategic Services during World War II, and, for ten years, the president of the Foreign Bond Holders Protective Council. Yet, always, from New Haven, from Washington, from Europe, Mr. Rogers returned home to his Colorado mountains. He bought an historic house in Georgetown and twice served as mayor of that mountain community. At present he is chairman of the Board of the State Historical Society of Colorado and still studies maps, collects information on the names of mountains, and generously shares his knowledge with others who play the name-game.

What happened to the other members of the Colorado Geographic Board? Hugh Steele continued to tell tales of early Colorado until his death in 1923. Jerome Smiley went home to his native Ohio— practically nothing is known of the personal life of this man who contributed invaluable books to the history of Colorado. Harriet Vaille married Judge Francis Bouck of Leadville in 1917, then returned to Denver where Judge Bouck sat on the bench of the Colorado Supreme Court. They brought up three daughters in the traditions of Colorado history and mountain climbing.

Ellsworth Bethel continued longest in the business of nomenclature. Between the years of 1914 and 1917—after his retirement, aged 51, from teaching at East High School, and his appointment as plant pathologist for the U.S. Forestry Deparment—Bethel spent much time establishing names for mountains. Weekend after weekend found him riding the Fisherman's Special up the South Platte Canyon. The engineer would let him off anywhere along the' line, even where neither fishing hole nor raspberry patch was in sight, the usual reasons the engineer was asked to stop the train. Shouldering his heavy pack, the fragile-looking Bethel covered the hills, checking maps for contours and altitudes, interviewing local people for names, camping out on Saturday night to continue his work next day. On Sunday night the engineer of the Colorado & Southern narrow gauge train watched for him standing beside the track and stopped the train for this little man with his pack full of rocks, his hand full of flowers for his wife, and his head full of names.

Bethel was science director of the State Historical and Natural History Society of Colorado. (This was before the Denver Museum of Natural History took over the science part of the State Historical Society.) In his 1919-20 report he wrote of two manuscripts concerning Colorado mountain names that he planned to deposit in some library. So far an extensive search for these documents has failed. Perhaps in them are recorded the meaning of various names added to the map of Colorado that are merely mentioned in the minutes of the Colorado Geographic Board, are not on file in Washington, and are not in the clear memory of James Grafton Rogers.

After Bethel's death in 1925 his friends both in and out of The Colorado Mountain Club asked the U.S. Board on Geographic Names to name a peak near Loveland Pass for him. Mt. Bethel is a fitting memorial to a man who signed his letters, in a clear Spencerian script, "Yours for a more beautiful nomenclature, Ellsworth Bethel."

NAMERS SINCE 1915

Since the time of the Colorado Geographic Board names have been added to the Rocky Mountain National Park and its environs, sometimes spasmodically, but with three concerted efforts. Roger Toll made the first effort. As Park Superintendent from 1919 to 1929 he climbed most of the mountains, named many of them, and christened lakes and creeks and glaciers. He amassed an extensive collection of local maps which, bound, are in the Park headquarters library. The card file of names there also probably dates from Toll's regime.

In 1942 the staff of Rocky Mountain National Park under Superintendent David H. Canfield spent a profitable winter revising names. And before 1961 another official committee, headed by a summer ranger named Phillip Ritterbush, suggested names and changes. The results appeared on the accurate and beautiful 1961 map of Rocky Mountain National Park published by the U.S. Geological Survey. All the names on that map and names selected from the Indian Peaks to the south and the Lake Granby area to the southwest comprise the 428 distinctive names listed in this dictionary. The names reflect the interests of various people, the efforts of various groups, and are really a history of the northern Front Range of the Colorado Rockies, the Rockies that were once known as the Shining Mountains.

How To Name A Mountain

Anyone may suggest a name for a mountain. Just send the suggestion to the U.S. Board on Geographic Names, Washington, D.C. Thereupon the Board will go into its routine based on more than 75 years of experience in dealing with names. If the name is approved it is published in the Board's quarterly decisions list and thereafter is used on maps of government make, such as those of the Geological Survey and the Forest Service.

The Board on Geographic Names, born in 1890, has grown until it is now a part of the Department of the Interior. It consists of one member from each of the Armed Services, and one each from the Departments of Agriculture, Commerce, Interior, and State, from the Central Intelligence Agency, the Government Printing Office, the Post Office Department, and the Library of Congress. Its executive staff is divided into two sections, one for domestic names and one for foreign names. Staff work for the Domestic Geographic Names Committee is done by the Geological Survey.

The section on Domestic Geographic Names deals not only with new names but with problems involved in trying to bring order out of the chaos of names already on the map of America. It studies maps and endeavors to give a range of mountains the same name in its entire length. It traces a river backwards from its mouth to its source, giving it the same name the whole way. For tributaries of rivers it usually prefers distinctive names rather than directional names like the West Branch of the North Fork of the South Platte River.

The Board must study etymology. Although it knows the derivation of a name, it usually retains names that have been corrupted by usage rather than restoring them to their original form. This has little application in Rocky Mountain National Park where names are too young to have been corrupted, but applies to the Picketwire River in southeast Colorado, derived from Purgatoire.

The Board must have a sense of history, and states that it "retains euphonious and suitable names of Indian, French, and Spanish origin." It complains, however, that "the transliteration of Indian names has everywhere been a fruitful source of difference in spelling, inasmuch as no two persons understand alike or render into the same English characters the obscure sound of Indian names."

The Board's efforts at style editing are aimed at simplification. It shortens—Arapaho instead of Arapahoe; burg instead of burgh. (It has not, however, taken the *h* out of Pittsburgh, Pa.) It drops the apostrophe—Longs Peak instead of Long's Peak. It avoids hyphens

12

and combines two words into one—Oldman Mountain, Flattop Mountain. It shuns long and clumsy names, but was helpless in the face of established names on lakes in upper New York State.

All these are rules by which the Board makes decisions on old names. What about a new name? When someone sends a suggestion to the Board, it sends back a printed set of guidelines for naming geographic features. The closer the name adheres to the Board's guidelines, the better the chance of its acceptance.

Logically, the Board divides names into two classes—the first for names suggested by the peculiarities of the topographical features, the second for personal names. Under the first come names derived from the form of the feature—Notchtop; from vegetation—Mertensia Falls; or from animal life—Ptarmigan Point. The last two may be given either because of abundance or scarcity, either because so many orchids grow near Calypso Cascades, or because one lone bear was seen near Bear Lake. The rules of the Board do not mention imaginary, literary, poetic, or whimsical names. They are acceptable to the Board if appropriate, but frequently fail to pass the acid test of local approval.

The other class of names recognized by the Board is that of personal names. The Board's printed *Statement of Policy for Applying Names of Persons to Natural Features,* mailed to anyone suggesting a personal name, covers three pages of fine print, divided into rules for major features, secondary features, and minor features, covering in a reasonable way most contingencies. The most definite of these rules requests that the name of a living person should not be proposed for a major feature, or even a secondary feature. Because of the fleetness of fame, this rule eliminates most political names. Minor features may honor living persons; of the two such names in the area today, honoring retired Rangers Jack Moomaw and Melvin Potts, one is so minor it is called a puddle.

In honoring deceased persons, the Board diplomatically suggests that a distinction be drawn between honorable fame and mere notoriety. It also suggests that the size of a geographical feature be commensurate with the stature of the person to be honored. So we have a massive mountain in Alaska about to commemorate Sir Winston Churchill, and a 10,486-foot mountain in Estes Park honoring A. Q. MacGregor, a local rancher. Lake names seem, by custom, to be reserved for birds, flowers, and "the little woman."

To christen an unnamed mountain is easy compared to trying to exchange an old name for a new name. "Over my dead body," shout most of the people who live near the mountain. Therefore the Board refuses to change an existing name unless it is (1) a duplicate, (2) inappropriate, or (3) unworthy of perpetuation. Concerning duplicates, the various people who have named features in the Rocky Mountain National Park have done a remarkable job of avoiding repetitious names on the same kind of feature. Beaver Brook, Beaver Creek, Beaver Meadows, Beaver Point, and even Beaver Mountain, yes, but not two Beaver Creeks. Of the 20-odd Bald and 10 Baldys in the state of Colorado, not one—not even one—is on the maps accompanying this dictionary.

The inappropriate rule is usually applied when someone wishes to name a secondary feature after a person who had no connection whatever with the area. If the Board had been in operation in the 1880's, Fairchild Mountain would not bear the name of a governor of Wisconsin who never saw this mountain.

For the third rule, the best Colorado example of a name considered unworthy of being perpetuated is near the town of Breckenridge. Nigger Hill has officially changed to Barney Ford Hill, after a negro prominent in early Breckenridge history.

Nothing is to be named—and here the Board thunders its edict— against the wishes of local residents. As an example, Copeland Mountain was not changed to Mt. Clarence King. This seems a simple rule, but the wishes of local residents are seldom simple and never unanimous. The war of Tahosa vs. Elkanah Valley demonstrates this.

The U.S. Board on Geographic Names is not a group of disembodied bureaucrats sitting in judgment in Washington. The proof of this statement lies in the Board's strenuous efforts to find out if a name is acceptable to local residents. It writes people like postmasters, mayors, forest service men, geological surveyors, National Park rangers and interested organizations like The Colorado Mountain Club. The Board bases its final decisions on the suggestions submitted by these on-the-spot investigators as well as on the suggestion submitted by the original proposer of the name, who should submit a full description of the feature and biographical information if the name proposed is a personal one.

All information that can be obtained is assembled by the name researchers and presented to the Board for consideration. When approved, the name is published in the Board's quarterly decisions list. This pamphlet is mailed to agencies, libraries, and interested organizations. An entry looks like this:

Gravel Mountain: mountain with an elevation of about 11,769 feet, about 2.5 miles west of Porphyry Peaks in Arapaho National Forest; Grand County sec. 22, T.4.N., R.77.W. Sixth principal meridian. 40° 16' 30" N., 105° 59' 40" W. Not: Bennay Mountain [former decision].

The "Not:" is always interesting, followed as it is by the names that have been collected, considered, and vetoed by the Board. In the example, the last phrase indicates that this decision is a reversal of a former decision by the Board. This demonstrates that the Board is amenable to correction and changes names for good and sufficient reasons. This Gravel Mountain, for instance. (It lies too far west of Grand Lake to be included in the present dictionary.) In 1914 the Colorado Geographic Board, on its Indian spree, named this mountain after some Indian named Bennay, specifying neither who nor why. Before 1914 local people had called this Gravel Mountain, because it had gravel on it, and they continued to call it Gravel Mountain despite the official name on the maps. Finally someone, probably a Forest Service official, told the Washington Board about this. The Board reversed its decision in accordance with its policy of respecting local opinion.

Perhaps these selections from the workings of the U.S. Board on Geographic Names are enough to show that it exerts an efficient and reasonable control over innumerable suggestions that might add up to chaos. It will remain effective in direct proportion to the amount of help it receives from ordinary people, alone or organized. The excellent nomenclature of Rocky Mountain National Park and environs is an example of satisfactory cooperation.

PLEASE NOTE!

Five maps published by the U.S. Geological Survey have been used as authority for the spelling of names and the altitudes of mountains: Allens Park (1957), Isolation Peak (1958), Monarch Lake (1958), Rocky Mountain National Park (1961), and Ward (1957). The nine maps in this book are sectional reproductions of these five maps. Each section is named according to its most prominent feature: Estes Park, Forest Canyon, Glacier Gorge, Grand Lake, Indian Peaks, Lake Granby, Mummy Range, Never Summers, and Wild Basin. These sectional maps will be found at the end of the book, arranged alphabetically, with the key map on the last page.

Each name in this dictionary is keyed to the map or maps on which the name appears, thus:

Flattop Mtn. 12,324'   GLACIER GORGE, GRAND LAKE

This means that Flattop Mountain is 12,324 feet above sea level, and appears on both the Glacier Gorge and Grand Lake maps in this book. It appears on two maps because the sectional maps were designed to overlap.

Hayden Creek, Gorge, Lake, Spire   FOREST CANYON

All the features named Hayden are on the Forest Canyon map; the U.S. Geological Survey does not record the specific altitude of Hayden Spire.

Beaver Creek—NEVER SUMMER; **Beaver Brook, Meadow Point**—ESTES PARK; **Beaver Mtn. 10,491'**—FOREST CANYON

The various features named Beaver are grouped together, with the map on which each appears indicated.

Olympus Mt.— (East of Estes Park Village)

This means that Mt. Olympus is not on a map in this dictionary, but it is located east of a feature that is on one of the maps.

Horse Creek   WILD BASIN

No text follows this or about 60 other names in the dictionary. We have listed these even though we know nothing about why, when, or by whom they were named. We hope our readers will write their own notes, and supply us with the information.

Note: 1914 Arapahos.

This expression, used frequently in the dictionary, does not mean a tribe numbering 1,914 Indians, but refers to the visit in 1914 of three Arapaho men brought to the Estes Park-Grand Lake region by The Colorado Mountain Club.

Dictionary of Names

A

Achonee, Mt. 12,649'

The Colorado Geographic Board left no record of its reason for choosing this name. Research has produced two possible sources, one Ute, one Arapaho. Among the Uncompahgre Utes who now live near Randlett, Utah, Achonee is a family name pronounced A ka wa' na, to rhyme with Lackawanna. The word means red edge or red line, a description that fits Mt. Achonee no better than the Ute pronunciation of the word fits its English spelling. The Utes cannot trace the name to any prominent man in their history.

A sub-chief of the Arapahos, whose name was spelled almost the same—Ochanee or Ochinee—was well-known to whites. He was one of the unsuspecting Arapaho and Cheyenne Indians camped on Sand Creek on November 29, 1864, when Colorado troops under Colonel John M. Chivington attacked at dawn. About this fight the granddaughter of Ochinee, Mary Prowers Hudnall, wrote:

> Grandfather Ochinee (One-Eye) escaped from the camp, but seeing that all his people were to be slaughtered, he deliberately chose to go back into the one-sided battle and die with them rather than survive alone. . . . Mother, father, and I were out at Big Timbers when we heard of the massacre. . . Mother was always very bitter about the Sand Creek Massacre. A number of years later, while she was attending a meeting of the Eastern Star in Denver, a friend brought Chivington over to introduce him to mother, saying, "Mrs. Prowers, do you know Colonel Chivington?" My mother drew herself up with that stately dignity peculiar to her people, and ignoring the outstretched hand, remarked in perfect English, audible to all in the room, "Know Colonel Chivington? I should. He was my father's murderer!"

Ochinee's daughter was named Amache. In 1861, when she was 15 years old, she married the handsome Missourian John Wesley Prowers, trader at Bent's Fort, who is credited with bringing the first cattle into Prowers County. During World War II the relocation center where Japanese were interned was named Amache Relocation Center. Thus on the map of Colorado a mountain (Achonee), a town (Amache), and a county (Prowers) commemorate an Arapaho Indian, his daughter, and his son-in-law.

Acoma, Mt. 10,508' GRAND LAKE, LAKE GRANBY

The ancient pueblo of the Acoma Indians sits on a mesa in Valencia County, New Mexico. F. H. Hodge, in his classic *Handbook of American Indians,* states that the word comes "from the native A kóme, 'People of the White Rock,' now commonly pronounced A' co ma." Denver people, often criticized for accenting the name of Acoma Street on the second syllable, may be reverting to the original. The mountain was named by the Colorado Geographic Board, as proposed by Ellsworth Bethel.

Adams Falls GRAND LAKE

In 1886 Jay E. Adams of San Antonio, Texas, began to build a small cabin on a large rock on the southeastern shore of Grand Lake, accessible only by boat. He sold it in 1891 to Stephen D. Cook. Later it became a ghost house; youngsters rowed across the lake to picnic near "The House on the Rock." In 1946 Dudley Abbott of Denver bought and rebuilt it.

Jay Adams built two more, much larger, houses on the eastern shore of Grand Lake. In 1917 he entertained the Grand Lake community with a sumptuous shore picnic, then asked his replete guests to suggest a name for a nearby waterfall. They voted unanimously to name it Adams Falls. Before this it had been known as Ouzel Falls, although Judge Wescott and his young friends called it Minnehaha Falls. (See Mt. Wescott.)

Adams Lake; Adams, Mt. 12,121' GRAND LAKE, LAKE GRANBY

This name may commemorate the same Jay E. Adams of San Antonio. Enos Mills, however, thought the mountain honored another Adams family, year-round residents of Grand Lake. Alexander and Louise Adams bought the Garrison House, built in 1881 south of the outlet of Grand Lake, and renamed it the Grandview House. Here they ran a pleasant resort until 1901, when the hotel with its fine furniture and gay rugs burned. Mrs. Adams thereafter lived in a cottage close by until her death in 1940 at the age of 101. Mrs. Adams' granddaughter, Mrs. E. E. Gemmill, now has a house on the site of Grandview House.

Adams Tunnel GLACIER GORGE, GRAND LAKE

The official name for this tunnel is the Alva B. Adams Tunnel. Senator Adams, Democrat from Colorado, introduced into the United States Senate, in June 1937, the bill that authorized the Colorado-Big Thompson Project. Water collected in Lake Granby, Shadow Mountain Lake, and Grand Lake flows through the Continental Divide in the Adams Tunnel to empty into the Big Thompson River. Water first rushed through the tunnel in 1947, flowing 13.1 miles from the intake below the surface of Grand Lake to the Emerald Mountain Outlet.

18

Agnes, Lake   NEVER SUMMER

John Zimmerman changed the name of Island Lake to honor one of his two daughters. In the clean Swiss tradition, Agnes and Eda Zimmerman were housekeepers for their father's famous Keystone Hotel on the upper Poudre River near the town of Home. The three-story brick building housed contented fishermen who gladly paid $10 a week for clean rooms and ample cooking. In 1946 the State of Colorado bought the hotel, razed it, and turned the area into a fish-retaining pond.

Alberta Falls   GLACIER GORGE

Named by Abner Sprague for his wife.

Albion, Mt. 12,609'   INDIAN PEAKS

Albion is a Celtic word related to alp, meaning white or snowy. Poets use Albion as a name for the main British Isle. Following this custom, when homesick men from the lowlands of Scotland located the pioneer lead-silver vein in the Snowy Range Mining District, they called their lode Albion. Although discovered in 1864, the mine was not recorded until October of 1879. From the name of the mine, a town and a mountain and a lake were all called Albion.

Starting in 1881 the Scottish Mining and Smelter Company with headquarters at Salina, Kansas, worked the claim, and later the Cashier Mining and Milling Company drilled the Snowy Range Tunnel.

Today's Mt. Albion was in mining days known as Sheep Mountain. The miners knew Mt. Albion as the higher peak, farther west, which appropriately towers over Lake Albion. This peak the Colorado Geographic Board renamed Kiowa Peak, in line with their efforts to call all the snowy summits north of the Arapaho Peaks after Indian tribes. Changing old Mt. Albion to Kiowa Peak and Sheep Mountain to Mt. Albion upset mining records. Kenneth I. White of Boulder, whose father and grandfather both were officers in the Scottish company, is not the only mining man who still complains in vain about the change.

Alice, Mt. 13,310'   GRAND LAKE, WILD BASIN

Who was Alice?

The first record of this name for the mountain seems to be on Enos Mills' map published in the 1905 edition of his *Story of Estes Park*. The map is based on notes by A. E. Sprague, and if either Mills or Sprague knew who Alice was, he did not record it in any available records.

Mt. Alice next appears on the Cooper-Babcock map of 1911. W. S. Cooper made the first detailed survey of Wild Basin in 1908. On his map the U.S. Board on Geographic Names based some of their decisions, including Mt. Alice. Dr. Cooper, however, stated in 1965 that he merely accepted the name in general use in 1908, that he did not name Mt. Alice, nor did he know who the lady was.

In the spring of 1914, when Ellsworth Bethel was trying to fasten the names of Indian tribes on the snowy peaks between the Arapahos and Longs Peak, he wished to change the name of Mt. Alice to Shoshone Peak. The U.S. Board on Geographic Names refused the change. Bethel wrote back pleading his cause. He said he had been unable, after much research, to find out about Alice, but that "saloonists and lewd women camped near Longs Peak and named mountains." Despite his appeal, the U.S. Board on Geographic Names retained Mt. Alice.

Many suggestions about the identity of Alice have been made. One candidate is Mrs. Kirkwood, the mother of the Hewes boys of Hewes-Kirkwood Inn. The name, however, predates her advent into the Park region, and her name was Mary Catherine Palmer Hewes Kirkwood (1850-1920).

Alice Hutchinson, wife of the English dentist who lived at the mouth of the Big Thompson Canyon west of Loveland in 1872, has been suggested. Here Isabella Bird visited the Hutchinsons—she called them Hughes in her published book—and wrote of Alice, greatly beloved, who died in 1874, aged 33. Dr. Hutchinson buried her at the ranch, married the Swiss nursemaid, and took her and the children to New Zealand. The theory that Alice Hutchinson left her name on Mount Alice seems improbable chiefly because of the great distance between Wild Basin and the mouth of the Big Thompson Canyon.

Many people theorize about Alice Roosevelt Longworth, daughter of President Theodore Roosevelt. She was America's darling around the turn of the century, but to date no publicity about naming a mountain for her has been discovered in old newspapers, and one cannot imagine such a political move made without headlines.

The town of Alice northwest of Idaho Springs was named for a girl of that locality, surely too far from Wild Basin to be pertinent.

A romantic theory is that the mountain was named for the childhood sweetheart of Elkanah Lamb, Longs Peak's first guide. (See Lambs Slide.) Eleanor James Hondius of Elkhorn Lodge was irritated when Parson Lamb, in the presence of his second hard-working and faithful wife, referred frequently to this girl he left behind in Indiana as the one great love of his life. Lamb wrote in his memoirs that this early affair of the heart left "a shadow over my life which more than 50 years cannot efface." Such undying devotion could well have been memorialized by Elkanah Lamb, who was early in that part of the Longs Peak area from which Mount Alice is most conspicuous. The two catches in this logic are: (a) One who talked about the girl so often would surely have climaxed his story by pointing to the mountain he named after her; (b) No one knows the girl's name.

Perhaps the mountain was named for Alice in Wonderland?

Allens Park   WILD BASIN

In 1859 Alonzo Nelson Allen came to Colorado. He established his family in Burlington, a plains town on the St. Vrain River. While Mrs. Allen ran a stage station, her husband prospected all the way from the Dakotas to southwestern Colorado. In 1871, during one of his visits home, he helped move the hotel, along with the rest of the town of Burlington, from its original site to a new location two miles north (present Longmont).

During his first siege of mining fever, Alonzo Allen prospected in the hills around Allens Park, but his few prospect holes were disappointing. He stayed long enough to build in 1864 a cabin about two miles east of the present town of Allenspark (the post office is spelled as one word) and helped blaze a trail from his Park to Ward. The cabin's fireplace still stands on the north side of Highway 7. This name—Allens Park—is the only one on the 1961 Rocky Mountain National Park map that dates from the gold rush days of the 1860's.

Alpine Brook   GLACIER GORGE

Andrews Creek, Glacier, Pass, Tarn   GLACIER GORGE, GRAND LAKE

Edwin B. Andrews was the widower of Abner Sprague's wife's sister. In 1897 Sprague and Andrews climbed to the glacier hanging from the Continental Divide at the head of Loch Vale. Because of this feat, but more because Andrews was one of the area's best fishermen, Sprague named the glacier. By association near-by features bear the Andrews name.

Andrews Peak 12,565'   GRAND LAKE

This peak, which stands about three miles from Andrews Pass, was definitely not named for Edwin B. Andrews. Abner Sprague in 1915 and Edwin B. Andrews himself in 1936 both disclaimed any connection. This was after the 1915 Longs Peak quad map appeared with Andrews Peak labeled. The name was approved by the U.S. Board on Geographic Names in 1932.

Then who was this other Andrews? A likely candidate is Darwin M. Andrews, the founder of the Rockmont Nursery in Boulder, where gardeners secured mountain plants. From 1893 Darwin Andrews botanized in northern Colorado hills, sending his specimens to the famous botanist, Aven Nelson, for identification. Although Darwin Andrews' name would grace a mountain, his son Philip in 1965 averred he had never heard that one was named for his father. (See Arapaho Glacier.)

Apache Peak 13,441'   INDIAN PEAKS

The word may mean "knife-whetters" or "enemies," for the various branches of Apache Indians were indeed enemies of the encroaching white men. They produced leaders like Cochise, Victorio,

21

and the great Geronimo. Ellsworth Bethel in 1914 proposed Apache as one of the Indian peak names.

On various maps Apache Peak and Mt. George have exchanged places several times. The U.S. Geological Survey, on March 6, 1961, finally fastened Apache securely to the higher peak, the one on the Continental Divide, with Mt. George to the southwest.

Apiatan Mtn.— (Six miles west of Grand Lake)

Apiatan, a Kiowa chief, had earned the right to carry the feathered wooden ceremonial lance called an *apiatan.* In 1890, because of his standing, his tribe sent him to Nevada to investigate a new religion which was spreading through the western tribes. A Paiute Indian there was prophesying that the earth would be restored to the Indians, that the buffalo would come back, and that the dead would be resurrected if all Indians joined in the Ghost Dance. Apiatan's son had recently died, but the Paiute, Wovaka, was unable to help Apiatan communicate with the dead boy. Disillusioned with Wovaka and the Ghost Dance, Apiatan returned to his tribe. The Kiowas turned to the religion known as the Native American Religion which makes use of peyote to induce dreams of happier times.

When Apiatan was an old man, head chief of the Kiowas, his cousin, Hiamovi of the Cheyennes, brought a white woman named Natalie Curtis to see him. For her he sang the oldest songs of his tribe. Recorded in written music, they were published in 1908 in a book called *The Indian's Book.* When Harriet Vaille was looking for Indian names for mountains, she must have studied it. No other source has been found for names of two Colorado peaks—Apiatan and Hiamovi.

Arapaho Bay   LAKE GRANBY

Arapaho Indians left their names on Colorado scenery, like glaciers, passes, and peaks; on a Colorado county and a National Forest; on streets in various Colorado towns; and most recently on Arapaho Bay on Lake Granby. The Arapahos were typical plains Indians, depending for their life on the buffalo, and friendly enough to white men until they realized the whites were taking away their livelihood. The Arapahos considered places like Estes Park on the eastern slope of the northern Colorado Rockies their personal hunting ground, but stepped over the Divide into Middle Park when they wanted better hunting or a small war, usually with Ute Indians, the tribe that belonged to the western mountains of Colorado.

After the white men came, the Arapahos divided into three sections. One was the Gros Ventre of the Prairies on the Milk River in Montana; one was the Southern Arapahos on the Canadian River in

22

Oklahoma. In between, in Wyoming, the third group settled in 1874 on the Wind River Reservation next to their traditional enemies, the Shoshones. These Northern Arapahos (presently numbering about 2,200) are considered the mother tribe because they hold the sacred objects of the Arapaho nation, including a pipe whose smoke acts like truth serum.

Etymologically, the word Arapaho presents problems both in its derivation and meaning, even to the Arapaho people themselves. They call their nation *Inunaina* (our people). A chief of the Southern Arapahos in 1897 said that he did not know the meaning of the word Arapaho but he did know it was a white man's word. One proof of white origin lies in the lack of the letter *r* in the Arapaho language; early Arapaho Indians pronounced the word N'appaho. If it is a white man's word, could it be derived from *arrapo* or *harapo,* two Spanish words meaning rag or tatter?

Both the Pawnees and Crows used names for the Arapaho Indians that resemble Arapaho in sound, and have different meanings. The Pawnees said *Tirapihu,* or *Harapihu,* meaning traders, which the Arapaho people were. The Crow word means "lots of tattoos"; the Arapaho Indians often tattooed scattered designs over their breasts. In sign language, the *lingua franca* of the plains, the speaker touched his breast in various places to indicate Arapahos.

Another problem connected with the word Arapaho is its spelling. Arapaho or Arapahoe? The old way was usually with the *e,* although in 1847 G. F. Ruxton, an English army officer traveling in the West, wrote Arapahó, with an accent. The sovereign state of Colorado still uses the *e* in Arapahoe County, and Denver has an Arapahoe Street. The U.S. Board on Geographic Names, in its 1920-23 report, officially dropped the *e.* Both the Geological Survey and the Forest Service have heeded the edict, though not always happily. When the rule was first enforced, one of the Arapaho National Forest Service men complained that people in his district thought he could not spell!

The plural spelling presents an additional problem: potatoes— Arapahoes; solos—Arapahos. The U.S. Board on Geographic Names recommends simplicity.

Arapaho Creek   INDIAN PEAKS, LAKE GRANBY
When Monarch Lake was constructed, the names of the two largest creeks that flowed into it were the East Fork and the South Fork of the Grand River. Below the lake, the stream that ran eight miles to the river was the South Fork. Now all the names have changed. The river is the Colorado, the East Fork is Buchanan Creek, and the South Fork, even the half-mile remnant of the stream between Monarch Lake and Lake Granby, is Arapaho Creek.

23

Dates are important in discussing Arapaho Glacier.

1874—Surveyor James P. Maxwell subdivided the township on which this glacier is located, but he did not recognize it as a glacier.

1897—Darwin Andrews (see Andrews Glacier) was botanizing on the east side of Arapaho Pass with his brother-in-law, H. N. Wheeler. They noted a large snowbank, and the more they looked at it the more convinced they became that it was a glacier. This they reported to Junius Henderson of the University of Colorado.

1900—Willis T. Lee wrote the first description of Arapaho Glacier, a report that caused almost as much excitement in glacialogical circles as the discovery of Hallett Glacier in 1884. (See Rowe Glacier.) Also in 1900, Eben Fine of Boulder claimed to have discovered Arapaho Glacier.

1903—When H. N. Wheeler took lantern slides of Arapaho Glacier he carefully stated that this was a return trip, his first having been made in 1897.

1903-1912—Junius Henderson made annual measurements of the movement and shrinkage of Arapaho Glacier.

1919—Junius Henderson discovered the glacial characteristics of the ice bank north of Arapaho Glacier, which was named Henderson Glacier, though it is not named on the 1958 quad map.

This Junius Henderson (1865-1937) was a delightful lawyer-scientist of Boulder, called "Judge" by his friends because he was County Judge while teaching part time in the law school of the University of Colorado. Gradually he gave up the practice of law for enthusiastic activities in the field of natural history. He was the first curator (without pay) of the natural science museum, now housed in the Henderson Building. First a teacher of paleontology, then, from 1919, Professor of Natural History, he contributed to magazines both popular and technical. He helped discover and name Fair and Isabelle Glaciers in 1910. He worked on the Colorado Geological Survey with R. D. George—perhaps he named Mt. George? Henderson's book, *Extinct and Existing Glaciers of Colorado,* published in 1910, is still the definitive work on the subject.

Laymen as well as scientists were excited about Arapaho Glacier. Boulder County and the U.S. Forest Service planned to build a road to the southern edge of Arapaho Glacier, continuing it with a Figure-Eight Trail, equipped with hostels, which would cross the Continental Divide at Arapaho, Pawnee, and Buchanan Passes. After national publicity and the appropriation of $56,000 from the Forest Service, the Maxwell Road was built as far as Rainbow Lakes in 1924. Then lack of funds cancelled the project, but the city of Boulder is known as "The

Gateway to the Glaciers," and is the only city in America, according to its Chamber of Commerce, that drinks glacial water.

Arapaho National Forest INDIAN PEAKS
This forest was established by Theodore Roosevelt on July 1, 1908. Its acres—over a million—include lands adjacent to the Rocky Mountain National Park on the west and southwest. From undesirable exploitation it protects the western slope of the Indian Peaks.

Arapaho Pass 11,906' INDIAN PEAKS
About 1900, Boulder County and Grand County felt the need of a road connecting Nederland and Hot Sulphur Springs. They planned it to cross the Continental Divide at Arapaho Pass, and Boulder County thereupon built a road up the eastern slope of the Pass. On the 1915 Longs Peak quad map it appears as a secondary road. Today it is a pack trail running above the tunnel entrance of the Fourth of July Mine and passing the mine's shaft house.

Atop the windy pass, the traveler must choose between two trails which lead down the Western Slope on either side of Satanta Peak. One goes west, past Lake Dorothy, then utilizes a cut in the scree slope that was obviously the beginning of a road at one time. This was Grand County's effort to live up to its agreement to build a road on the west side of Arapaho Pass. Roughed out, the road was never completed. The trail that follows its proposed route leads to Caribou Pass, then via Caribou Trail to the old roads made by lumbermen when miles of wooden flumes scooted logs down to mills in Sawmill Meadow.

The other trail from Arapaho Pass plunges north to Caribou Lake. The traveler, eyeing the switchbacks, thinks twice before he starts zigzagging down. Once he enters the timber, he follows Arapaho Creek for miles and miles to Monarch Lake.

Old-timers claim the Indians used Arapaho Pass. One wonders which route they chose, and by which route Gordon and McHenry, two road builders of the 1860's, planned to have their road descend the Western Slope. Theirs was to be a military road connecting Boulder City and Middle Park. Proceeding via Sunshine and Four Mile Canyons, it actually ended in the valley of North Boulder Creek.

Arapaho Peaks: North Arapaho Peak 13,502';
South Arapaho Peak 13,397' INDIAN PEAKS
Who named the Arapaho Peaks, and when? No one seems to know. Certainly the German W. E. Andree and his two Hungarian companions, prospectors, who climbed one of them in July 1861 did not name them—they thought they were on Longs Peak!

The Arapahos had at least one other name. On Case's map of Colorado Territory, dated 1862, the name for the mountain at the head of Boulder Creek appears as Mt. Edmunds. On June 21, 1862, a

25

reporter for the *Rocky Mountain News* wrote that Surveyor Francis Case had, in his handsome office in Denver, a crayon sketch of Mt. Edmunds, 50 miles south of Longs Peak, "painted by the General [Case] in his artistic manner and the mountain christened by him in honor of his friend, Edmunds, Commissioner of the General Land Office in Washington." One suspects that Commissioner Edmunds recommended Case to President Lincoln for the job of Territorial Surveyor of Colorado, and therefore naming the mountain was paying a political debt. Mt. Edmunds appeared on the Pierce map of 1863, on Colton's 1872 and 1874 maps, and Clarence King's Atlas of 1876.

But F. V. Hayden, surveyor of western territories, stated that the name Arapaho for this mountain was in common use before 1873, and used it in his 1877 atlas. Thayer's map of Colorado used Arapaho in 1873. Since then it has remained on the peaks, sometimes spelled differently, and now used in the plural. Unsolved is the problem of who named the Arapaho Peaks and when.

Arch Rocks FOREST CANYON

Below The Pool on the Fern Lake Trail are these arching rocks, probably named by guests of near-by hotels, such as Fern Lake Lodge or the Brinwood.

Arikaree Peak 13,150' INDIAN PEAKS

The Arikaree tribe now lives in North Dakota near Fort Berthold. The name means "horn," used because Arikaree men wound their hair around two pieces of bone on either side of their heads. The Board on Geographic Names gave official sanction to Arikaree Peak in October 1914, when it was suggested by the Colorado Geographic Board at the request of Ellsworth Bethel. However, the name had been used for some time before this in a collective sense. Before each of the summits in the snowy range north of the Arapahos was given a distinctive name, Coloradans referred to them all as The Arikarees. (Some old-timers still do.)

Arrowhead GLACIER GORGE

This and Spearhead, on the opposite side of Glacier Gorge, were named at the same time by the Colorado Geographic Board, approved by Washington in 1916. The shape of an arrowhead on this mountain is especially obvious on a contour map.

Arrowhead Lake FOREST CANYON

This, the largest of the Gorge Lakes, looks from Trail Ridge Road as if it might slope downhill; seen from the cliffs of Mt. Ida its shape resembles a large arrowhead. The name was suggested by Dr. W. J. Workman of Fern Lake Lodge or by Julian Hayden. (See Gorge Lakes.)

The shape of the arrowhead would have been considerably altered if the 60-foot dam started by Henry Heinricy of Loveland had raised the level of the lake 15 feet, as he hoped. Heinricy planned a fishing resort at this out-of-the-way lake and was ready to file on water rights, when the establishment of Rocky Mountain National Park in 1915 ended his venture.

Aspen Brook ESTES PARK

The aspen tree's Latin name *Populus tremuloides* means a poplar that trembles. The leaves shake in the slightest breeze because their flat stems are set at right angles to the leaves. Nicknamed "popples" by Wisconsin lumbermen, westerners call them quaking aspens, or simply quakers.

Aspens tend to sprout following a fire, hurrying to cover the unsightly burn. (See Butterfly Burn.) On poor soil they grow scrubby and deformed and their boles are yellowish; on good soil they grow tall and straight. Their trunks, covered with white powder, have almost as many modulations of white as Chinese porcelain. Aspen groves arrange themselves on open hillsides in patterns. In winter they look like smoke against the snow. When the miniature leaves first show in the spring, the effect is yellow-green; all summer they provide a fresh contrast to the dark conifers, then blaze into gold in the fall. Botanists still puzzle as to why most aspen leaves turn yellow, others rose or red.

On white aspen trunks animals record that they have passed this way. Look for scratches left by bears who sharpen their claws on aspen trunks higher than you think they possibly could be—even a small bear can stretch and climb. Aspen boles that are black toward the bottom, like those in Horseshoe Park, show that wintering elk have nibbled the bark. Wherever aspens grow near streams, beavers leave signs. They leave pointed stumps where they have felled aspens with their sharp incisors, and paths through the forest where they have dragged logs to the water to use for food or dams or houses.

Audubon, Mt. 13,223' INDIAN PEAKS

John James Audubon (1780-1851) painted pictures of hundreds of birds and of many wild animals. His prints still rank high as nature portraits, and are priced even higher as collectors' items. Audubon was born in Haiti, lived in France, Kentucky, Louisiana, England, New York City, and is buried in that town's Trinity Churchyard.

Although Audubon never came to Colorado, two of his admirers did. Dr. C. C. Parry, botanist, and Dr. J. W. Velie, zoologist, arrived in Denver on June 2, 1864, were shocked at the devastation of the Cherry Creek flood, then proceeded to the mountains of the northern Front Range to botanize. (In August they joined William Byers in an attempt to climb Longs Peak.) Camping a few days west of the present

27

town of Ward, Parry reported that they observed a "smooth rounded peak" which they climbed despite deep snow, "supposing it was Mt. Edmonds." (See Arapaho Peaks.) "At the suggestion of my companion, Dr. J. W. Velie, we concluded to affix to this well marked elevation the name of the distinguished naturalist, Audubon."

In 1914, Ellsworth Bethel must have been torn between his admiration for Audubon and his systematic scheme to label with Indian names all the peaks between the Arapahos and Longs. The naturalist won out. Bethel recommended the retention of Audubon, named 50 years before, even though it did stand right in the middle of the Indian Peaks.

Azure Lake   Forest Canyon

Named by Dr. W. J. Workman in color contrast to Inkwell Lake just below it. (See Gorge Lakes.)

B

Baker Gulch, Pass; Baker Mtn. 12,397'   Never Summer

Two distinctive peaks finish off the southern end of the Never Summer Mountains—Bowen and Baker. Grand Lake people link their names together—Bowen 'n Baker—just as mountain climbers say Grazentorreys for two peaks near Georgetown.

Baker Mountain may be the one called Upper Grand Valley Peak by the Hayden Survey in 1875, located by them "in the remote southeast corner of North Park, where the Continental Divide separates from the Medicine Bows." The Continental Divide takes a right angle turn to the west near Baker Mountain.

John Baker is said to have been the first white man to climb the peak that bears his name. Originally from Fort Wayne, Indiana, he wandered from place to place in Colorado in the 1860's. He and a man named Bartholomew bought a ranch halfway between Baker Gulch and Grand Lake from a Mr. Hartzell who was operating a sawmill there. This was Green Mountain Ranch, now a guest ranch still bearing that name.

In 1878 John Baker brought his widowed daughter, Mary Jane Young, and her two children to settle at Grand Lake. She filed on a homestead near the western shore where, in 1879, her kindly neighbors held a house-raising party for the widow-woman. In one day they

28

erected Fair View Hotel for her. A bronze marker now stands near the site of this hostelry because here, on July 4, 1883, four men killed each other in a political squabble.

South of Baker Mountain is Baker Gulch, notable as the upper terminal of the Grand Ditch and for its snowslides. Here Jules Harmon, superintendent of the Hidden Treasure Mine, was killed in a snowslide; in 1881 three more men met the white death in Baker Gulch. A fourth man lay beneath the snow for 24 hours before he was rescued alive.

Battle Mtn. 12,044′ GLACIER GORGE

The keen eye of naturalist Enos Mills noted the effects of wind and snow and fire on this mountain, and named it after the battles of nature. For the same reason, he named nearby Storm Peak. Abner Sprague stated that the fire on Battle Mountain, the effects of which are still obvious today, occurred before he came to the area in 1875.

Bear Lake GLACIER GORGE

Horace Ferguson, early rancher, saw a bear at this lake and, because very few bears frequent the area, he named the lake after the bear. No grizzly bears live in Rocky Mountain National Park now, so Ferguson's bear probably was a black bear, a deceptive name because black bears may be colored cinnamon brown or blonde. When down on all fours these bears stand about three feet high, may weigh up to 500 pounds. They live on their fat in the winter, hibernating lightly. The cubs are tiny, weighing less than a pound at birth. Twin cubs playing in the springtime are charming to watch, but the mother bears guarding them are unpredictable and can be vicious.

Beaver Creek—NEVER SUMMER; **Beaver Brook, Meadows, Point—**ESTES PARK; **Beaver Mtn. 10,491′—**FOREST CANYON

Beavers do not live on mountains, so this mountain indubitably derives its name by association with Beaver Brook. The same hill was once called Brinwood Mountain, named for Brinton Woodward, chancellor of the University of Kansas in 1893, who owned land at its base.

The beaver is the largest rodent in the Park. He works at night, and may sometimes be seen in the twilight hours. The sound of his flat tail hitting the water as he dives is unmistakable. Evidence of his presence is in every aspen grove near water, where one may see pointed aspen stumps, felled aspen trees, trails where he dragged logs to water, dammed-up streams, and beaver huts in the ponds made by his dams.

Bench Lake GLACIER GORGE

This early-named lake lies on a bench, or shelf, on the side of a mountain. Such lakes on shelves left by glaciers are known to geologists as hanging lakes.

29

Bennett Creek

Joe Bennett grazed cattle in this territory, trailing them up Long Draw from the Poudre.

Bierstadt Lake, Moraine

Bierstadt was suggested as a name for this moraine by the Colorado Geographic Board in 1914, officially accepted in 1961; but Bierstadt Lake was named fifty years before.

The Earl of Dunraven was never content with the small or second-rate. He wanted all of Estes Park as his hunting preserve, and he wanted the hotel he built for his friends to have the best possible view of Longs Peak. To pick the site he imported one of America's top artists, Albert Bierstadt (1830-1902), renowned for his romantic interpretations of western scenery covering square yards of canvas. Bierstadt made periodic trips west for inspiration, his first in 1858 with surveyors in Wyoming. In December 1876 Lord Dunraven brought him to Estes Park, and the artist returned in the next summer. The Earl's Number One factotum, Theodore Whyte, drove Bierstadt around the park behind a matched four-in-hand, and named a lake admired by the artist for the artist. Abner Sprague gave Whyte the credit for thus naming Bierstadt Lake.

Though Bierstadt admired the lake that bears his name, it was not here that he chose the perfect site for Lord Dunraven's hotel. For this he merely corroborated the taste of Joel Estes and Griff Evans, recommending the hotel be built a little south of their cabins. Back in Philadelphia, Bierstadt executed a large oil painting of Longs Peak, for which the Earl is said to have paid $15,000. Shipped to Ireland, the canvas hung in Dunraven Castle to remind the Earl of the rugged American pioneers who thwarted his plans for an American hunting preserve. (See Mt. Dunraven.)

When the Denver Public Library moved into its new building in 1956, Roger Mead, contractor for the structure, presented the Bierstadt painting of Longs Peak to the library. With a simpler frame replacing the carved gilt original, Bierstadt's magnificent canvas now hangs in the Western History Room of the library, from whose northern windows Longs Peak itself is visible.

Big Meadows

Early literature of the Park describes the western descent from Flattop to Grand Lake via the Big Meadows. The 1914 Arapaho name was Tonahutu—meaning Big Meadows.

Big Owl Road

Charles Edwin Hewes published a verse in 1922 telling of the "Big Owl of Big Owl Hill." As an introduction to the poem he wrote:

The Big Owl of Big Owl Hill is a subject both interesting and romantic to the dwellers of the Vale of Elkanah. It was discovered, as the poem describes, in 1907, by the Poet himself, on the afternoon of an early fall day as he was locating his homestead in the south end of the Vale; which tract, however, did not include the Big Owl's domain, but which locality was subsequently patented as a homestead by Miss Katherine Garetson.

It is believed at this writing, 1921, there are at least two pairs of these birds in the Vale, their species being the Western horned owl, large magnificent nocturnal fowl whose low soft notes are the invariable accompaniment of every quiet evening.

Big Thompson River   Estes Park, Forest Canyon, Mummy Range

The 1914 Arapahos called this "The Pipe River," because they sat on its shore to carve pipes out of stone they probably had brought with them from some other place.

Many theories surround the name Thompson, the one provable fact being that it dates back to the 1830's when fur traders left written records using the name. The most likely tale seems to be that the river was named for Philip Thompson who was trading mules at Fort Vasquez in the 1830's. He was, however, more intimately connected with Browns Hole, in the northwest corner of the state.

Another story, quite elaborate, tells that a man named Thompson was killed by Indians on this river. He was a big man with a small brother—hence Big and Little Thompson. Another theory is that the name honors David Thompson of the Northwest Fur Company, though he probably never came this far south.

Bighorn Creek—Estes Park, Mummy Range; **Bighorn Lake**—Never Summer

Bighorn Flats   Forest Canyon, Grand Lake

This great expanse of high country north of Flattop Mountain offers good grazing to bighorn sheep. The flats are part of a geological peneplain. (See Flattop Mountain.) When Indians wanted to cross from Bear Lake to the Kawuneeche Valley, they climbed to the Divide, then angled northwest across these Bighorn Flats. The trail they made is now crossed by a ditch built to collect water from this rolling plain. It empties into Spruce Canyon. Henry J. Heinricy of Loveland constructed this ditch in 1902, with $2,000 he secured from Greeley men when Loveland men were not interested. Later the City of Loveland bought the ditch and its water rights for more than $2,000.

Bighorn Mtn. 11,463'   MUMMY RANGE

Sprague states that Pieter Hondius named this mountain. (See Hondius Park.) It may have been called Dome Rock earlier. Bighorn sheep, sometimes called Rocky Mountain sheep, are the world's most skillful mountaineers. The lambs start rock climbing before they are a week old. The rams grow powerful curved horns with which they battle for their harems. Racing at each other, they leap into the air for the final impact, which sometimes can be heard a mile away. Listen for it in November during the mating season. This splendid creature, chosen for the symbol of The Colorado Mountain Club in 1912, has recently become the official state animal of Colorado.

Abner Sprague wrote that bighorns were decimated by scabies about 1878. Recently bands of bighorns have been observed in the Park area. (See Rams Horn Mtn.)

Black Canyon, Black Canyon Creek   MUMMY RANGE

Black this canyon looks with its steep sides and thick timber. The name was probably used even before the MacGregor family settled there. Later F. V. Hayden noted that "from a black gorge, Black Canyon Creek brings water," the present water supply of the village of Estes Park.

Black Lake   GLACIER GORGE

The Glacier Gorge Lakes (not to be confused with the Gorge Lakes) bear the names of colors—Black, Blue, and Green. They appear as early as Enos Mills' 1905 map.

Black Pool   FOREST CANYON

Blue Lake—GLACIER GORGE; **Blue Lake**—INDIAN PEAKS

Bluebird Lake   WILD BASIN

Two kinds of bluebirds summer in the Park region, the western bluebird and the mountain bluebird. The western bluebird usually nests in holes in dead ponderosa pines. Like its eastern cousin, it has a reddish breast and blue wings, but it also has red on its back; sometimes it is called the chestnut-backed bluebird.

The mountain bluebird nests in the lower meadows of the Park and in burned areas near timberline. After the young leave home, usually in early August, the birds migrate vertically to meadows above timberline where they flash their true blue for a few weeks, then descend to the plains to migrate horizontally south.

William Cooper in Wild Basin in 1908 must have seen both varieties of bluebirds, but probably the mountain bluebird, all-over blue, was new to him, and he had it in mind—perhaps in eye—when he named Bluebird Lake. As he walked upstream from Ouzel Lake, already named by Enos Mills, Cooper named the next lake Ptarmigan,

32

the small pond higher up he called Bluebird, and the highest Pipit Lake. On their 1915 map the U. S. geological surveyors changed Ptarmigan to Bluebird, ignored the pond, and retained Pipit; in 1961 they named Lark Pond.

Bluebird Lake had a name before Cooper went to Wild Basin—Arbuckle Reservoir #2. Frank P. Arbuckle was a Denver man, prominent in business and in the Democratic Party, who also owned a ranch six or seven miles above Lyons on the North St. Vrain River. (His death in New York in 1896 made the front page of the *New York Times* not only because of his importance but because of the unanswered question—was he murdered?) At his death his widow, Emma, ran a resort on the St. Vrain ranch until 1903 when, according to the *Lyons Recorder,* William A. Welch became the new owner of the "Arbuckle summer resort, known as the Dale St. Vrain."

In 1902 Mrs. Arbuckle, searching for water after a dry summer, her 24-year-old son, Frank, and the caretaker of her ranch, Jabez Billings, filed on five reservoirs in Wild Basin and started to build dams on two of them. Within two years they sold out to a group of Longmont business men organized as the Arbuckle Reservoir Company. In 1933 the Reservoir Company sold its rights in these reservoirs and in another Wild Basin reservoir (Sandbeach Lake) to the city of Longmont for $92,000. To this day Longmont city officials refer to Bluebird, Pear, and Sandbeach as "the three Arbuckles."

Of the original five Arbuckle filings, Pear Reservoir and Bluebird Lake are the only two on which dams were built in 1902. Between 1912 and 1919 the Arbuckle Reservoir Company constructed a larger dam on Bluebird Lake. Rolley Neely, one of the rodmen on the survey, recalled details of that late summer job. The men packed in with two mules, their bread on the lead mule; arrived in camp they found no bread. The second mule, following closely, had eaten every bit. The rodmen threw together a raft of sorts to measure the depth of the lake. The engineer in charge declined to board but the two boys put to sea, their soundings showing a depth of 50 feet in one place. For triangulation points the party used Ouzel Lake, which they called Lily Lake; Mahana Peak; and "a mountain to the south." The country was so rough Neely wore out three pairs of shoes in eight days, and came out in a September blizzard with wet, cold feet.

The next summer, 1914, the construction of the dam started, accompanied by problems in transportation. The reinforcing steel was chained in bundles to the axle beam between two wagon wheels, one end left dragging on the ground. The driver balanced on the axle and urged four straining horses up the narrow trail.

Donkeys packed sacks of cement to Bluebird Lake, but no sand was there to mix with it. Plenty of granite—mountains of granite. The contractor undertook to make sand out of granite. Three days the men worked to take a rock-crusher apart, load it on mules, drive the mules to camp, and reassemble the crusher. For power they used an old automobile engine packed in the same way. Cal Maier of Longmont, water commissioner since 1934, recalled in 1965 that "the granite was not very fine, not much cement, but for 40 years the dam held together pretty good."

Boulder Brook, Field   GLACIER GORGE

The Boulder Field, the famous hazard on Longs Peak, marks the end of the horse trail now as it did in 1873 when Isabella Bird rode "as far as what, rightly or wrongly, are called the 'Lava Beds,' an expanse of large and small boulders, with snow in their crevices." William Byers called the Boulder Field "a rocky plain tilted upward," and in the late 1880's F. H. Chapin wrote, "On this Bowlder Field, covering perhaps a hundred acres, are strewn great slabs of granite,—some as much as 20 feet in width and 30 feet in length,—and between them are heaped bowlders, great and small." Whatever he calls it, the climber on the Boulder Field of Longs Peak prays for balance as he leaps from rock to shifting rock, and is tantalized by water running beneath the boulders far out of reach.

Boulder-Grand Pass   GRAND LAKE, WILD BASIN

The name refers to the counties joined by the pass. Jack Moomaw proves his theory that Indians used the pass by showing various kinds of rocks he picked up on the pass which are not indigenous to the area. Who else but Indians would have imported them?

Bowen Gulch, Mtn.—Two miles southwest of Baker Mtn.

All that is recorded about Jim Bowen is that he was a prospector who discovered the Wolverine Mine on the side of Bowen Mountain. The present road, hardly fit for a donkey, that ascends Bowen Gulch to the Wolverine Mine, continues to North Park. This was a wagon road in the 1880's connecting Teller City and Gaskill at the foot of Bowen Gulch.

Box Canyon   NEVER SUMMER

Many canyons in the Rockies bear this name. Visitors feel that the stream is so boxed in by cliffs that neither they nor the water will ever find an exit.

Box Lake   WILD BASIN

This name appears on a reservoir filing, but Jack Moomaw called it Pit Lake.

Bridal Veil Falls 9062'   MUMMY RANGE

Bryant, Mt. 11,034'
Grand Lake summer people suggested the name Mt. Commodore for this peak, but the Colorado Geographic Board preferred Mt. Bryant. The two names refer to the same man—Commodore William H. (Harry) Bryant, a lawyer, graduate of the University of Virginia, who lived in Denver but summered at Grand Lake. Why the nautical title, 2000 miles from an ocean? Because Bryant was the first Commodore of the Grand Lake Yacht Club, the highest (according to the local Chamber of Commerce) yacht club in the world. Organized in 1901, it held its first race the next year. Harry Bryant in a flat-bottomed scow raced Richard Crawford Campbell in a rowboat, both crafts being rigged with sails.

In 1912 the Grand Lake Yacht Club built its club house on the north shore of Grand Lake on land donated by J. N. Pettingell. (See Pettingell Lake.) Sir Thomas Lipton gave a $1,500 silver loving cup, which is still passed around to the winner of the yacht races held during the August Regatta Week. The modern skipper must cope not only with the vagaries of mountain breezes but with the hazards of high-powered motor boats, a contingency undreamed of by Commodore Harry Bryant in his flat-bottomed scow. Mrs. Bryant was the daughter of Governor Routt, and Mrs. Routt was the sister-in-law of Bayard Craig. So one family of summer cottagers has three names on the map—Mt. Bryant, Routt National Forest and Mt. Craig.

Buchanan Creek, Pass
Buchanan Creek flows from beautiful Buchanan Pass. The trail across the pass appears as a wagon road on Nell's maps of Colorado from 1899 to 1907, and before that the route, like almost every other pass over the Front Range of the Rockies, was surveyed for a possible railroad route. The history of the name Buchanan is probably recorded in some obvious book but the authors of this dictionary have failed to find it. Our guess is that Buchanan was a railroad surveyor, and we wish some railroad buff would write a history of the many surveys of the Front Range passes. Or Buchanan might have been a pioneer—Captain Buchanan hunted out of Left Hand Creek, and a Buchanan homesteaded in Big Elk Park.

The name of the pass is usually credited to James Buchanan, who defeated Fremont to become the pre-Civil War President of the United States. If this is true (but we have found no documentation to prove it) the name is more relevant than most political names on western maps because Buchanan was the president who signed the bill creating Colorado Territory on February 28, 1861.

An earlier name for Buchanan Creek was the East Fork of the Grand River, just as Arapaho Creek was originally the South Fork.

Buck Creek—Estes Park; Buck Gulch, Lake—Wild Basin

The historian would like to attribute this name to one of the earliest residents of the Estes area, Hank Farrar, called Buck by Milton Estes, Buckskin by Enos Mills, but doubtless Buck Creek, Gulch, and Lake were named for the male deer. When a buck comes to a lake to drink, the sight of him lifting his antlered head from the water is reason enough to name a lake for him.

Bulwark Ridge 10,890'   Mummy Range

Butterfly Burn   Estes Park

About 1929 fire destroyed the lodgepole pines that covered this slope of Twin Sisters Peak. Ruth Ashton Nelson, Park naturalist, immediately started a year-after-year ecological study of the burn. Aspens started to grow immediately since their roots had not been killed by fire. In a few years the aspens covered an area shaped like a butterfly, green in summer, yellow in autumn—the Butterfly Burn.

C

Cabin Creek   Wild Basin

According to Joe Mills, who must have heard the tale from Elkanah Lamb, Kit Carson spent a winter (probably in the 1840's) on the eastern slope of Longs Peak, and in the spring bargained with Indians to help him carry out his furs. Parson Lamb pointed out the remains of an old cabin at the foot of Cabin Rock as the Kit Carson cabin. This impressed young Joe Mills, and for his own cabin he selected a location near Cabin Rock. In 1926 Joe Mills recorded in his book *A Mountain Boyhood* that "the walls, the hearth, and part of the stone chimney still mark the site of that stone cabin" built by Kit Carson. In 1966 a pile of rocks remains. Cabin Creek is named on the 1882 Township Survey, and subsequent maps; Cabin Rock is located on the 1911 Cooper-Babcock map.

Cache la Poudre River   Mummy Range, Never Summer

This name is one of the few of French origin in Colorado, stemming from the French-speaking Creoles of St. Louis. In 1836 fur trappers, caught in an early fall snowstorm, dug a hole beside a stream, not far from present Bellvue, in which they deposited some of their supplies, including black powder. Carefully they restored the surface of the ground above their cache to its natural look, even burning wood over it—an old Indian trick. The next spring, happily, they found their cache intact. They referred to the river thereafter as the hiding place of the gun powder—"La Cache la Poudre."

Ever since then, innumerable changes have been rung on the spelling and the pronunciation of the name of the river. The most ingenious of many spellings was by L. J. Eastin in his *Emigrant's Guide to Pike's Peak,* published in Leavenworth, Kansas, March 1, 1859. He wrote "Cochela Padre." To the Coloradan, the pronunciation of this name presents no problem. Just call it "The Pooder."

Cairns, Mt.   GRAND LAKE

James Cairns came from Canada in 1881 to establish the first store in the village of Grand Lake. When Cairns was the oldest living inhabitant, Abner Sprague named a collection of mountains between the North and East Inlets for him—Cairns Mountains. Maps from 1905 used this label, in the plural, until the U.S. Geological Survey in 1915 changed the name to Mt. Cairns and confined it to the mountain marked by cliffs rising above the north bank of the East Inlet.

Calypso Cascades   WILD BASIN

In Greek mythology, Calypso was a sea nymph whose charms detained Ulysses on her island for seven years. *Calypso bulbosa* is the Latin name for the charming fairy slipper, one of the 22 orchids that have been identified in Colorado. Because he was a botanist, young William Cooper knew and used the name when he surveyed Wild Basin in 1908. He gave the name to the Calypso Cascades on the Cony Creek trail that runs through a series of large patches of fairy slippers. Usually, the flower-lover is lucky if he sees more than three or four blossoms in one spot.

Cameron Pass   NEVER SUMMER

This pass was named for a peripatetic gentleman of early Colorado, General Robert A. Cameron (1828-1894). "I went to Indiana," he wrote, "when it was a wilderness, and to Chicago when it was a mud hole, and now I want to go to Colorado." This he did in 1870, as vice-president and superintendent of the Union Colony (present Greeley), in charge of greeting and locating colonists. In 1872 he organized an agricultural colony at Fort Collins; and then he became the vice-president of Fountain Colony, now Colorado Springs, where Camerons Cone bears his name. From there he moved to Canon City as warden of Colorado State Penitentiary.

Cameron explored the headwaters of the Poudre River in 1870. The pass was named for him by Union Pacific Railroad surveyors. It first saw use in 1881 as the route of a toll road to Teller City in North Park. Forty-five years later the automobile road across Cameron Pass was dedicated. Today, near the top of the pass, each summer Sunday, services are held in a church with the sky for a roof.

37

Caribou Lake; Caribou Pass 11,851' INDIAN PEAKS
Caribou is the name for northern reindeer, but that does not mean that Colorado was ever host to these animals. It was host to a man who had probably seen caribou herds in the North Country. The story is that George Lytle, one of the men who filed on the Caribou Lode in August 1869, said the Middle Boulder Creek country reminded him of the Cariboo Mountains in Alberta Province, Canada, and why not name the mine Cariboo?

It was a lucky name. The Caribou Mine produced silver by the ton. In 1873 when General U.S. Grant visited Central City, he walked from his carriage to the Teller House on a sidewalk paved (for the occasion) with silver bricks from the Caribou Mine. In 1872 a Dutch syndicate (the town of Nederland commemorates their nationality) bought the Caribou for three million dollars and made enormous profit.

But the Caribou Mine and Caribou town are far to the east of Caribou Lake and Caribou Pass. True, but a trail leads from the town across the Continental Divide and down to Middle Park, called the Caribou Trail. It crosses Arapaho Pass, which sometimes was called Caribou Pass. The 1958 Geological Survey map of the Monarch Lake quad specifies a point as Caribou Pass about a mile and a half northwest of Arapaho Pass, and not on the Continental Divide. (See Arapaho Pass.)

What about the spelling—Cariboo or Caribou? This was settled on June 27, 1871, as reported in the *Central City Register*. The U. S. Post Office Department decided to spell the name Caribou for two reasons: 1) Caribou was the accepted French spelling of the Indian name of the animal, Cariboo being a corruption; 2) Caribou would make a distinction "between two or three Cariboos up north."

Cascade Creek—INDIAN PEAKS; **Cascade Creek**—MUMMY RANGE; **Cascade Falls**—GRAND LAKE; **Cascade Lake**—ESTES PARK, MUMMY RANGE

Castle Lake, Lakes WILD BASIN
The rocks on an island in Castle Lake looked like a castle to Ranger Jack Moomaw, who named the small lake; Castle Lakes, less than a mile to the south, are really just ponds.

Castle Rock—FOREST CANYON; **Castle Mtn. 8834'**—ESTES PARK

Chaos Canyon, Chaos Canyon Cascades, Chaos Creek GLACIER GORGE
Though sometimes this canyon is called Otis Gorge, Abner Sprague thought Chaos appropriate because of the jumble of boulders.

Chapin Creek, Pass; Chapin, Mt. 12,454'

This mountain is named on Mills' map of 1905. At least three stories tell why the mountain is named Chapin. Dr. Homer James, son of the founders of Elkhorn Lodge, gallantly said he named it for his wife whom he married in 1905. Jennie Chapin and Elizabeth Foote were partners in a small general store in Estes Village.

But his sister, Eleanor J. Hondius, heard her mother say this:

> Mr. Chapin, for whom Mt. Chapin was named, was a guest one summer, and occupied one of the little bedrooms. He always kept his window open, and every day a hen would come in through the window and lay an egg on his bed.
>
> In those days, eggs were hauled in each week by wagon from the valley; when they arrived, half were broken, and the other half should have been. So Mother kept a few hens at the ranch.
>
> She didn't want Mr. Chapin to know about the hen laying an egg on his bed each day, so she would listen carefully for the hen's cackle, then hastily remove from Mr. Chapin's bed the egg and any feathers the hen might have lost. Each morning Mr. Chapin had a fresh egg for breakfast without ever suspecting where the egg had been laid.

The third and most probable candidate for Mt. Chapin stayed at the Highlands, H. W. Ferguson's hotel, in the fall of 1886 and for two succeeding summers. (Perhaps he stayed at the Elkhorn Lodge some other summer, and is the same Chapin as mentioned in Mrs. James' story.) Frederick Hastings Chapin of Hartford, Connecticut, came, with his wife, to climb the Rockies with other members of the Appalachian Mountain Club. W. L. Hallett, a cattleman who had a cottage on Marys Lake near the Highlands, acted as their guide. In 1887 Chapin named Hallett Peak; in 1888, so the story goes, Hallett named Mt. Chapin.

Chapin wrote up his Colorado climbs for the magazine of the Appalachian Mountain Club. Collected and enlarged, these were published in book form by the Club in 1889, with the title *Mountaineering in Colorado: the Peaks about Estes Park.*

Chasm Falls

Originally called Horseshoe Falls, these falls on Fall River were renamed by the father of Minnie March Service to avoid confusion with the Horseshoe Falls on Roaring River. The water of Chasm Falls drops 25 feet into a whirlpool where revolving stones are gradually enlarging a pot hole in the canyon floor.

Chasm Lake

Elkanah Lamb thought Chasm Lake occupied the crater of a

volcano. "No doubt," he wrote, "this lake occupies the opening caused by internal forces—throwing up and bursting through." Actually the lake lies in a glacial cirque. With the East Face of Longs Peak as a background, the name Chasm is appropriate and seems to have been used in pioneer times. Perhaps in 1873 it bore another name—Gold Lake. That year Captain Edward Berthoud, Colorado's engineer after whom Berthoud Pass was named, wrote this tale:

> One lake near Long's Peak is Gold Lake, which is noted, not only for its clear cold water, but is fabled by the Indians and old trappers as the resort of some *lusus naturae*, which the following legend illustrates:
>
> In Gold Lake, Indian tradition recites that there dwells, in its deep cold waters, an animal but rarely seen. It is described by them as biformal in shape, having a human head, arms and body to the waist, while the rest is the body of a horse. Rarely seen, it approaches the shore only in the evening. The resemblance of this animal is ludicrously like the classical Centaur of the Greeks. . . . Is this an evidence of Indo-Greek tradition revived by a lousy Arapahoe near Long's Peak? or is it tradition repeating itself? We pause!

Chasm View   GLACIER GORGE, WILD BASIN

From this point the climber on the Cable Route can look down, down, down the East Face of Longs Peak to Chasm Lake—definitely a chasm view.

Chickadee Pond   WILD BASIN

This is one of the bird names given to lakes in Wild Basin by W. S. Cooper. The mountain chickadee lives in the northern Rockies all the way to timberline, winter and summer. It is a little thing, grayish, with a black bib and cap, and a white stripe running above each eye. It is friendly, especially around cabins, where it will perch its featherweight on a patient hand offering doughnut crumbs. Along trails and in the forests it chirps its friendly call—chick-a-dee-dee.

Chickaree Lake   GRAND LAKE

Chickarees are the common, chattering tree squirrels of the mountains, sometimes called pine or Fremont squirrels. They are gray with rusty yellow on the back. Small, alert, agile, they run up and down tree trunks in the spruce and fir forests, leap from tree to tree, chatter incessantly in winter as well as summer. They eat seeds from the cones of evergreen trees, piling up debris sometimes to a depth of a foot or more. The tuft-ear or Abert squirrel lives lower than the chickarees in ponderosa pine country.

Squirrels carry their bushy tails high over their backs. This habit was observed by the Greeks; the word squirrel comes, by a circuitous

40

route, from two Greek words that mean shaded rear-end. The way most Americans pronounce the word squirrel is so difficult to imitate that suspected spies are sometimes asked to pronounce it to prove their nationality.

Chiefs Head Peak 13,579' GLACIER GORGE, WILD BASIN

This name was well established before Cooper used it on his 1911 map, although on the 1910 Burlington map it appears as Mt. Barrett. In 1915 Bethel complained that he could not find out who Barrett was, and wanted to call it Comanche Peak. The U.S. Board on Geographic Names refused this request, probably for two reasons: 1) Comanche had already been used for a peak by the 1876 King Survey, northwest of Hagues Peak; 2) they preferred the already established local name, Chiefs Head. The 1914 Arapahos called it Head Mountain since they saw in it the profile of the head of an Indian, complete with war bonnet, just as we see it today. The war bonnet lies to the south, the face has a long forehead, a distinct nose and chin, and even an eye when the snow stays late into the summer. Some imaginative people can see the outline of the chief's body stretching north.

Chipmunk Lake MUMMY RANGE

The stone walls provided as guard rails by the Park Service at parking areas on Trail Ridge Road, like Many Parks Curve and Farview Curve, serve as dining tables for little animals and birds who demand handouts from human visitors. Chipmunks and ground squirrels stuff their expandable cheeks with peanuts or bread and whisk off to eat or store them. To tell which is a chipmunk, which a ground squirrel is easy. Chipmunks have stripes on their cheeks, and down the middle and sides of their backs; ground squirrels are larger and have stripes only on their sides. Also chipmunks scurry a bit faster than the larger ground squirrels.

The word chipmunk comes from two Ojibway Indian words meaning headfirst and mouth, the idea being that these little creatures—about six inches long with a five inch tail—lead with their mouths, which they certainly do when a handout is possible. Chipmunks build long tunnels below the frost line and live in rooms enlarged in the tunnels. One is a bedroom furnished with a grass mattress; others are pantries. Their worst enemy is the weasel, who can insinuate his body into their holes.

Chiquita Creek, Lake; Chiquita Mtn. 13,069' MUMMY RANGE

In 1902 a book was published called *Chiquita, An American Novel; the Romance of a Ute Chief's Daughter.* It was written by Merrill Tileston (see Mt. Tileston), published by Merrill in Chicago.

The novel reads no better today than in July 1902, when Ellis Meredith, literary reporter for the *Rocky Mountain News*, reviewed it.

41

She headed her article, "This is the place for the Scalping Knife." She even punned on the "B-Uteful Chiquita."

The story tells that Jack, a stalwart American, camped in the White River country of the Utes. Chief Yamanatz had a beautiful daughter, Chiquita, who longed to be educated so that she could help her tribe. When Jack mentioned that a college education cost money, Yamanatz took him to the California Desert where they scooped up enough gold from the floor of the Blazing Eye Mine to send Chiquita to an eastern woman's college. She prepared to help her people by studying French, Spanish, German, Russian, Greek, Latin, elocution, and music. Jack married a white girl; Chiquita, home with her tribe, died young. Included in the book are accounts of the Meeker Massacre, a climb of Longs Peak, and a poem commemorating the death of the eccentric New Englander, Carrie J. Welton, the first woman to die on Longs Peak.

Enos Mills may have been responsible for naming the mountain after the book. (Maybe he liked the author.) It appears on Mills' 1905 map, which is based on information furnished by Abner Sprague; but Sprague disclaimed naming it.

The mountain might have been named, not for the novel, but for Chipeta, wife of Chief Ouray of the Utes. Her name had variant spellings, such as the Spanish diminutive Chiquita, and Sabeta, a peak in the San Juan mountains which Henry Gannett stated was named for Ouray's wife.

Cirque Lake   MUMMY RANGE

When glacial ice pulls away from a mountain, it may pull rocks with it, leaving steep walls in the form of an amphitheater, usually with a lake at the bottom. This recess is called a cirque. The Park contains many cirque lakes, the two most noted being Chasm Lake and Iceberg Lake.

Cirrus, Mt. 12,797'   NEVER SUMMER

Meteorologically speaking, cirrus is the name for the highest clouds, isolated, feathery, and rather filmy. Four of the peaks in the Never Summer Mountains are named for cloud forms. This pleasant invention was the brain child of James Grafton Rogers who named Mounts Cirrus, Cumulus, and Nimbus in 1914; in August 1921 Roger Toll added Mt. Stratus. (See Mt. Howard.)

Cleaver, The   GRAND LAKE, WILD BASIN

This marks the termination of the distinctive, slender, granite ridge extending from Isolation Peak. It was named because of its shape by Phillip Ritterbush and his committee of five of the Park staff who made up names for the 1961 Geological Survey map.

Colorado River

The word is Spanish, meaning rusty red. Anyone who sees the muddy water of the Colorado as it flows through the Grand Canyon in Arizona knows why it is called red. In the southwest, the stream has had other names but has been called the Colorado River since Spanish times. Upstream, above the confluence with the Green in Utah, the river has had many names. In 1776 Father Escalante spoke of the Rio San Rafael, a name retained on the San Rafael Swell in Utah. To Fremont in 1843 it was the Grand River, but ten years later the Gunnison-Beckwith report called the present Gunnison River the Grand, and said it "joins the Nah-un-kah-rea, or Blue River of the Indians and mountain men, which rises in Middle Park, and is erroneously called Grand River on some of the most correct maps."

By the 1860's, on most maps, the river names had sorted themselves out. A stream rising above Breckenridge was the Blue. The water that rises in the inverted U made by the Continental Divide in the northwestern corner of the Rocky Mountain National Park, and leaves the state of Colorado below Grand Junction, was definitely the Grand River. Hence Grand Lake, and Grand Junction where the Gunnison River makes a junction with the Grand. Below Moab, Utah, as geography students learned by rote, the Grand and Green formed the Colorado.

So matters stood until Edward F. Taylor (1858-1941) arrived in Glenwood Springs in 1887. From that time, first as state senator, then as powerful U.S. Congressman, he campaigned to change the name of the Grand River to the Colorado River. But he reckoned without his neighbor states. Arizona felt it was bad enough to explain that the Grand Canyon of the Colorado River was in Arizona, not Colorado, but to change the name of the upper river to Colorado was too much! Utah rose to defend its Green River—it was longer than the Grand. This was true. Colorado replied, equally truthfully, that the Colorado branch produced more water. In 1921 the Utah Legislature introduced a bill to change the name of the Green River to Colorado, but failed to vote on the measure in that session. The astute politician, Ed Taylor, knowing that the Utah Legislature did not meet again for two years, encouraged the Colorado State Legislature on March 24, 1921, to pass a bill renaming the Grand River. Seething neighbor states asked the U.S. Board on Geographic Names for a decision. The Board declined. The matter went to Congress. Here Utah did not complain, probably because of some political move of Ed Taylor. On July 25, 1921, President Harding signed the bill into law, presenting the pen with which he signed it to Representative Taylor of Colorado. The name became officially the Colorado River from La Poudre Pass to the Gulf of California.

Columbine Bay, Creek—GRAND LAKE, LAKE GRANBY; **Columbine Falls** —GLACIER GORGE; **Columbine Lake**—GRAND LAKE; **Columbine Lake**— INDIAN PEAKS

The type specimen of the Colorado columbine was found in 1820 by Dr. Edwin James, Colorado's first botanist and climber, south of Elephant Rock near Palmer Lake. This was about the first of July, the height of the columbine season for the 8000-foot altitude. From the foothills to alpine meadows, from June to September, one can follow columbines in the Rockies. It is as ubiquitous as it is lovely. It was made the official state flower of Colorado in 1899. DO NOT PICK!

The word columbine comes from the Latin word for dove, but its scientific name—*aquilegea coerulea*—comes from a larger bird. *Aquilegea* is akin to "eagle," because the flower has spurs like an eagle's talons. *Coerulea* means cerulean blue—azure—like the Colorado blue sky at its deepest. When Dr. Edwin James saw blue flowers above timberline on Pikes Peak in 1820 he wondered if their proximity to the sky had any relation to their color. The Colorado columbine ranges in color from lavender through the blues to all white, but is never yellow or red like the garden varieties. True, July on the Western Slope produces a red columbine, but it lacks the petal skirts of the blue variety.

In the Rocky Mountain National Park columbines have left their names on bays, creeks, falls, lakes, but not on a mountain. This seems a pity because the rare dwarf columbine, intense blue, sometimes rewards the exhausted climber on the very summit rocks.

Comanche Peak 12,702'   MUMMY RANGE

This peak was named on King's Atlas of 1876. There must be a story behind the name, else why would a mountain here be named for a tribe of plains Indians who lived mostly below the Arkansas River? Their savage treatment of Texans earned them an evil reputation. (See also Mahana Peak.)

Coney Creek, Lake, Upper Coney Lake   INDIAN PEAKS

The dictionary accepts two spellings for the name of this little animal—cony and coney—as does the U.S. Geological Survey. Perhaps to distinguish the two creeks, it labels the one that runs into the Middle St. Vrain as Coney Creek; the one that runs into the North St. Vrain as Cony Creek. (See Cony Creek.)

Continental Divide

All visitors to the early West endeavored to explain the Continental Divide. "Water-parting," a succinct and accurate term, was seldom used; the explanation in nine out of ten books of travel went into poetic detail thus: If two drops of water fall within an inch of each other on either side of the line that marks the division of the drainage systems of the Americas, one drop ends in the Atlantic Ocean, one in the Pacific. "So close in infancy, so far separated at their watery grave," added Crofutt in his 1881 *Grip-Sack Guide to Colorado.* It was a relief in the 1930's when Thomas Hornsby Ferril produced another version in his poem "Old Men on the Blue":

> Up where the Mississippi River ends
> And the bodies of the frozen dragonflies
> Begin to float to the Gulf of California.

Geological forces did not leave a simple straight line on the map of the Americas to divide the waters of the Atlantic Ocean from the Pacific; the Continental Divide is erratic. Look at what it does in the northwestern part of the Rocky Mountain National Park, where it makes an inverted U-turn around the little creeks that flow into the North Fork of the Colorado River. Then it twists generally southeastward, at Sawtooth Mountain reaching its most easterly point in North America. Farther south it makes a right-angle turn, so that between South Arapaho Peak and Mt. Neva it runs due west.

Moreover, geological forces put only two of Colorado's 53 fourteen-thousand-foot peaks along "The Hump," a colloquial term for the Continental Divide; these two, Grays and Torreys Peaks, stand squarely on it. You don't believe that Longs Peak is not on the Divide? Trace the water that flows from it. It is all collected by the Big Thompson or the St. Vrain en route to the Atlantic Ocean by way of the South Platte, the Missouri, the Mississippi, and the Gulf of Mexico.

Cony Creek—Wild Basin; **Cony Lakes**—Wild Basin, Indian Peaks; **Cony Pass**—Grand Lake, Wild Basin

A cony is a small animal of great personality and many names, including two spellings—cony and coney. Another name—pika (pronounced pie' ka) —comes from the Mongols of the Ural Mountains. The cony's high-pitched squeak earns him the name of Eek, and Joe Mills called him Little Chief Hare.

"If you pick a cony up by his tail his eyes will fall out," mountain guides have been known to tell children. The cony is quite safe from this fate, however, not only because he has no tail but because he moves much too fast for a child to catch; so fast that he can usually dodge the talons of swooping hawks by disappearing under rocks. He has more trouble eluding vicious weasels, especially the white and hungry weasels of winter. The cony lives in rockpiles, usually above timberline, but the rugged climate does not force him to hibernate. As summer draws to a close, he frenetically collects grasses to cure and store beneath the rocks for his winter hay stacks. Mountain climbers like to watch these characters though they have difficulty seeing them because conies are the color of rocks—in fact they never would see them if the conies were not so vociferous. (See also Coney Creek.)

Cooper Peak 12,296' INDIAN PEAKS

On the 1958 Isolation Peak quad map this peak appears as Copper Peak, but on the 1961 map of the Rocky Mountain National Park this name is spelled Cooper—a typographical error to be corrected on the next edition, an embarrassed Geological Survey man of Denver stated. That will make eight Colorado mountains called Copper. The name on this mountain reflects abortive attempts to make copper mining pay in such mines as the Copper King and the Fourth of July. But the name Cooper has significance in this country, too. William S. Cooper named what we know as Ogalalla Peak for his father. So now we have by chance and temporarily a Cooper Peak just south of the one previously so named.

Copeland Falls, Lake, Moraine WILD BASIN

For a man who has left his name on these features as well as on a mountain, little is known about John B. Copeland. A man of that name pioneered in Central City in the 1860's and was still there in the 1870's. Starting in 1889, "Old Man Copeland," as Lon C. Allen of Longmont remembers him, homesteaded 320 acres near Copeland Lake. He proved up on the homestead March 4, 1896.

On February 2, 1900, *The Denver Times* reported that the Colorado State Game and Fish Department had brought suit against John B. Copeland for "keeping fish in his lake without first securing a license." The license cost $10 for two years; the fine for violation was $10 to $500. How the pioneer must have sputtered that in the old days he could have kept his own fish in his own lake without asking anybody's permission, much less pay $10 for a license, and he would not have had to buy a fishing license to catch his own fish from his own lake for his own dinner, either. Something, perhaps the sputtering, softened the heart of the Game and Fish Department. They agreed to withdraw the case "if Copeland will pay costs and take out a license. It is the intention of the officers to prosecute future cases to the end, however."

The lake into which Copeland dumped the fish that got him into trouble was a small lake in a moraine, fed by springs. Copeland dug a ditch from the North St. Vrain Creek to his lake, enlarging the pond by an earthen dam. He still owned the land in 1903 when William H. Davis of Denver filed with the State Engineer's office his intention to build a million dollar Copeland Park Reservoir. Other than surveying it and entering it on the records nothing came of this scheme.

In 1902 and 1903 the State Business Directory lists "Copeland Park, J. B. Copeland, Mgr." Does this mean that Copeland was running a resort? By 1910, Copeland or somebody else had built Copeland Lake Lodge, because the 1910 Burlington map shows it plainly on the exact spot where a lodge was built in 1914. What happened to the earlier lodge, and what happened to John B. Copeland?

In the late fall of 1913 Burns Will together with Walter McCaslin and an auto dealer in Longmont named Wylie formed a company to start Copeland Lake Lodge. They opened for business in the spring of 1914 in a building east of Copeland Lake, beside the road. Two other Longmont men, Walter Coulehan and Frank Richart, were concerned in the venture, either then or a couple of years later, when the company dissolved. Burns Will and his wife built another hotel south of Allenspark.

In 1913 the City of Longmont bought 129 acres surrounding Copeland Lake and filed on a reservoir. No million dollar scheme this—the dam was expected to cost only $63,000 and be only 43 feet high. The dam was built, the water right secured, and Longmont uses the water. From Copeland Lake it flows into the North St. Vrain, down to the diversion dam about six miles above Lyons, and from there through a conduit to Longmont.

The Copeland dam washed out in 1934. Longmont rebuilt it, erecting another earthen dam. Longmont has done nothing about exercising its priority to enlarge the dam to hold 20 times the present amount of water.

Copeland Mtn. 13,176′ WILD BASIN

Copeland Mountain is a sturdy mountain quite capable of withstanding assaults from factions that have tried to change its name. Bethel reported that an earlier name than Copeland had been Rosa, after either Monte Rosa, the high mountain in the Alps, or a girl. The Stapp family of Stapps Lake Lodge knew it as Mt. Mack, after an early rancher; the 1882 township map locates Mack's Ranch. Enos Mills wanted to call it Mt. Tyndall. (See Tyndall Glacier.)

The heaviest campaign to change the name of Copeland Mountain was conducted by admirers of Clarence King (1842-1901), who had many admirers. King was head of the 40th Parallel Survey, debunker of the Great Diamond Hoax, first director of the U.S. Geological Survey, a gifted writer, and a charming man. Also, he actually had been in Estes Park. On August 5, 1871, he headed for the uplands west of Greeley "in a light 4-wheeled buggy over a track hardly fit for a commissariat mule," wrote his biographer Wilkins. In Estes Park King lodged with Griff Evans, where he met Bostonian Henry Adams. They began a life-long friendship by climbing Longs Peak the next day.

The war for changing Copeland Mountain's name to Mt. Clarence King was triggered by William S. Cooper, who wrote the name on his map of 1911. He argued with the Board on Geographic Names for years, backed by people like Ellsworth Bethel, who wrote the Washington bureau that "Copeland, pioneer of Allenspark, was probably a worthy man, but it is one of the unfortunate names in the Allenspark region." The Board continued to refuse to sanction the change. One of the reasons was that features in other states bore King's name; another was that they approved of local names. All this time the local people, headed by Burns Will, ignored the furor over changing the name. Copeland Mountain it was to them, Copeland Mountain it is today.

Copper Peak—See Cooper Peak

Corral Creek, Park   NEVER SUMMER
Remnants of the fence of a corral may still be seen in this park. Perhaps beaver trappers built it to keep their horses from wandering where Indians could steal them, but definitely lumbermen used it for their horses. These men cut railroad ties and floated them down the Poudre to the plains. Cowboys and sheepherders were grateful for the old corral when they grazed their cattle in this park.

Cow Creek   MUMMY RANGE
This predates 1882, because the township map of that year notes the Cow Creek Stock Ranch.

Coyote Park   INDIAN PEAKS
Ancient Indians of Mexico called this animal *coyotl;* modern Americans pronounce coyote with either two or three syllables. From the prairies almost up to timberline, the coyote yelps, wails, bays the moon from hunger or loneliness, or calls to his mate. Sometimes mistaken for a small wolf—even at times called a prairie wolf—he looks much like a dog, with yellowish-gray coat and bushy tail. He is cunning, adaptable, and prolific, so that, although man continuously wages war on him (outside the National Park) the coyote survives and multiplies. He eats everything—rodents, vermin, carrion, an occasional sheep. He hunts down jackrabbits and the swift antelope by chasing them in relay teams. Indians endowed coyotes with supernatural powers, admiring them for their tricky wisdom; mountain men regarded them with superstition; modern ranchers consider them an annoyance. The coyote, always present, inevitably leaves his name on the land.

Cracktop   FOREST CANYON, GLACIER GORGE
In the early 1950's, Cheley Camp counselors named this mountain for the crack in its crest, easily seen from Trail Ridge Road.

Crags, The   ESTES PARK
The name was already established before the Cooper map of 1911.

48

Craig Mt. 12,007' GRAND LAKE

This rounded mountain stands squarely in the middle of most photographs of Grand Lake; the 1914 Arapahos called it Middle Mountain. It had other names. In 1874, W. H. Jackson, photographer of the West, called it Round Mountain. H. H. Bancroft's *History of Colorado* (1890) speaks of "Grand Lake in the immediate shadow of Round Top," and to some Grand Lake people this mass at the head of East Inlet will always be Roundtop, to balance Flattop at the head of North Inlet. Other old-timers call it Baldy, or Old Baldy, because its pate is treeless, and others call it Mt. Wescott, thinking it absurd that it does not memorialize Judge Joseph L. Wescott who looked across the lake from his cabin to the mountain for 47 years—1867 to 1914. Bert A. Goodman, a Forest Service man, reported the year Judge Wescott died that "Rev. Craig had named the mountain after himself. I believe that it should be called Mt. Wescott because that was its original name and is most favored by the natives."

These many names persist in spite of the official name given by Grand Lake villagers. A Denver magazine, *The Colorado Graphic* for August 18, 1888, reported that "Rev. Bayard Craig of this city feels altitudinous since the admiring citizens of Grand Lake have named a mountain for him. Mount Craig sounds well."

William Bayard Craig, Canadian-born graduate of Yale Divinity School, came west in 1882 at the age of 36. Since his sister-in-law was Mrs. Governor John L. Routt of Denver, he had good connections. He was pastor of Central Christian Church in Denver both before and after 1894-1902 when he served as chancellor of Drake University. Though he visited Grand Lake only a few summers, he is remembered as a man of forceful character. He dealt in real estate around Grand Lake; Craigs Point north of the outlet of the lake was once his property; and he sold the Barbee-Warren cabin to Dean H. Martyn Hart of St. John's Cathedral, Denver, also a man of character. The town of Craig also bears his name, courtesy of his influential friend, railroader David Moffat.

Crater, The; Crater Gulch—See Specimen Mtn.

Crater Lake INDIAN PEAKS

At the base of the spectacular spire of Lone Eagle Peak lies Crater Lake, not in a volcanic crater but in a glacially formed basin. The Colorado Geographic Board was pained by this scientific inaccuracy; they recommended the name be changed to Hyslop Lake, a name used by old-timers.

Crystal Lake, Little Crystal Lake MUMMY RANGE

Cub Lake   FOREST CANYON

Abner Sprague named this lake, not because he had seen a bear cub there, but because it was little, just a cub of a lake.

Cumulus, Mt. 12,725'   NEVER SUMMER

This is one of the peaks of the Never Summer Mountains that James Grafton Rogers named for cloud forms. The dictionary defines a cumulus cloud as "a massive cloud form having a flat base and rounded outlines often piled up like a mountain. It commonly appears in the early afternoon on warm days, and may afford rain or thunder gusts." Cumulus clouds piled high in the east are often the most spectacular part of a summer sunset.

Cutthroat Trout Bay   LAKE GRANBY

Native trout, commonly called "cutthroat" because of the blood-red markings on the lower jaw, were the only trout the first white men found in Colorado. The committee of local men who named the various features of Lake Granby after kinds of trout—Kamloop Bay, Rainbow Bay, Lochleven Cove—wisely added the word Trout to Cutthroat Trout Bay; Cutthroat Bay might not entice fishermen.

D

Dark Mtn. 10,859'   MUMMY RANGE

The staff of the Rocky Mountain National Park proposed this name in 1942 because the mountain is covered with dark conifers and is near Black Canyon.

Deer Island—LAKE GRANBY; Deer Ridge—WILD BASIN; Deer Ridge, Deer Mtn.—ESTES PARK

In 1880 Chapin used the name Deer Mountain, probably an old name then. In 1912 or 1913 the ladies of Estes Park, who later organized as the Estes Park Woman's Club, built a trail to the top of Deer Mountain.

The kind of deer in the Park is the mule deer. He has big ears like a mule, a small rump patch, and his white tail waves a black tip. The fawns, often twins, wear spots for camouflage. Deer are curious and may stand watching a passer-by as long as the passer-by quietly watches them. Usually anyone on a trip into the park who really looks for deer will see them.

Desolation Peaks 12,949'   MUMMY RANGE

Climbers gave this anthropomorphic name to these rocky summits, according to the National Park Service who recommended the name in 1961.

Devils Gulch— (Northeast of Estes Park)
The Devils Gulch road belies its name as it gently rises northeast of Estes Park to an elevation of 7980 feet. Then it sinks 600 feet in about a mile to the floor of West Creek, a branch of the North Fork of the Big Thompson. Perhaps it earned its satanic reputation from the way the clouds boil up from it, like smoke spewing out of Hell, long after the sun has burned off the clouds on the higher slopes. Hayden labeled this Devils Cañon in his 1877 atlas, and indicates no trail dropping down it. Eventually a trail was built, and then a wagon road which was used by early automobiles but with difficulty. George Dennis, who homesteaded at the foot of Devils Gulch, was the road overseer for the North Fork of the Big Thompson. In his Model-T Ford he took an hour to drive to the top of Devils Gulch, a ten-minute drive today (but the road still involves a precipitous hairpin turn).

Hayden's designation of Devils Cañon probably changed to Devils Gulch by popular western usage; not *gorge,* which word is western but derives from an Old French word meaning *whirlpool,* nor *gully* which is cousin to *gullet,* also French, but *gulch,* a purely western word. Webster's Dictionary gives it no lineage, suggests it perhaps imitates the sound of gushing water, and ends the discussion with "Orig. Western U. S."

In contrast to Devils Gulch, quiet Glen Haven lies near its foot, a community originally sponsored by the Presbyterian Assembly Association.

Dickinson, Mt. 11,831'   MUMMY RANGE
A rancher named Dickerson lived near this mountain; the mountain was not named for him, local opinion to the contrary, but for a visiting lady. Enos Mills suggested the name Dickinson to the Colorado Geographic Board about 1914. The lady so honored was the first woman on record to climb Longs Peak. The date—September 1873.

Miss Anna Dickinson was 31 years old, attractive, dynamic, with a flexible voice, artfully controlled, with which she thrilled audiences as a lady lecturer. When just out of her teens, Anna lectured, by invitation, the senators of the United States, inspiring them to finish the Civil War. She was for the Union, against slavery, and for woman suffrage. Between engagements as a lecturer, she went on the stage as a tragedienne.

Miss Dickinson had many beaux; the one she was interested in was Whitlaw Reid, in 1872 the editor-in-chief of Greeley's *New York Tribune.* Another beau was Ralph Meeker, son of Nathan Meeker who founded the Union Colony at Greeley, Colorado. Ralph worried when in 1873 Anna had a fit of depression. He persuaded her that the Colorado climate would invigorate her. Correctly chaperoned by her clergyman brother, Anna came west. Ralph was right; she was invigorated sufficiently to ride burros up Pikes, Grays, and Lincoln Peaks. For Mt. Elbert she borrowed a government mule and guide from a survey party. Presumably she was the first woman to gain the top of this, at present the highest mountain in Colorado. (In 1873 the honor of being the highest vacillated between Mt. Lincoln and Sierra Blanca.)

By September 1873 Miss Anna thought climbing was over for the season, but in Estes Park she met F. V. Hayden and James Gardiner, surveyors. She noted that Hayden's eyes were blue and he had soft brown hair; Gardiner's eyes were amber and his hair was gold. Doubtless the gentlemen noted Miss Dickinson's small but shapely appearance. What Gardiner later wrote about Miss Anna, however, referred not to her charms but to her political influence, she being "in" with the powerful *New York Tribune*. Gardiner needed her influence. The surveyors of the West each winter had to wheedle appropriations out of Congress for the next summer campaigns, and Gardiner wrote that Miss Dickinson was "no mean power to enlist in a cause." His method of enlisting her support was to ask her to climb Longs Peak with the survey party.

This, the largest group up to that time to attempt the ascent of Longs Peak, included Anna, Hayden and Gardiner, and Anna's brother, the Reverend Mr. John Dickinson; her admirer, Ralph Meeker; William Byers, the mountain-climbing editor of the *Rocky Mountain News;* and seven others. Longs was one peak to whose top Anna could not ride a burro, but she got there with the aid of a lemon. ("Never climb without a lemon," was her advice to mountaineers.) She carried to the summit a yard-long, spring tape measure, a puzzling piece of mountaineering equipment. On its metal case she scratched her name and left it on the peak. Abner Sprague saw this on the summit of Longs Peak in July of 1874, but on his next visit the metal case and records of other climbs, including those of the 1868 Powell first ascent, had disappeared except for pieces of a photograph of Powell which had been riddled with bullets.

After the climb, camping below timberline, the Hayden party sat by the fire kept blazing "with heaps of whole trunks of dead trees," and talked "of all things that touch the brain and soul," Anna wrote. From this discussion came decisions to name two mountains near Longs Peak: one, Mt. Meeker for Nathan Meeker of the Union Colony; the other, Mt. Lady Washington.

Anna's record of being the first woman to climb Longs Peak was a narrowly won distinction, since her party met, at the foot of the mountain, three women in another group about to ascend. They may not have made the summit, but the next month dumpy Isabella Bird of the magic pen climbed to the top. She started out in boots loaned her by Griff Evans, her host, but discarded them in favor of a pair of small overshoes she found in the boulders of the "Lava Beds," presumably left by Miss Dickinson. In July of 1874, the next year, the *Rocky Mountain News* reported that Longs Peak climbers "near the tip-top. . . found a cloak folded in the crevice, just where the redoubtable Anna Dickinson had left it, forgetfully, last September when she climbed to that dizzy pinnacle. The garment was forwarded."

Dorothy, Lake 12,061' INDIAN PEAKS

Henry Lehman had a granddaughter named Dorothy, and she is the only Dorothy that has been mentioned as a possible explanation of the name of this lake. The Lehman Ranch was on the South Fork of the Colorado River below Monarch Lake, and the Lehmans rode over Arapaho Pass whenever they came to Denver. On the east side of the pass the trail skirted Lake Dorothy.

Doughnut Lake FOREST CANYON

Dr. Workman or Julian Hayden, on the fishing trip which resulted in naming the Gorge Lakes, thought of doughnuts because the lake is small and round and has an island in the middle. This may be the lake The Colorado Mountain Club intended to call Terra Tomah Lake. (See Gorge Lakes and Terra Tomah Mountain.)

Dove, The GLACIER GORGE, WILD BASIN

Paul Nesbit, whose love affair with Longs Peak resulted in a pamphlet telling all about it, reports that The Dove is the obvious name for the snowbank lying above the Keyhole which resembles "a white bird flying downward with wings outstretched, that is, until the right wing melts away in late summer."

Dragons Egg Rock WILD BASIN

Named about 1921 by Ranger Jack C. Moomaw.

Dream Lake GLACIER GORGE

Dream Lake was once known as Emerald Lake, and Dr. Workman of Fern Lake Lodge called it Lake Ursula, not for a girl but for *ursus,* the Latin word for bear, because it was near Bear Lake. George Barnard named this Dream Lake during The Colorado Mountain Club's second annual outing in 1913. Barnard was chairman of four of the first five outings of the Club, generously making it possible for others to share his ability to penetrate into high country, especially of the northern Front Range. He led the 1913 outing to Bear Lake, the 1914 outing from Grand Lake to Fall River, and the 1916 outing to Wild Basin. (The Colorado Mountain Club returned to Wild Basin in 1919 and to Shipler Park, with Roger Toll as leader, in 1921.) On these trips and many others, by himself or with Jim Rogers, Barnard worked for the Colorado Geographic Board in its search for suitable names for the Rocky Mountain National Park terrain.

George Cooper Barnard (1876-1947) was born in Michigan, lived in California, and came to Denver in 1897. He worked for the Colorado & Southern Railroad until 1910; then, as contractor, built many Park Hill homes. In 1922 he entered the real estate and insurance business. His remarkable ability to interest young people in mountains has inspired succeeding generations to do likewise.

Dry Gulch ESTES PARK

Dunraven, Mt. 12,571' MUMMY RANGE

The Irish Earl of Dunraven's name was Windham Thomas Wyndham-Quinn (1841-1926). His titles included Fourth Earl of Dunraven and Viscount Mount Earl and Adair. Fortunately the Colorado Geographic Board decided against using his full name in 1914 when they recommended Mt. Dunraven.

Besides being titled, the Irishman was a millionaire and a sportsman. In 1867, the Earl of Dunraven was a war correspondent in Abyssinia. H. M. Stanley (who later found Dr. Livingstone in darkest Africa) was also there as a reporter. One account states that the Earl and Stanley tented together. Perhaps Stanley told Dunraven about hunting in Colorado; Stanley had been in Colorado the year before. In fact, he borrowed $50 to build a raft so he could float down the Platte River to get out of Colorado.

In the winter of 1872, Lord Dunraven and two titled friends arrived in little Denver, hired a hunting guide, and, two days after Christmas, descended on Griff Evans in Estes Park. Griff put them up in one of his well-ventilated log cabins and Mrs. Evans fed them.

The hunting was superb. The next winter the Earl of Dunraven returned and by 1874 decided he would acquire the whole of Estes Park for his private hunting preserve. The Earl hired Theodore Whyte as resident manager, and acquired 10,000 to 15,000 acres of land, sometimes by purchase, more often by bribing men to declare they had homesteaded, or by using fictitious names on homestead papers. (Many of the large land holdings in early Colorado were acquired this way.) His Lordship announced in the *Rocky Mountain News* that admission to Estes Park, his game preserve, was by invitation only. But keeping people out of the area was impossible, as the Earl noted in his memoirs:

After a time people began to wander in. . . . It became evident that we were not to be left monarchs of all we surveyed. Folks were drifting in prospecting, fossicking, pre-empting, making claims; so we prepared for civilization. Made a better road, bought a sawmill at San Francisco, hauled the machinery in, felled trees, and built a wooden hotel, and did pretty well with a Chinese cook who could make venison and anything else out of bogged cow beef.

This hotel, usually called the English Hotel, operated from 1877 until it burned in 1911. The summer it opened a reporter wrote an article thanking "the noble earl" for building the hotel and for fencing thousands of acres of land "lest objectionable parties interfere with the freedom and comfort of the guests at the hotel." Dunraven last visited the Park in the middle 1880's, but before that he and his sporting friends had gay times, once so gay that the hotel manager put the noble earl and his actress companion out of his Lordship's own hotel. (Was her name Alice, as in Mt. Alice?)

South of the present Lake Estes, Dunraven's agent, Theodore Whyte, built not only the hotel but also ranch houses, stables, and a home which still stands. On George's 1913 map of Colorado this community had a name—Mountearl. Remember the Irishman's full title that included Viscount Mount Earl? Here Whyte ran what western cattlemen would call "a big spread," meaning a large cattle ranch; and he did his best to protect the Earl's claims, some spurious, to almost all of Estes Park. Whyte irritated the settlers by fencing land claimed by others, by running his cattle on other people's territory, and by threatening the neighbors in a high-handed way. Eventually, the Americans went to court. They proved that Dunraven had acquired 21 parcels of land from five or six men, none of whom had lived on the land or made improvements as specified in the homestead laws.

This troubled the Earl in Ireland. He wrote:

> People came in disputing claims, kicking up rows; exorbitant land taxes got into arrears; we were in constant litigation. The show could not be managed from home, and we were in danger of being frozen out. So we sold what we could get and cleared out, and I have never been there since.

The absentee landlord disposed of his Estes Park holdings—about 6,000 acres, in 1907. B. D. Sanborn and F. O. Stanley bought the land.

Dunraven's name remains in Estes Park though he was there less than a dozen visits, but his manager's name, Theodore Whyte, who lived in the Park at least twenty years, is not memorialized. Once there was a lake named Whyte's Lake; Bierstadt painted a picture of it. Perhaps it was the lake, made by damming Fish Creek, that stood in front of the English Hotel. W. H. Jackson took pictures of it. When the dam was allowed to break, the lake disappeared.

Theodore Whyte was not only the local representative of the Earl of Dunraven and his whipping boy but he put his heart and money (his own and his wife's) into trying to make a success of ranching. He raised alfalfa and pedigreed oats to feed his pedigreed Herefords and imported horses, never letting his stock graze on unfenced land, a point of disagreement with his American neighbors. He not only irritated the settlers by trying to protect what he considered land belonging to the Earl, but continually amused them with his British ways. He hunted the fox in pink coat with cries of "yoicks" to encourage his imported hounds, and jumped gates and fences. To supervise the estate, he drove a four-in-hand, and always returned home in time for tea.

Theodore Whyte grew up in Devon, then came to the Canadian Northwest where he trapped for three years with the Indians for the Hudson Bay Company. When he was 26, in 1872, he came to Colorado. As the Earl of Dunraven's agent, he lived in the white house that still stands in Estes Park, which his second wife, Lady Maude Ogilvy, made attractive with embroidered hangings and English silver. After his bankruptcy in 1896 he returned to England to manage an estate. In 1950 two of his daughters were living together in Scotland.

Dunraven, Lake   Mummy Range

This lake lies north of Mt. Dunraven, on the headwaters of the North Fork of the Big Thompson. The name on the lake may antedate the mountain, and certainly Dunraven Park and Dunraven Glade, lower down the North Fork on the Dunraven Trail, were in use long before the Colorado Geographic Board recommended the name of Mt. Dunraven. The Irish Earl fancied hunting on the North Fork. He had a lodge built there, equipped it with supplies, and sent servants to it when he and his guests wished to use it. Today visitors still look for the case of whisky said to be buried beneath the frost line awaiting the return of the Earl. The site of this hunting lodge was upstream from the present North Fork Ranger Station.

Later the land around the lodge was homesteaded by Fred and George Simonds who sold to Fred and Alta Sprague. Fred, who was Abner Sprague's brother, ran a resort here as late as 1909. Then the place became known as the Deserted Village. The site is now occupied by the Cheley Boys' Camp.

Dutch Creek   Never Summer

Little and Big Dutch Creeks remind us of eight Germans who formed a clique in Lulu City, as did groups of Irishmen and Swedes. Each nationality had a nickname, the Germans being known as Dutch. One night the Dutchmen, home from a spree at Grand Lake, started a free-for-all in Lulu. When the smoke cleared away, the townspeople found much damage, including a broken arm on a respectable woman. Blaming the Dutchmen, the majority of citizens ordered them out of town. The Germans climbed to the west, settling two miles above

Hichens' claims on Big Dutch Creek. The villagers still held their grudge, expressing it by climbing to a point above Dutchtown in order to shoot down on the Germans. Finally a border line was agreed on— a small ridge between Hitchens Gulch and the North Fork. The story, as told by Lloyd Redburn of Grand Lake, concludes that Dutchtown lasted longer than Lulu City.

E

Eagle Cliff Mtn. 8906'   Estes Park
The golden eagle, dark, with a seven-foot wing spread, is occasionally seen in the Park. The bald eagle, America's emblem, rarely visits the Park, and then only in winter.

Eagle Lake   Wild Basin
This is overshadowed by the Eagles Beak.

Eagles Beak   Wild Basin
Ranger Naturalist Ferril Atkins, who is studying the historic sites in Rocky Mountain National Park, has a record showing that this rock was once known as Pipit Rock. It does not stand near Pipit Lake, but is certainly more the size of an eagle than of a pipit. The Cheley Camp boys and girls have called it Eagles Beak since the early 1950's.

East Face   Glacier Gorge, Wild Basin
The East Face of Longs Peak drops vertically 1630 feet. A Princeton professor named J. W. Alexander made the first ascent of this cliff on September 7, 1922, followed in three days by Dudley Smith of Denver and Estes Park with six climbers, one a woman. Since then technical climbers laden with ropes and jangling hardware have spent hours and days on the East Face, finding new routes or essaying old ones in various kinds of weather. The smoothest part of the cliff, high and to the right, is known as The Diamond because of its shape. Two California climbers made the first ascent of The Diamond in August 1960, spending 52 hours on the job.

Longs Peak has a guidebook all its own, by Paul Nesbit. In it he lists the names of various routes and ledges of the East Face not named on the 1961 Geological Survey, such as Alexanders Chimney, Fields Chimney, Stettners Ledges, Kieners Route, and the narrow walkway known as Broadway.

A word of warning—the East Face is for technical climbers only. They must register with the Park authorities before attempting the

57

climb, and report back after the climb. This seems reasonable since the Park rangers must rescue those in trouble on the East Face.

East Inlet   GRAND LAKE
Two creeks feed Grand Lake—East and North Inlets. They have no other names, but are known only as Inlets from their beginnings on the Continental Divide to their ends in the Lake.

Echo Creek   GRAND LAKE

Elephant Island   GRAND LAKE, LAKE GRANBY
The Lake Granby businessmen who named this island must have had a reason for the name. It may be that at high water the island is only as big as an elephant; or that at low water it looks like an elephant; or that on it grow little red elephants. These flowers always amuse the young in heart, whether in Greenland or Colorado, because each blossom on its upright stem comes equipped with an elephant trunk.

Elk Tooth 12,848'   WILD BASIN
On the southern rim of Wild Basin stands Ogalalla Peak with its great arm stretching eastward. On this arm the most prominent rock was called Elktooth in location claims for mines and in an early survey for a reservoir. W. S. Cooper in his 1911 map of Wild Basin labeled this Mt. Caroline after his mother. In 1965 Dr. Cooper remarked that he was happy the name had not survived, since the highest point his mother ever reached was the top of Oldman Mountain, 8310 feet above sea level, on the usual stroll from Elkhorn Lodge.

When the Colorado Geographic Board was trying to connect ridges with their parent mountains—like Paiute, Paiute Horn—they called the point Ogalalla Horn, but the U.S. Board on Geographic Names decided in favor of the original name, but spelled it in two words, Elk Tooth.

This is the only geographic feature in the Park region that bears the name of elk; sheep aplenty—Sheep Rock, Sheep Mountain, Bighorn Flats, Rams Horn Mountain—but this is the lone elk. Abner Sprague stated that when he came to the region in 1875 he saw elk by the thousands. From the west, they crossed the Divide about Christmas time and descended into the meadowlands, there to be met by hunters with repeating rifles and four-horse teams. Hauled to Denver, the carcasses sold for three or four cents a pound. Each year thereafter fewer and fewer elk appeared. After 1880 the butchers conducted their slaughter in North Park. In the 1880's and 1890's when men were naming so many geographical features in the National Park region, they did not see elk around, so used the name but once.

About 1913 or 1914 the Forest Service brought from Yellowstone

58

National Park two railroad cars full of elk destined for the Estes Park region. At Lyons these animals were transferred to motor trucks, then released in the Park. Today the progeny of these elk gather in the fall, the mating season. The bull elks bugle their challenges across Horseshoe Park and other meadows, heedless of people who gather to hear their falsetto screeches.

The elk is a member of the deer family, kin to the English red deer sometimes called elk, the variety hunted by Robin Hood in Sherwood Forest. To distinguish between the two, our elk is called the American Elk, or Wapiti. This is an Algonquian word, accented on the first syllable by naturalists, on the second by Colorado miners who dug flakes of pure gold out of the Wapiti Mine near Breckenridge.

Embryo Lake   GLACIER GORGE
William Hickox, a fine photographer from Rochester, New York, spent three summers in Estes Park. He prized his picture of this little lake, and, deciding it needed a caption, called it Embryo Lake.

Emerald Lake   GLACIER GORGE

Emerald Mtn. 9237′   ESTES PARK
Early delegates to the Y.M.C.A. camp called this Green Mountain. Abner Sprague said in 1923 that he had long preferred Emerald Mountain. The Park rangers, wishing to avoid commonplace names, adopted Emerald for the hill.

Emmaline Lake   MUMMY RANGE
Emmaline Lake was named by Frank R. Koenig for his mother. (See Hazeline Lake and Ramsey Peak.)

Enentah, Mt. 10,781′   GRAND LAKE
The 1914 Arapahos called this *Enetah-Notaiyah* (man-mountain) because near its summit a fringe of pine trees made it look like a man's head. The Colorado Geographic Board decided on the spelling Enentah, with accent on the second syllable.

Estes Cone 11,006′   ESTES PARK, GLACIER GORGE
The 1914 Arapahos knew this and the Wind River Cliffs as the Three Buttes. The name Estes Cone predates Hayden's 1877 atlas. Geologically, a cone is an isolated remnant of erosion, conspicuous despite its relatively low height.

Estes, Lake   ESTES PARK
This lake was made and named when the Colorado-Big Thompson Project brought water through the Alva B. Adams Tunnel to fill it.

Estes Park   ESTES PARK
The word park used in connection with today's National Parks

means a tract of land kept in its natural state, but to early Colorado travelers it meant a high valley surrounded by mountain ranges, and without exception their books devoted paragraphs to the explanation of North, Middle, and South Parks (spelled parcs by the French). Smaller tracts of land surrounded by mountains were also called parks, like Estes Park, though the 1914 Arapahos expressed the same idea by calling it "The Circle."

Estes Park was named for Joel Estes (1806-1875), a Missourian, who had tried his luck in California, returned from its mines with a sizable stake, farmed in Missouri, and had then come west with the Colorado gold rush. He went into the cattle business near Fort Lupton on the South Platte River. About the middle of October 1859, he and one of his sons, Marion, Milton, or Joel, Jr.—in later years each claimed the honor—followed the Little Thompson River into the hills looking for a place to graze cattle. In 1929 Milton wrote:

> I shall never forget my first sight of the Park. . . . We stood on the mountain looking down . . . where the Park spread out before us. No words can describe our surprise, wonder and joy at beholding such an unexpected sight. It looked like a low valley with a silver streak or thread winding its way through the tall grass, down through the valley and disappearing around a hill among the pine trees. This silver thread was Big Thompson Creek. It was a grand sight and a great surprise. . . . In 1860, the year after the discovery of "The Park," as we called it from the day we came in there, we built two houses and corrals for the stock. We then returned home and drove the cattle from the Platte River ranch to the Park. Father said it would not take much, if any time, to herd the cattle, if we fenced the trail at a place before it entered the Park. . . . By 1863 father and I had made sufficient preparations to move our families to the Park.

Of Joel Estes' 13 children, three sons and a daughter were still living at home. Milton's family consisted of his wife and two babies. Milton's memoirs tell of wholesale hunting and fishing, and trips to Denver every two or three months to sell wild meat and hides. "The women of our families, my mother, sister and wife, cheerfully shared with us the rugged life of the pioneer. With dutch-ovens, iron kettles hanging over open fire places, they cooked food that could not be surpassed."

Visitors to the park agreed with Milton's opinion of the food. In April 1864, John T. Prewitt ate a beaver-tail supper at the Estes home. "That Mrs. Lady was a mighty fine cook," he wrote, and boarded with her three days. He found Joel Estes, whose slight speech impediment

60

Copeland Mountain from Copeland Lake

Photo—Willis T. Lee, U.S. Geological Survey

cott's cabin built in June 1867. Note burned trees.

GRAND LAKE

This undated photograph of Grand Lake (below) shows the wooden bridge over the outlet. Today this bridge is concrete and steel, and sportsmen fish from power boats.

(Above) Mt. Toll, Paiute Peak, and Mt. Audubon from Niwot Ridge, August 16, 1894.

Photo—Denver Public Library Western Collection

INDIAN PEAKS

LONGS PEAK

from Airplane

Taken August—1921, from Curtiss
"Standard J-1" plane. Alt. 14,500 ft.

Thomas F. Fanton

THE BOULDER FIELD

This shelter house stood from 1927-1937 in the Boulder Field on Longs Peak.

Photo—Glenn Gebhardt

The Keyhole above the Boulder Field.
Photo — William Henry Jackson, courtesy State Historical
Society of Colorado

LONGS PEAK FROM TRAIL RIDGE ROAD

Photo—Elwyn Arps

Baker Mountain and Green Knoll showing the course of the Grand Ditch.

NEVER SUMMER MOUNTAINS

Mt. Richthofen, named for a German baron.

A close-up view of Arrowhead Lake, the largest of the Gorge Lakes.

FOREST CANYON

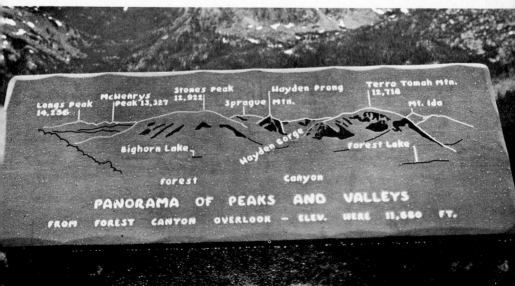

Longs Peak 14,256 — McHenrys Peak 13,327 — Stones Peak 12,922 — Hayden Prong — Sprague Mtn. — Terra Tomah Mtn. 12,718 — Mt. Ida

Bighorn Lake — Hayden Gorge — Forest Lake

forest Canyon

PANORAMA OF PEAKS AND VALLEYS

FROM FOREST CANYON OVERLOOK — ELEV. HERE 11,680 FT.

Photo—Willis T. Lee, U.S. Geological Su

Chapin, Chiquita, and Ypsilon mountains above Horseshoe
Park. Horseshoe Inn was designed in 1907 by Frank Lloyd
Wright.

MUMMY RANGE

(Left) Spectacle Lakes seen from the
"Y" on Ypsilon Mountain.

Photo—Elwyn Arps

(Right)-**GLACIER GOR**

Hallett Peak and Tyndall Gla
Emerald Lake in foreground

Photo—Willis T. Lee,
Geological S

GLACIERS—
REMNANTS OF
THE ICE AGE

A member of The Colorado Mountain Club looks at Andrews Glacier in July 1913.

(Right) A member of The Color: Mountain Club looks at Arap: Glacier in October 1958.

North Face of Lone Eagle Peak
July 26, 1940

**FOR
TECHNICAL CLIMBERS
ONLY!**

The Sharkstooth

added charm to his vivid way of expressing his thoughts, as interesting as he found hunting above timberline on Longs Peak.

William Byers, editor of the *Rocky Mountain News,* named Estes Park in an article he published on September 22, 1864, about a month after he, George Nichols, Dr. C. C. Parry, and Prof. Velie had failed to climb Longs Peak. He stayed two nights with the Estes family and named the park for them. His diary, which is disappointingly succinct, records his trip. He left Denver August 16, 1864, spent the night in Boulder with the Nichols family, and camped the next night

> six miles in the mountains at the upper crossing of the St. Vrain Creek. Long's Peak covered with new snow this afternoon. Aug. 18. Reached Estes Park and stayed for the night at Mr. Estes. A rough wagon road but can easily be made good. Left wagon 5 miles back. Aug. 19. Moved up to timberline on the north side of Long's Peak and in the evening climbed to the foot of the Peak. . . . Aug. 20. Ascended the east peak [Mt. Meeker] and found the west, or loftiest, was inaccessible. Returned to Estes in the evening. Fine day. Aug. 21. Returned to Mr. Franklin's at foot of mountains. Pleasant day. Expenses: Bill at Estes $2.20.

Mrs. Estes and her daughter-in-law were lonesome despite running a boarding house for occasional droppers-in, and Joel disliked the deep snow of the winter of 1865-66. On April 15, 1866, he left the park and moved his family to New Mexico. Today a bronze plaque on a granite boulder marks the spot where the Estes family lived, east of Lake Estes near a ragged pine tree.

How much Estes received for the sale of his holdings in the park seems to be a matter of opinion. Milton Estes wrote, "Father sold the Park, with all his right, title and interest in the same, and in consideration of one yoke of oxen. Michael Hollenbeck and a man whose real name we never knew, but who went by the name of 'Buck' made the purchase."

In June 1904 Mr. Hollenbeck of Highlandlake recalled for the *Lyons Recorder* that Estes traded his interest in Estes Park to him for one 3-year old steer. "Estes took the steer and moved out," said Hollenbeck. Enos Mills wrote:

> The Estes abdicated their scenic throne for one of the following considerations: Fifty dollars, a yearling steer, or yoke of oxen. It is impossible to say which one of these is correct, but had Michael Hollenbeck given them all these he had become a monarch dirt cheap.
>
> In a few months a Mr. Jacobs gave $250 for the claim, but in a short time it was acquired by a regular Robinson

77

Crusoe of a character called Buckskin. [A trapper named Hank Farrar.] Late in 1867 the Estes claim came under the control of Griff Evans, and in due course lost its identity by becoming some of the acres of the Earl of Dunraven. . . . Griff Evans founded the first permanent settlement by coming to stay—and by staying for nearly a score of years.

Though nothing is named for Griffith Evans in the Estes Park region, his name and hospitality are spread across the pages of almost every account written by visitors to the area in the 1870's and early 1880's. Isabella Bird noted the Evans family as "jovial, hearty Welsh people from Llanberis, who laugh with loud, cheery British laughs, sing in parts down to the youngest child, are free hearted and hospitable, and pile the pitch-pine logs half way up the great rude chimney."

Griff Evans worked hard for this reputation. How he got to Estes Park was told in the *Lyons Recorder* for December 22, 1921, by Captain George W. Brown, an early rancher near Longmont. He remembered that Mrs. Griff Evans came to tell him of the splendid opportunity they had to go to Estes Park and acquire the ranch of Jacobs, but they had no way of getting there. Captain Brown, because he had never been to Estes, offered to take them. The Evans furnishings were not a heavy load—"a broken cook stove, two chairs past using, a table with one leaf gone, and a few pieces of bedding." After the wagon turned over a few times on the rough road, the furnishings were less useful. Before he left the Evans family at the Jacobs' cabin, Captain Brown divided his bullets and powder with Evans, his flour and potatoes with Mrs. Evans. Until Griff Evans acquired a horse, he carried saddles of venison on his shoulders to the John Reece place on the South St. Vrain to trade for supplies. But sometime before 1873, Griff Evans had prospered enough to bring a piano to his cabin, on which Isabella Bird played hymns on Sundays.

Griff Evans sold his property to the Earl of Dunraven on November 7, 1878, for $500. When he left the park, with a reputed $18,000 in his pocket, he lived in the large red sandstone house that still stands near the entrance to the North St. Vrain Canyon just west of Lyons.

Eugenia Mine   GLACIER GORGE

On Battle Mountain, a short walk from the Longs Peak Trail, tumbled-down buildings mark the site of a mine dug into the mountain about 1000 feet. Not old for a Colorado mine, the Eugenia lode was recorded in September 1905—which probably means it was not named for the Empress of France, since by that time the Napoleonic fever had cooled. The company was incorporated by Carl P. Norwall and Edward A. Cudahy of Chicago. (Is this one of the meat-packing Cudahys of that city?)

78

Carl P. Norwall lived near the tunnel of the Eugenia Mine, not in a mine shack but in a comfortable home. He had two daughters and one piano, three reasons why young guides from Longs Peak Inn and Hewes-Kirkwood Lodge spent many pleasant evenings at the Norwalls.

One of these young men was Harold Dunning, a professional guide on Longs Peak in 1911-1912, from whom the information about the Eugenia Mine came. He has lived in the St. Vrain country all his life, driving his itinerant grocery van regularly from Longmont to Raymond and Allenspark. From this pleasant way of making a living, he has collected historical objects to deposit in the Loveland Historical Museum, and a vast store of historical data, which he publishes in a Loveland newspaper column and later collects in book form. His writings are a rich mine, producing more worth in authentic information than the Eugenia Mine ever produced in metal.

F

Fair Glacier   INDIAN PEAKS
Fred Fair, Boulder County surveyor and mountaineer, went into the Crater Lake country west of Pawnee Pass and discovered this small glacier in 1908. Junius Henderson of the Science Department of the University of Colorado named it Fair Glacier, and named the glacier on the east of the Divide after Fred's wife, Isabelle. (See Arapaho Glacier; Lone Eagle Peak.)

Fairchild Mtn. 13,502'   MUMMY RANGE
Lucius Fairchild (1831-1896), son of the first mayor of Madison, Wisconsin, was three times governor of his state, and the Fairchild home was the social center of Madison. In 1878 President Rutherford B. Hayes sent Fairchild to Paris, in 1880 made him minister to Spain. He was a militant veteran of the Civil War, saying, when President Cleveland, Democrat, ordered the Confederate flags returned to the southern states, "May God palsy the hand that wrote that order." In 1886, Fairchild, as commander-in-chief of the Grand Army of the Republic, traveled with thousands of other veterans to the G.A.R. convention in California. He and his daughter were headlined in the Denver papers when they stopped there and rode the narrow gauge train to Colorado's greatest tourist attraction, the Georgetown Loop.

Some of Fairchild's admirers, climbing in Estes Park, named Fairchild Mountain, one of the few purely political names in the area. Chapin mentioned Fairchild Mountain in 1888; in 1908 Ellsworth

Bethel recommended to the U.S. Board of Geographic Names that the name be retained.

Falcon Lake WILD BASIN

Falcons are small hawks, measuring from 9 to 20 inches, with pointed wings. Of the four varieties found in the Park, the prairie falcon, pigeon hawk, and peregrine falcon are less common than the sparrow hawk, which nests along the lower borders of the Park and in late summer seeks food at the elevation of Falcon Lake and above timberline.

Fall Creek; Fall Mtn. 12,258' MUMMY RANGE

Fall Creek rises on Fall Mountain and runs north to the Poudre. The creek was probably named first, and then, by association, the mountain. This is a common pattern in mountain nomenclature.

Fall River ESTES PARK, MUMMY RANGE

Indians walked up Fall River to the Pass, then down to the North Fork of the Colorado River. The 1914 Arapahos called this route the Dog Trail because they had used dogs to pull travois over it, especially when snow covered the ground. Beaver trappers used it, as did the earliest prospectors.

About 1911 various counties were building roads into the mountains, and an automobile road was planned up Fall River. In September 1913, "Tom Tynan's boys," convicts from the state penitentiary at Canon City, moved into cabins at the foot of Fall River, working on the road that year and the next.

Then someone got the idea of continuing the road across the Divide to Middle Park. Credit for this thought is usually given to Dick McQueary, a contractor in Middle Park. In 1915 Grand County Commissioners had hired him to build a road from Grand Lake to Squeaky Bob's place on the North Fork. (See Squeak Creek.) He thought—why not continue to the top of the Divide and join the Fall River road? He and Franklin I. Huntington, the engineer who blazed the North Inlet Trail down from Flattop, surveyed the road from Squeaky Bob's to the Pass in one day. They found that to hold the road to an eight per cent grade they needed nine switchbacks in five and a half miles.

Dick went to Denver where he won the enthusiastic support of Governor Ammons and of Frederick Bonfils of *The Denver Post*. Enos Mills threw his influence behind the idea. After a substantial appropriation had been secured from the State of Colorado, Dick McQueary bid $49,000 for the contract to build the western slope part of the road. He started construction in August 1917, finished the next June. In all essentials this is the route followed by the present Trail Ridge Road on its western descent.

A contractor named J. N. Jacobson finished the eastern side of the road up Fall River. In September 1920 the opening of the first automobile road linking Estes Park and Grand Lake was celebrated in Grand Lake village. The Fall River side was a test for motor cars and drivers. In one place the drivers had to back and fill to negotiate a switchback, and many a Model-T Ford was backed up the road because its reverse gear had more power than its low gear. Nevertheless the Fall River road was well-used by adventuresome motorists covered with dusters and disguised by goggles.

After Trail Ridge Road opened, traffic on the Fall River road was confined to one way—up. Now the road is closed to wheeled vehicles above Chasm Falls.

Fall River Pass 11,796′ MUMMY RANGE

There sits Fall River Pass at 11,796 feet. Four miles down the road, over 1000 feet lower in altitude, is Milner Pass. Fall River Pass does not span the Continental Divide, Milner Pass does. What does Fall River Pass cross? The divide between the waters of Fall River which flows east and the Poudre which flows north, and they both reach the South Platte River.

Fan Falls WILD BASIN

Named by Ranger Jack Moomaw.

Farview Curve NEVER SUMMER

The view extends from the Never Summer Mountains and their Grand Ditch, down the Colorado River toward Grand Lake and Middle Park.

Fay Lakes MUMMY RANGE

C. E. Fay of Tufts College climbed in this area with Chapin in 1888. Fay was later the first president of the American Alpine Club.

Fern Creek FOREST CANYON

Many walkers along Fern Creek look for an exceptionally lush growth of ferns that might have given the creek its name. This is futile because the creek was named for either trees or a lady. Take your choice:

1. Abner Sprague said he named Fern Creek because the trees in the canyon through which it runs sway in the wind like giant ferns.

2. A younger daughter of Dr. W. J. Workman said he may have named it for one of the earlier of his four wives; she was not sure, however, that one of his wives had been named Fern. Since Dr. Workman's first child was born in 1873 and his last in 1918, the younger daughter may be forgiven for not knowing definitely the name of the earlier wife.

Fern Falls   FOREST CANYON

Dr. Workman called these Lulu Falls after one of his wives, but Fern Falls became its official name.

Fern Lake   FOREST CANYON

Abner Sprague thought he named Fern Lake as well as Fern Creek. Another authority states that Mr. Turck of Denver, a friend of Dr. Workman, named Fern Lake. Yet another source gives Dr. Workman as the namer of this lake. When he first saw it he thought it was the birthplace of Fern Creek, later finding Odessa Lake higher up. Fern Lake appears on a Forest Service map of 1910, the year Dr. Workman started to build Fern Lake Lodge.

Whether or not he named the lake, Dr. Workman's lodge (enlarged by subsequent owners) made the area one of the best known beauty spots in northern Colorado. At the end of a five-mile trail, Dr. Workman built a series of cabins and a central building that housed a living room, dining room, and kitchen. The living room floor was made of cross sections of logs, sawed smooth and laid flat, with pounded dirt between. The dining room demonstrated the doctor's inventiveness by its large Lazy Susan table. Here he entertained his guests by spinning fish stories. The kitchen was well supplied by packhorses from the end of the road in Moraine Park.

Dr. William J. Workman came to Denver from his home in Ashland, Kansas, about 1900. In the winter he practised his profession, living at 1057 Race Street, Denver; but he managed to spend at least five months a year in Estes Park, fishing. He built Fern Lake Lodge in 1910 and sold it five years later so he could devote his whole time to fishing, which he did skillfully despite a withered arm. When some one asked him if he had climbed Longs Peak he looked surprised and said, "Hell, no! There are no fish up there!"

Starting in 1915 and continuing until the middle 1930's, Fern Lake Lodge was opened many winters for about two weeks for the winter outing of The Colorado Mountain Club. Supplies were laid down in the fall, with fresh food carried in by the lodge owners. Ranger Jack Moomaw, one of the sturdiest of skiers, brought in cases of eggs, and added a modern touch in 1925 by packing in a radio. The outings lasted sometimes for ten days, with capacity crowds of 45. A history of the art of skiing in Colorado could be written by observations of the skiers on the Fern Lake Trail. In 1915 they used snowshoes, some of the young men carrying skis. Soon many walked up the trail on skis, with ropes or canvas bags fastened to the skis to prevent slipping. Coming down the trail only the most expert made the corners without falling. The highlight of winter outings, whether one skied well or not, was the moonlight trip to Odessa Lake.

Fifth Lake   GRAND LAKE

The highest of the five lakes on the East Inlet of Grand Lake.

Finch Lake 9912'   WILD BASIN

Spruce and fir trees around this lake house the Cassin's finch, with its rosy red head, breast, and back. It is the only finch in the forested parts of the Park.

A related bird, the brown-capped rosy finch, nests in cliffs above timberline, where his rosy wings flash against the snowbanks as he snatches insects. This finch, indigenous to Colorado and New Mexico, winters in the foothills on the edge of the plains. Ornithologists have been known to come to Colorado just to see this rosy native.

Finger, The   ESTES PARK

Fish Bay   LAKE GRANBY

Fish Creek   ESTES PARK

Fish Creek now runs into Lake Estes, but in the days of the English Hotel it was dammed to make a lake near that resort. When the Estes family settled near Fish Creek in 1863, their second location, Joel Estes, Jr., became the fisherman of the family. His older brother, Milton, wrote that it was the duty of this youngster

> to drive up the cows, look after the horses and catch the fish the family used. . . . The largest trout that any of the family caught weighed three and one-half pounds. . . . We fished with grasshoppers or with artificial flies, which we made; and we would change the flies, until we found the color that suited the fish. . . . We kept the fly on top of the water and kept it moving, and the fish would jump after the fly. . . . It was a regular Paradise for the fisherman in those days in the Park.

Flat Top Mtn. 11,355'   NEVER SUMMER

To distinguish this mountain from the better publicized Flattop between Bear Lake and Grand Lake, the authorized spelling is in two words.

Flatiron Mtn. 12,335'   MUMMY RANGE

Frank R. Koenig, looking at this mountain from the north, thought it resembled his wife's flatiron.

Flattop Mtn. 12,324'   GLACIER GORGE, GRAND LAKE

The Park Service maintains a trail from Bear Lake to the top of Flattop Mountain. Then the trail branches. The longer branch first swings north across the Bighorn Flats, then descends by Tonahutu Creek to the North Fork of the Colorado River. Indians used this trail;

the 1914 Arapahos called it the Big Trail. The shorter branch, made by white men in 1901, descends the North Inlet to Grand Lake.

When W. L. Hallett guided Chapin to Flattop Mountain in 1887, they called it Table Top Mountain. It stands on the plateau that gently rolls along the 12,000-foot level west of the Continental Divide from Bighorn Flats south to Andrews Glacier. It has given its name—Flattop Peneplain—to a vast geological feature of the northern Colorado Rockies.

Peneplain is a hybrid word geologists manufactured by adding the English word *plain* to the Latin word for *almost*. Geologists explain the Flattop Peneplain by telling of two sets of mountains—maybe more—that rose and were washed away before the present Rockies were formed. Each was flattened to almost a level plain just above sea level. Following the creation of the present Flattop Peneplain near sea level, great forces within the earth's crust irresistibly lifted the whole plateau to its present position, over two miles above sea level. The plain originally included Trail Ridge and continued to the north; traces of it can be found as far south and west as Berthoud Pass. In the Park region, Trail Ridge and Bighorn Flats once had no Forest Canyon between them; Mounts Ida, Julian, Terra Tomah, and perhaps Stones Peak, were all one mound. Then the glaciers and streams started to cut back, back, back from the east to carve the spectacular scenery motorists on Trail Ridge Road admire across Forest Canyon.

Flint Pass   Mummy Range

Because he found chips of flint on this pass, indicating that Indians had made arrowheads here, Roger W. Toll named it in 1927.

Forest Canyon   Forest Canyon

First known as Willow Canyon, Forest Canyon earns its name from the heavy stands of conifers along the slopes of the upper Big Thompson River valley. Abner Sprague thought he named this canyon, but so did the fishing party who named the Gorge Lakes.

Forest Canyon Overlook   Forest Canyon

For a good look at Forest Canyon, park your car and walk to this lookout point. The dark green forest is deep below you, at the foot of the great peaks that form the Continental Divide opposite the Overlook. To help you identify the mountains, the Park Service has drawn an outline of the view with each peak named.

Forest Canyon Pass   Never Summer

Forest Lake   Forest Canyon

Fourth Lake   Grand Lake

The Fourth and Fifth Lakes on the East Inlet of Grand Lake deserve names, not numbers.

84

Fox Creek—MUMMY RANGE; **Fox Creek**—WILD BASIN

Theodore Whyte, the Earl of Dunraven's resident manager, hunted the red fox behind imported Irish hounds. The few foxes these hounds pointed for their pink-coated masters could not have affected the fox population of the Park as much as the trap lines set out by men who made their living selling fur; fox pelts were especially valuable. In the 50 years since the National Park banned hunting and trapping, the fox population has increased so that one is occasionally seen today.

The red fox is smaller than a coyote, some say not as cunning. It runs chiefly at night. Usually its coat is reddish-gold, but cross-breeding produces heather mixtures, with various colors in one litter.

Fox Park   INDIAN PEAKS

This valley at the western foot of Buchanan Pass was known to local people as Paradise Park. The 1958 Isolation Peak quad labels it Fox Park.

Frigid Lake   WILD BASIN

A record in the file of the Rocky Mountain National Park states that Roger Toll named this in 1924 because he found ice on it in mid-August. Another note states that the lake may have been previously called Isolation Lake. Perhaps from this name Colonel Allen S. Peck derived the name for Isolation Peak.

Frozen Lake   GLACIER GORGE, WILD BASIN

Roger W. Toll in 1922 observed three small ice fields, not glaciers, above this lake. The lake is frozen most of the year.

G

Gable, The   FOREST CANYON

A gable, according to the dictionary, is the vertical triangular portion of the end of a building. The rock called The Gable that stands above Fern Lake is somewhat triangular and certainly vertical and has snow cornices in the winter.

Gabletop Mtn. 11,939′   FOREST CANYON

This mountain extends back from The Gable. South of it two other tops decorate the skyline—Knobtop and Notchtop.

Gash, The   GLACIER GORGE, GRAND LAKE

Gaskil (Site) (i.e. Gaskill)   NEVER SUMMER

Captain L. D. C. Gaskill (spelled with two l's) was the manager of the Wolverine Mine in Bowen Gulch, and his is the name commonly used for the town at the foot of the gulch, although the 1884 Colorado Business Directory gives Auburn as an alternative name. Gaskill was headquarters for the Wolverine Mine, the most important mine not only in Bowen Gulch but probably in the North Fork region. Nothing is left of Gaskill's buildings, not even of its Rogerson Hotel. Today a large and symmetrical blue spruce grows out of a hole in the ground to mark the cellar of a saloon, once lined with cobblestones.

Gem Lake   ESTES PARK, MUMMY RANGE

Gem Lake, one of the few lakes in the Park not formed by glacial action, has neither inlet nor outlet. Its waters come from Heaven or seepage, and flow nowhere. Israel Rowe, the bear hunter who first visited Rowe Glacier, discovered Gem Lake.

George, Mt. 12,876′   INDIAN PEAKS

We have no documentary proof that this mountain was named for R. D. George, but most Boulder people think it was. Dr. Philip G. Worcester, his associate for many years, wrote in 1965, "It is probable that Mt. George was named for R. D. George, yet I . . . never heard of a mountain being named for him."

Russell D. George (1886-1955) deserved to have a mountain bear his name. He was Professor of Geology at the University of Colorado from 1903 to 1934. As Colorado State Geologist from 1907 for about 20 years, his word became law on matters geological. In 1913 he published a topographical and a geological map of the state. His interest in oil shale dated back to 1917; in 1966 some of his prophecies on the importance of that source of oil are materializing. Dr. George, as state geologist, was a member ex-officio of the Colorado Geographic Board.

Near Mt. George is Apache Peak. On maps, these two peaks switched places every now and then, the Forest Service and the Geological Survey disagreeing on their respective locations. This so confused the Boulder Group of The Colorado Mountain Club that when they wanted to announce a climb of what they thought was Mt. George they would add "or Apache Peak," and vice versa. At this moment, the name Apache is on the Continental Divide, as most of the other Indian tribal names are, and Mt. George is the peak a little south of west.

Gianttrack Mt. 9091'

The 1914 Arapahos recalled that the Indians knew that giants had left footprints in the rocks of this mountain, but that no one cared to investigate. The footprints are still there, in the form of deep potholes, sometimes called bathtubs because they usually contain water. Two of them are six to eight feet deep, ten to twelve feet wide. No wonder the Arapahos did not care to investigate!

On this mountain in 1876 the artist Bierstadt sat to sketch Longs Peak. Gianttrack Mountain was probably called Sheep Mountain then, as it was until the decision by the Colorado Geographic Board recalled the giants.

Glacier Basin
ESTES PARK

When in 1877 a friend of Abner Sprague, Frank G. Bartholf, particularly admired this valley and playfully claimed it as his own, Sprague named it Bartholf Park. The two men were still friends in 1904 when Bartholf was the president and Sprague the engineer of a proposed electric railroad, the Loveland and Estes Park Railroad Company. The line did not materialize, but the name Bartholf remained on the Park until the U.S. Board on Geographic Names changed it, for the 1961 map, to Glacier Basin "to agree with common usage." The original name is still retained by geologists who call the ancient glacier that formed the basin Bartholf Glacier.

Glacier Creek, Falls, Gorge, Ridge; Glacier Knobs 10,225'
GLACIER GORGE

Many features of the Park bear the word glacier. This is appropriate; glaciers carved the Park. Geologists theorize that about a million years ago the climate of the northern part of the earth grew cold, and snow fell, packed, and turned to ice. As the earth warmed after the Ice Age, or Pleistocene Era, heavy ice moved down the valleys, scooping them into U-shapes. Ice plucked rock from mountain walls leaving cirques. Ice pulverized stones as it moved, so that water flowing from glaciers looked like milk, and high country lakes looked like cream-of-turquoise soup. Remnants of this tremendous force remain in the Park—moraines, cirques, and lake basins; living glaciers still grind rocks.

87

Glass Lake (i.e. Lake of Glass) GLACIER GORGE

Everybody but the U.S. Board on Geographic Names calls this Lake of Glass. Abner Sprague heard with his own ears Robert Sterling Yard name it so, when Sprague was guiding that National Park official around the area. Local residents correct you if you speak of Glass Lake —"Oh, you mean Lake of Glass," they say. The Park trail signs direct you to the Lake of Glass.

The Board on Geographic Names may have invoked their rule for simplification when they approved Glass Lake in 1932; perhaps they will reconsider according to their system of abiding by well-established local names, and will give official sanction to Lake of Glass.

Gore Range Overlook MUMMY RANGE

The blue mountains far to the south of this parking place on the Trail Ridge Road form part of the southern rim of Middle Park. They bear the name of an Irish baronet who predated the Earl of Dunraven by some 20 years. Sir St. George Gore hunted in the West, starting in 1855, mostly on the upper Missouri. Many tales are told of him. His equipment included what today we call a camper—a bedroom built into a wagon. Each day his valet supervised a bucket brigade who filled his portable bathtub. When the Irish sportsman felt too lazy to mount a horse but wanted to shoot, he sent his retinue, numbering about 40, to act as beaters; they herded the game toward his tent door where he could shoot without rising. In the evening, so runs the tale, he read Shakespeare aloud to Jim Bridger, mountain man and guide.

Historians can prove that Bridger guided Gore, but have not yet documented the tale that the first road into the Gore Range was made for his wagons, nor that the Irish lord slaughtered game to such an extent that the animal population in the Gore Range has never returned to normal.

The two highest peaks in the Gore Range are named Powell and Eagles Nest. Major John Wesley Powell climbed Mt. Powell after he had made the first ascent of Longs Peak. In the can in which they left their names on Mt. Powell, his college boy companion also left a biscuit. The one-armed Major had made the biscuit, and the boy was sure it was hard enough to last for eternity.

Recently a movement has started to rename the higher portion of the Gore Range, leaving the Irishman's name only on Gore Pass, but calling the mountains Eagles Nest Range.

Gorge Lakes FOREST CANYON

The gorge in which these lakes lie has no name; it should not be confused with Glacier Gorge. Credit for naming most of the Gorge Lakes goes to a fishing party. Perhaps Al and Julian Hayden organized this group of five fishermen. They had previously investigated Hayden Gorge with Abner Sprague, the time he named Hayden Spire and Mount Julian. Ed Andrews, of Andrews Glacier, was with them, and their engineering partner Bob Larimer of Chicago, and, of course, the dedicated fisherman of Fern Lake Lodge, Dr. Workman. When they found no fish in the high lakes, they spent the day climbing and naming lakes. Julian Hayden named Arrowhead and Doughnut Lakes for their shape. Dr. Workman was so struck with the contrasting color of the lake above Inkwell that he forgot his compulsion to name lakes for girls and called it Azure Lake. These names have remained on the map, but two other names given by Dr. Workman on this trip have been changed—Glacier Lake to Highest Lake; Primrose Lake to Little Rock Lake. The other Gorge Lakes are Forest Lake, Love Lake, and Rock Lake. A collective name sometimes used for the Gorge Lakes is Paternoster Lakes, because they resemble beads strung on a string.

Gourd Lake   INDIAN PEAKS

Grace Falls   FOREST CANYON, GLACIER GORGE
Grace Workman (Mrs. H. C. Hansen) was one of Dr. Workman's daughters by his second wife.

Granby, Lake 8280′ (spillway elevation)   LAKE GRANBY
As part of the Colorado-Big Thompson Project, the water level of this reservoir goes up and down—up when rain falls or snow melts, down when farmers or cities need water. The name comes from the nearby town of Granby named for Granby Hillyer, U.S. district attorney for Colorado at the time David Moffat built his Denver & Salt Lake broad-gauged railroad across Middle Park.

The skyline of the Indian Peaks seen from the western shore of Lake Granby is almost identical with the view of the same skyline seen from the plains near Longmont (in reverse, of course). From the west, youngsters personify the outline of the Indian Peaks, calling it the Old Man of the Mountains, or Old Abe Lincoln. Mt. Toll is the rugged head of the figure stretched along the skyline to the south. The Old Man even has toes, formed by rocks that look like Lone Eagle Peak but are not.

Grand Bay   LAKE GRANBY

Grand Ditch   NEVER SUMMER
The Grand Ditch collects water from the Never Summer Mountains and carries it across the Continental Divide to Long Draw Reservoir. Although technically the name is Grand River Ditch, the 1961 map uses Grand Ditch. This may be because the U.S. Board on Geographic Names tends to simplify names, or because the Grand River

has been changed to the Colorado River, or because of the need to distinguish this ditch from the enormous canal near Grand Junction known as the Grand River Ditch. Every name connected with the Grand Ditch since its inception in 1890 has been changed. The Never Summer Mountains were known as Rabbit Ears or the southern part of the Medicine Bow Mountains. The pass over which the ditch crosses the Divide was Mountain Meadow Pass, now La Poudre Pass. Even the name of the Poudre River has variations, as in the report in the *Denver Republican* for October 10, 1897, which states that A. G. Allen had spent the summer constructing "a large high-line feeder for the North Fork Ditch across the Continental Divide to the Cachula Poudre."

Various companies have been connected with the Grand Ditch. The company that now owns and operates it is the Water Supply and Storage Company, a non-profit farmers' cooperative with headquarters at Fort Collins, with the enviable record of financing its extensive operations without one cent of government aid.

Irrigation ditches seldom are built all at once and, no exception, the Grand Ditch inched piecemeal along the Never Summer Mountains until on September 1, 1890, the first segment started carrying water across the Divide. In 1894 three more miles were built, in 1897 another few miles. Then the ditch head rested at Opposition Creek in Hells Hip Pocket. On August 3, 1906, the District Court at Hot Sulphur Springs awarded the ditch company Priority #83. Total length of canal—11 miles, total number of headgates—12.

With this setup the company was satisfied for about 25 years. Then everybody on the plains east of the Rockies started talking transmountain diversion of water from the upper Colorado River. The Water Supply and Storage Company decided to acquire more water and lengthen its ditch. This literally took an Act of Congress, because in 1929 the Never Summer Mountains had been added to the Rocky Mountain National Park. With permission of Congress, the company built three additional miles of ditch at the reputed cost of less than $500 for machine labor, as against the reputed $375,000 it had paid for hand labor on the first 11 miles. The company also dammed Long Draw to create a reservoir.

Today most of the Grand Ditch is clearly seen from the Trail Ridge Road or from the floor of Kawuneeche Valley. Its scar on the side of the Never Summers looks like a lateral incision, and although it is 75 years old, the wound is still raw. The 14-mile ditch starts in Bakers Gulch and runs north to La Poudre Pass at an exact slant designed to keep the channel reasonably clean but not to wash out the banks (which it does in wet years). On the eastern side of the Pass the water flows into Long Draw Reservoir where it rests until late summer when the farmers around Fort Collins need it for the last irrigation of their sugar beets. Ditches like the Grand Ditch have turned what Major Long called the Great American Desert into the Sugar Bowl of America.

What stories the men who built the Grand Ditch could have told! John McNabb, for instance. He helped build almost every ditch that carried water into the Poudre—constructed the Michigan Ditch, rebuilt the road and bridges after Chambers Lake Dam broke, helped build the town of Walden in North Park, and as a tie-cutter won fame as the best ax-man on the Poudre, in all "a man to match the mountains," as his friend Norman Fry called him.

McNabb supervised the construction of many miles of the Grand Ditch. His men lived in two ditch-camps, one for Swedes, one for Chinese, the same nationalities, perhaps some of the same men, who, along with the Irish, built the western railroads. The coolies worked on the Grand Ditch in the summer of 1899. They were brought up from the plains by way of the Poudre, over the Divide and down to the ditch-camp, great quantities of rice being shipped to them by burro-back over the same route. With shovels and wheelbarrows, about 30 Chinese worked all summer moving rock and earth at a daily wage of 17 cents up to almost a dollar, depending on which report one reads.

For the Orientals the company built a large dining room and cabins. Whether or not they lived in the cabins is a matter of opinion. Some people claim that small groups of Chinese dug holes in the side of the hill, erected frame entrances, and lived in these caves. The holes are still there, both above and below the Grand Ditch, quite close to the present ditch-camp.

Others, including John Holzwarth, say the caves were for storing supplies. They were definitely used for that purpose when Holzwarth was a youth, some years after the departure of the Chinese. He remembers supplies being stored in the caves in the fall before the snow fell to be used in the spring by maintenance men on the ditch, where work began long before the snows melted enough for supplies to be brought in. One of John Holzwarth's winter chores was to ride up periodically from his father's ranch on the North Fork to check the temperature of the caves. One time it had fallen to 28 degrees, and he found 3,300 pounds of frozen potatoes! He also had to turn the eggs in five cases, a quarter of a turn each trip. He remarked that by spring the eggs were pretty stout. Somewhere by the ditch-camp, he added, rests a ton of sledge hammers, a lost cache.

Grand Lake 8367'   GRAND LAKE

     "White man, pause and gaze around,
      For we tread now on hallowed ground!"
     So said a chief to me one day,
     As along the shore we wound our way.

"Tell me chieftain," then I said,
"About this fight so fierce and red;
For I have often heard before
Of a desperate fight in the days of yore."

So begins Judge Wescott's saga of "The Legend of Grand Lake," commemorating a fight between a Cheyenne-Arapaho band and Ute Indians. To protect them from the enemy, the Utes put their women and children on rafts and sent them to the middle of Grand Lake. One of the sudden storms for which Grand Lake is notorious drowned them all. Most of the Ute men were killed in battle. Thereafter Indians avoided this lake, calling it Spirit Lake because it is haunted by the souls of the dead. If you do not believe this tale, get up early some summer morning as the sun reaches the eastern shore of the lake. You will see spirit-like vapors rise into the air.

So runs the legend according to Judge Wescott. The 1914 Arapahos remembered only a minor battle, when they surprised some Utes on Sage Brush Flats, drove them to the ridge by the lake, then up the slopes of Shadow Mountain. They remembered nothing about a raft. The Ute fatalities were one man, one woman, and a baby.

On one point the two versions agree—the Arapaho names for Grand Lake included Spirit Lake, but their explanation of the name differs from Judge Wescott's version. The 1914 Arapahos said this:

Once the lake had nearly frozen over, so that only a little patch of water was left in the center of the lake. In the snow on the ice the Indians found many buffalo tracks. The tracks of one especially large buffalo seemed to come from the center of the lake and return there. The Indians concluded, therefore, that some enormous supernatural buffalo must live in the lake, from which they called it "Spirit Lake."

Grand Lake is the largest natural lake in Colorado, about two miles long. The name comes, of course, from the earlier name of the Colorado River. It has had other names. In 1863 an Irish writer, M. O'C. Morris, used Still-Water Lake. Phiminster Proctor, the artist who made the statues of the Indian and the Cowboy in Denver's Civic Center, spent much time at Grand Lake from 1875 to 1885. He remembered still another Indian name—"Meteor Lake, because of the number of meteors visible at certain times of year. The fool whites changed the name to Grand Lake."

Granite Pass   GLACIER GORGE

Green Knoll—NEVER SUMMER; **Green Lakes**—INDIAN PEAKS; **Green Mtn. 10,313′**—GRAND LAKE; **Green Ridge 8970′**—GRAND LAKE, LAKE GRANBY

Green Lake GLACIER GORGE, LAKE GRANBY

As a guide on Longs Peak, Paul Nesbit used to sit with his customers above Glacier Gorge and point out the three upper lakes; to him, geographically minded, they resembled the maps of Iceland, Italy, and South America. The lowest was South America, and for a time that name was in general use, but maps before and after have called it Green Lake.

Grouse Creek—LAKE GRANBY; **Grouse Creek**—MUMMY RANGE

The two creeks that bear this name are on opposite corners of the Park region—northeast and southwest—but both are in the 9000-foot altitude range. They run in country thick with conifers, just the place for dusky grouse to live. To avoid this duplication of names, one Grouse Creek might be changed to Fool Hen Creek, the name hunters call dusky grouse. The birds deserve the name; when they are disturbed on the ground, they noisily fly to the limbs of trees where they watch the hunters take aim and fire. If the first shots go wild, the fool hens remain sitting while the hunter fires again.

Another popular name for dusky grouse is blue grouse, a name that dates back to August 26, 1776, when Padre Escalante was startled by one in present Montrose County, Colorado.

Teenagers looking for new dance movements and drum rhythms should rise before dawn to see the courting dance of grouse. During their strutting the dusky grouse males inflate purplish sacs in their throats, then let the air out in a series of mellow pops.

Gull Island GRAND LAKE, LAKE GRANBY

Several species of gulls nest around Great Salt Lake and the marshes of the Great Plains, and then sail the skies of the West. The one most likely to be seen around Lake Granby is the ring-billed gull that nests near Salt Lake. Its bill looks as if someone had snapped a rubber band around it.

Over mountain valleys on the eastern slope of the Park the Franklin's gull may be seen. They nest in the marshes of the Great Plains. In late July hundreds of these graceful birds soar over the irrigated farmlands of northern Colorado and spill upland into the Estes Park region, feeding on schools of sawflies and other airborne insects. These plains birds winging over Glacier Basin seem incongruous.

H

Hague Creek   MUMMY RANGE

Hagues Peak 13,560'   MUMMY RANGE

The Hague brothers, James and Arnold, were Bostonians, grandsons of a sea captain, graduates of Yale University and scientific schools in Germany. They worked for Clarence King, also a Yale graduate, on the Survey of the 40th Parallel. The Hagues were his kind of men, quiet, scholarly, thorough. James Hague was one of the men who exposed the Great Diamond Hoax, and his report on the mining industry (Vol. II of the 40th Parallel reports) told all that in 1870 was known about western mining.

His younger brother Arnold (1840-1917), slight in build, not overly strong, was more intimately connected with the Estes Park region than was James. Arnold climbed Longs Peak with Clarence King and brainy Henry Adams in 1871, the year smoke from forest fires prevented topographical work. He may have used the top of Hagues Peak as a triangulation point, giving his fellow workers an obvious reason for naming it. Arnold Hague and S. F. Emmons wrote *Descriptive Geology*, the monumental opus published by the Survey in 1877. After 1883, Arnold Hague concentrated on the geology of Yellowstone, and wrote a number of treatises on its rocks and geysers.

Haiyaha, Lake   GLACIER GORGE

This was one of the Indian words suggested by Harriet Vaille, chairman of the Nomenclature Committee of The Colorado Mountain Club. She left no record of what it meant in what Indian language. F. W. Byerly said it meant rock; others thought it meant rainbow. In June 1932, the U.S. Board on Geographic Names favored rock, not rainbow, because great boulders were visible beneath the water.

Half Mtn. 11,482'   GLACIER GORGE

After glaciers finished slicing the rock on this mountain, only half a mountain was left.

Hallett Creek—GRAND LAKE; **Hallett Peak 12,713'**—GLACIER GORGE, GRAND LAKE

"The first difficulty which presents itself to the mountaineer in Colorado," wrote Frederick Chapin of the Appalachian Mountain Club, "is a lack of guides." The club members easily hired guides in the Swiss Alps, but in Estes Park in 1887 Chapin wrote:

The hunters object to climbing or walking; and although very familiar with the country, hunting as they do all around the peaks, it is rarely that they climb to the mountain tops.

94

One of their number, a dweller in an upper park, told me he
did not "see anything in the high mountains, and did not
know about the scenery." "Yes," said a listener, "he don't
know about anything but 'bar.'"

But our little company at Ferguson's was well provided
with a leader in the person of a gentleman who has a cottage
near this ranch, who spends all the summer months in the
mountains and knows thoroughly every trail and stream for
many miles around. To him I am indebted for all that I saw
of the Front Range, excepting my ascent of Long's Peak or
of some of the lower elevations. [Parson Lamb or his son
Carlyle guided Chapin up Longs Peak.]

The sharpest peak in the Front Range, as seen from the
valley of the Big Thompson Creek, which runs through Estes
Park, is a mountain near the centre of the range, to the left of
Table Top Mountain [Flattop]. It rises from the large snowfield which hangs like a true glacier [Tyndall Glacier] to a
steep ridge connecting the peak with Table Mountain. . . .
When our acknowledged leader proposed taking our little
company, consisting of a member of the Appalachian Mountain Club, the surgeon, and myself, over the mill trail to the
continental divide, I had no doubt that my plans would succeed.

The day fixed upon was late August. We were to have
been off at six o'clock, but it was half past six before we left
the ranch. We intended to take a barometer, but our leader
dropped it on the porch as we were packing, and it *fell* three
thousand feet. We rode off, however, in good spirits, thinking
ourselves fortunate in getting started even so early, for the
horses had to be "rounded up" for us; and Tom, the mule,
galloped all over the hillside before he was captured.

Chapin explained why he rode as far as possible up any mountain: he carried his photographic equipment, including bulky plates.
"The ideal way to climb mountains is to have nothing whatever to
carry,—no camera, no theodolite, no rifle—nothing to load one down
except perhaps a cracker and a bottle of cold tea." On this climb,
Chapin saw mountain sheep but had a bad case of buck fever when he
tried to shoot them with his camera.

The horsemen followed a trail, and then cairns, until they reached
Flattop. Here the leader waited with the horses while Chapin and Dr.
Otis climbed the sharp peak to the south. They found

a cairn on the summit, probably piled up years ago by some
indefatigable member of the Survey party. . . . We scanned the

depths of the gorges below, and all the rock-strewn waste of Table Mountain, hoping to have one more glimpse of the big-horn. . . . A wilder scene . . . they cannot find, nor better hiding-places, nor a more awful series of cliffs to wander among than the ravines of Mount Hallett.

Thus, simply, Chapin announced the christening of the mountain for their leader, William L. Hallett. That this photogenic peak in the Rocky Mountain National Park should be so named is appropriate, not only because Hallett was a summer resident of Estes Park from 1878, but because he was one of the first Colorado men to climb mountains for the sake of mountain climbing.

William L. Hallett and his mother came to Colorado in 1878 from Springfield, Massachusetts. They almost immediately went to Estes Park, staying first at the English Hotel, then with the Fergusons. Hallett went back to New York for his bride in 1879, and his idea of a honeymoon was a horseback trip from Estes Park to Grand Lake with Abner Sprague as guide. On three acres given them by Ferguson, in 1881 the Halletts built Edgemont, the frame house with the Victorian flavor that still stands near Marys Lake, and there his two daughters and four sons spent sun-drenched summers. In the winter they lived in Denver at 1200 Vine Street. (This is not the family of Judge Moses Hallett and his son Lucius who lived at 900 Logan, nor the Sam Halletts of Aspen and 847 Pearl Street, Denver.)

The mines of Leadville and Aspen, the Gunnison country, and the San Juan were clamoring for trained engineers in the late 1870's, but William L. Hallett, a recent graduate of the Massachusetts Institute of Technology, went into the cattle business. In Colorado Springs in 1882 he helped organize the Powder River Live Stock Company. In the fall of 1886, 24,000 head of cattle bearing their "21" brand grazed in Wyoming. After that incredible winter, the company gathered only 8000 head. Despite the $400,000 loss, the company stayed in business, but dissolved in 1893.

William L. Hallett had his own ranch west of Loveland, Colorado. He pushed his cattle to the high country of Estes Park for summer grazing. Unlike most cattlemen, he was interested in mountains not simply as feeding lots but as unexplored territory. His most publicized adventure was his fall into a crevice on a snowbank which turned out to be a crevasse in a glacier. (See Rowe Glacier.)

Hallett's friendship with Chapin and other dedicated mountaineers doubtless influenced him and 18 young men of Denver to form in 1896 the first climbing club in Colorado, the Rocky Mountain Club. Hallett was Vice-President and Chairman of Explorations. The club evidently considered him their star climber because they picked him to go with Italian climbers on the first ascent of Mt. St. Elias in Alaska, but, at the last minute, the Italians decided not to include any Americans. When the Rocky Mountain Club sent an expedition to climb the Grand Teton in Wyoming, Hallett was to be their leader. Members of the club collected $150 to pay his expenses, but, again at the last minute, he was unable to leave his job with the Arkansas Smelter at Leadville. Substituting as leader, Frank Spalding, later Episcopal Bishop of Utah, planted the flag of the Rocky Mountain Club on top of the Grand Teton on August 16, 1898.

After his adventures in cattle raising, William L. Hallett returned to his engineering profession, as smelter manager, then as an employee of the Denver Water Board. Three of his sons, graduates of the Colorado School of Mines, became practicing engineers. William L. Hallett died in 1941, at the age of 90.

Hallowell Park   Estes Park

George C. Hallowell's name was on this park as early as 1892 when the township map recorded it. Dan Griffith of Estes Park village remembered that Hallowell brought cattle from Loveland for summer grazing. He lived in a shack, known to cattlemen as a summer cabin, in the park that bears his name.

Hanging Valley   Forest Canyon

During the Ice Age a huge glacier over 1000 feet deep filled the valley of Horseshoe Park. Smaller masses of ice in the tributary valleys did not cut as deep as the principal glacier. When the ice melted, it left these side valleys hanging about 1000 feet above the glacial floor. Their streams have since cut their way downward, frequently forming sheer falls like Thousand Falls and Horseshoe Falls.

Harbison Meadow   Grand Lake

Harry Harbison built the Harbison Ditch to bring water to his Columbine Lake where he homesteaded. His two-story building still stands in Grand Lake village. He kept a store on the first floor, let the villagers dance to the tunes of three fiddlers on the second.

Another Harbison family settled on the North Fork of the Colorado. The two daughters, Annie and Kitty, took up homesteads, including the present Harbison Meadows. The homestead law stipulated residence on the land a certain number of nights a year. Each sister had a cabin in which she slept, the cabins being about ten yards apart on either side of the boundary line of their homesteads. The Harbison women were famed for their fried chicken dinners which summer residents of Grand Lake enjoyed on Sunday outings. The sisters had a brother named Robert who was not noted for his industry, but he did manage to deliver the milk from the Harbison dairy herd. This involved not only driving to the village but also rowing across the lake to summer homes on the southeastern shore.

The Harbisons were kindly people. When Henry Schnoor, who lived on the Green Mountain Ranch, was left with the rearing of his two baby girls, the Harbisons took the children. Schnoor was not a widower—his wife simply walked away from what she considered the God-forsaken country of the North Fork.

Harvey Island 8321' LAKE GRANBY
The waters of Lake Granby now cover the Jim Harvey Ranch, except for the hill called Harvey Island. The Circle H brand no longer sizzles the hide of Jim Harvey's cattle, but marks a restaurant on the shores of the lake. Harvey's daughter and son-in-law, the Frank Nortons, have turned from ranching to boating at the Norton Marina.

Hayden Creek, Gorge, Lake, Spire FOREST CANYON
Sprague named Hayden Spire for Al and Julian Hayden. (See Mt. Julian.) The creek and the gorge acquired the name by association. Though the Spire appears on the 1961 map of Rocky Mountain National Park, the Forest Canyon Lookout indicator, also official, specifies Hayden Prong.

Haynach Lakes FOREST CANYON, GRAND LAKE
The 1914 Arapahos used the word *haa' nach* to mean snow water. This name the Colorado Geographic Board modified for these lakes. John Holzwarth speaks for a number of North Fork residents when he says, "They are always the Murphy Lakes to me," but he does not add any information about Murphy.

Hazeline Lake MUMMY RANGE
About 1913, Frank R. Koenig married Hazel Ramsey, daughter of Hugh Ramsey of Pingree Park. (See Ramsey Peak.) Abner Sprague guided them on their honeymoon to this lake, which the young husband named for his wife, adding the *line* to rhyme with Emmaline Lake, which he had named for his mother.

Helene, Lake FOREST CANYON, GLACIER GORGE
Dr. Workman of Fern Lake Lodge was pestered by two girls who insisted he name lakes in their honor. To satisfy two at once he called this Lake Helmary. Later this pleasantry was superseded when Dr. Workman wished to honor Helene, daughter of a Denver lawyer, George Stidger, a summer cottager. (See also Two Rivers Lake.)

Hell Canyon INDIAN PEAKS
Surveyors for the Union Pacific Railroad in 1882 almost lost their lives before they were able to struggle out of this canyon during a storm. The name expresses their feelings about the canyon. (See Pawnee Pass and Mt. Irving Hale.)

98

Hells Hip Pocket   NEVER SUMMER

The pocket is an especially precipitous area drained by Opposition Creek. The name is credited to Squeaky Bob Wheeler of the graphic vocabulary acquired during his service with the Rough Riders of the Spanish-American War.

Hiamovi Mtn. 12,395′   INDIAN PEAKS

An undocumented source gives Hiamovi as derived from an Indian word meaning God. Was this the meaning Ellsworth Bethel had in mind when he proposed this name for the mountain that stands between Paradise Park and Hells Canyon? Or was it named for a Cheyenne named Hiamovi (High Chief) who helped Natalie Curtis collect songs, legends, and pictures for her book, published by Harper in 1908, called *The Indians' Book*? Hiamovi painted many of the illustrations and contributed an account of Cheyenne life before the white men came West.

Hichens Gulch—See Hitchens Gulch.

Hidden Cove—GRAND LAKE, LAKE GRANBY; **Hidden River**—FOREST CANYON

Hidden Valley, Hidden Valley Creek   FOREST CANYON, MUMMY RANGE

When the southern lateral moraine of the now-melted Fall River Glacier dammed Hidden Valley it forced the waters of Hidden Valley Creek to flow, not due north as its natural instincts would have led it, but due east along the south side of the moraine. Here beaver dams near the present road gave it the name of Beaver Dam Creek at one time. After about a mile the creek found a low place in the moraine, and cascaded down 400 feet to the bed of Horseshoe Park. This plunge from a platform gave it the name of Bench Creek at one time.

Anyone looking up the southern slopes of Horseshoe Park sees what appears to be an unbroken forest of trees to timberline. Hidden Valley is indeed hidden from this viewpoint. Now that it holds a road, a ski lodge and tows, it is not exactly a Hidden Valley.

Highest Lake   FOREST CANYON, GRAND LAKE

Dr. Workman called one of the Gorge Lakes, Glacier Lake; this 20-acre lake is probably the one since it lies at the foot of a permanent snowfield, under the crest of the Continental Divide at an elevation of about 12,500 feet. It is the highest not only of the nine named Gorge Lakes but, next to the lake at Rowe Glacier, the highest in the Park.

Hitchens Gulch (i.e. Hichens)   NEVER SUMMER

A prospector named Hichens (misspelled Hitchens on the 1961 map) located a vein here in the early 1890's. Over it he erected a shaft house and built a few other buildings, and here he lived and worked for years. When he was an old man, still coming to Grand Lake for supplies, he used to ask people what he should say when he met his three dogs in Heaven. "Each of them thought he was my best friend."

Hondius Park   Estes Park, Mummy Range

Pieter Hondius came from Holland to Estes Park for his health, and bought 2000 acres of land on Beaver Creek including Hupp's homestead. In 1914 the Arapaho Indians, camping on Beaver Creek, told of a big spring high on Deer Mountain near which stood a huge tree. Hondius knew the spring—he piped its waters to the cabins at Elkhorn Lodge—but not the tree. His belief in the stories told by the Indians was strengthened when he later found the rotting trunk of an enormous tree near the spring.

Hondius married Ella James, daughter of the owners of Elkhorn Lodge. She managed the Lodge in the summers while Pieter, retreating from asthma, spent many summers at Lawn Lake; an employee brought him supplies once a week. In the winters Mr. and Mrs. Hondius and their son sought warmer climates. In 1934 Pieter Hondius died at Palm Springs. The next year Mrs. Hondius built a $7,000 addition to the Estes Park library in memory of her husband.

Horse Creek   Wild Basin

Horseshoe Falls, Park, Little Horseshoe Park   Mummy Range

The flat valley of Horseshoe Park is the bed of a former glacial lake impounded by a terminal moraine. The name might come from the innumerable horseshoe bends Fall River makes as it meanders through the valley; or it might come from the shape of the valley, with the curved top of the horseshoe at the west end near Endovalley Campground.

Willard H. Ashton acquired land in Horseshoe Park in 1907. On June 4, 1908, *The Mountaineer,* an Estes Park newspaper that lived about four months, reported this about Ashton's new hotel:

> Frank Lloyd Wright, the famous architect of Chicago, drew the plans and has produced a building which seems a part of the beautiful landscape, rather than a mar upon it, as is so often the case with summer hotels.

Ashton ran Horseshoe Inn until 1915; the new owners sold it to the National Park in 1931, which razed the buildings. The bears which regularly tipped over the garbage cans outside the Inn's kitchen door were forced to look elsewhere for their dinner. Now Horseshoe Park has returned to nature, except for the Endovalley Camp Ground and the large parking lot designed for people who come to hear the elk bugle in the fall.

Horsetooth Peak 10,344'   WILD BASIN

The 1910 Burlington Railroad map labeled this Chisel Top; the 1911 Cooper-Babcock map called it Horsetooth Mountain; the 1961 Rocky Mountain National Park map changed it to Horsetooth Peak.

Hourglass Lake   FOREST CANYON, GRAND LAKE

Howard Mtn. 12,810'   NEVER SUMMER

We thought this an earthbound name for a mountain that stands high among the Cloud Peaks of the Never Summer Mountains, until we found that Luke Howard, early English meteorologist, was the first man to classify cloud forms. In 1803 he identified cirrus, cumulus, nimbus, and stratus clouds. Who but the erudite James Grafton Rogers of the Colorado Geographic Board, namer of the Cloud Peaks, would have named the highest after the man who christened cloud forms? This theory was exploded in a letter from Jim Rogers himself in 1965. "Your charming suggestion about Dr. Howard," he wrote, "has no footing in my memory." Then he cited a map published by Clason before 1913, before the birth of the Colorado Geographic Board, on which Mt. Howard was printed.

Who then was Howard? Rogers had a penciled note (when he penciled notes he distrusted the information) on his card for Mt. Howard stating, "Shep Husted says Sour Howard was a prospector living on Cinder Creek." (Where was Cinder Creek?) Three Howard families now live in North Park; perhaps they know the history of the name of Mt. Howard.

The *Rocky Mountain News* for July 15, 1880, refers to a Howard on the North Fork of the Colorado River—J. E. Howard (was his nickname Sour?). He and W. B. Baker (not the Baker of Baker Mountain) planned to spend the winter of 1879-80 at their mining claim near Lulu City. They managed to stay until February 20. Equipped with snowshoes, one blanket each, and "what chuck they could carry," they started for Estes Park, 25 miles away. Five days later they dragged into the village.

The article reported the exact location of Lulu City in relation to Lead Mountain, Howard Mountain, and Mt. Shipler. The article also cited Sheep Mountain near Lulu City, and one wonders whether this was an early name for Specimen Mountain which sheep so often frequent.

Hunters Creek   WILD BASIN

Where the trail to Sandbeach Lake crosses this creek, in 1908 Dean Babcock noted a carving on a wooden plank. It showed a party of white men hunting. He named the creek for the hunters.

Husted, Lake   MUMMY RANGE

Shepherd Husted came to Estes Park in 1898, passed the Forest Service examination in 1905, and served as ranger for two years before he became a professional guide and wrangler in the Estes Park region. He was one of the best. Through study and association with scientists he became an expert naturalist. As guide for the 1914 Arapaho Indians, his knowledge of every gulch and hill helped clarify their remarks, and his ability to fraternize with the jolly Arapaho, Sherman Sage, resulted in additional information. Husted's friendship as well as his skillful guide services were appreciated by such visitors to the Park as Chief Justice Charles Evans Hughes, Edna Ferber, Otis Skinner, and the Doctors Mayo.

Hutcheson Lakes   WILD BASIN

Henry Hutcheson was the contractor for at least three Wild Basin reservoirs—Bluebird, Pear, and Sandbeach. Originally from Michigan, Hutcheson arrived in Lyons in 1890 where he made his home until his death in 1941. He owned mining claims on upper Cony Creek, which probably led to the decision in 1950-1954 by the U.S. Board on Geographic Names to name four lakes—two in the Rocky Mountain National Park, two in Roosevelt National Forest—Hutcheson Lakes.

Not Hutcheson, but Hutchins, had been the name suggested for these lakes. In the early 1920's Charles Bowman Hutchins, known to many as "The Bird Man," lectured on birds and other natural history subjects, not only in northern Colorado but over the United States. He was a nature guide at Grand Lake, a militant bird-lover, an artist, and a musician of sorts, holding school children under the spell of his whistled bird calls and instant chalk sketches. Could it be that some member of the Park staff thought the Bird Man's name would rest appropriately among the bird lakes of Wild Basin?

Still another name had been proposed for these lakes. The Right Reverend Robert H. Mize, Episcopal Bishop of Kansas, from Salina, summered at Allens Park and tried earnestly but in vain to have the lakes officially called the Lakes of the Archangels.

I

Ice Field Pass   Mummy Range
Roger Toll, superintendent of the Park, named this in 1924.

Iceberg Lake   Mummy Range
A broad parking place on Trail Ridge Road encourages travelers
to leave their cars and peer down at this lake. Many walk down to
examine at close range the blocks of ice that never melt completely.
The reddish-brown cliff behind the lake is hardened lava, the result
of the same volcanic action that created Specimen Mountain.

Iceberg Pass 11,827'   Mummy Range
Roger Toll named this in 1924.

Icy Brook   Glacier Gorge
Icy Brook starts above Sky Pond which was named by an easterner,
Robert Sterling Yard. One suspects he also named Icy Brook, because
a westerner would call it creek, and probably pronounce it "crick."

Ida, Mt.   Forest Canyon
This name and that of Mt. Alice are examples of how frustrating
it can be to *cherchez la femme* while searching for name sources. Both
ladies have been impossible to trace. The one known fact about Mt.
Ida is that the name first appeared on 1915 maps. This late date is not
surprising because, except for the few people who rode horseback from
Estes Park to Squeaky Bob's over the Specimen Mountain Trail, who
was there to see Mt. Ida until the Fall River Road opened up the high
country at the head of the Big Thompson?

Possible, but certainly not probable, candidates for the honor are
Ida Webster, the first wife of Theodore Whyte, Dunraven's manager;
and Ida Lamb, a daughter of Elkanah Lamb. She died before he came
to Colorado, making this an even more tenuous theory than that he
named Mt. Alice for his childhood sweetheart.

Perhaps Mt. Ida is not named for a girl at all but for a Greek
mountain. But which Mt. Ida? The one on the Isle of Crete, birthplace of Zeus, or the Mt. Ida that looked down on the plains of Troy?
Was this Colorado mountain named by someone with a classical education like the school teacher who named Mt. Olympus far to the east
of Mt. Ida?

Or could Judge Wescott of Grand Lake have named the mountain
from his reading in mythology? From his cabin on the southwestern
shore of Grand Lake he must have constantly noted the sloping ridge
and abrupt drop-off of this mountain to the north, so often sprinkled
with snow after autumn showers. The cottagers who followed Judge

103

Wescott on that side of the lake usually called it Specimen Mountain. This bothered Charles Hanington, knowledgeable climber that he was, but without benefit of maps, he erroneously concluded it was Shipler Mountain.

Indigo Pond WILD BASIN

Named by Jack Moomaw in 1921.

Inkwell Lake FOREST CANYON

The fishermen who went to the Gorge Lakes about 1901 all noted the reflection in this lake of the great black wall behind it. To describe this effect, Al Hayden thought up the name Inkwell.

Inn Brook ESTES PARK, GLACIER GORGE

This creek, originating at the Eugenia Mine, runs by the Swiss Village which stands on the site of Enos Mills' famous Longs Peak Inn. Presumably the creek was named because it ran by the Inn, therefore named after Enos Mills had acquired Longs Peak House and changed the name to Longs Peak Inn. Enos Mills himself called the stream Evergreen Brook, and some records say it was called Sarah, or Sophia Brook, but Inn Brook is the name that survives.

Inspiration Point LAKE GRANBY

Irene Lake FOREST CANYON, GLACIER GORGE

The three lakes at the foot of Sprague Glacier were called Rainbow Lakes. On the 1961 map, one is Rainbow Lake, one has no name, and one, a dot of a lake, is called Irene. Since this is a recent decision, surely someone knows who this Irene is.

Irene, Lake NEVER SUMMER

Squeaky Bob named this for an eastern girl who stayed at his ranch. One of his neighbors remarked that since Bob stocked the lake he had a right to name it.

Iron Mtn. 12,265′ NEVER SUMMER

This mineralized mountain in the Never Summer Range makes compasses go wild.

Ironclads, The WILD BASIN

These rocks rise like fortress walls, appearing to have little vegetation, and when walked on, the jumbled mass of stone rings like metal.

Irving Hale Creek; Irving Hale, Mt. 11,754′ INDIAN PEAKS, LAKE GRANBY

The name of Hale, father and son, weaves in and out of Colorado history. The father, Horace, supervised the schools of Central City in the 1860's. In 1882 he produced $2,000 out of his own pocket to save the original Central City Opera House Association. Hale became the

104

second president of the University of Colorado, and Hale Science building on the Boulder campus bears his name.

The son, Irving, in 1878 decided to take the competitive examination for West Point. Needing money and time to study, he thought of an ingenious plan. He bought a covered wagon and a team of mules wise enough to pull the wagon while he studied. All summer long, back and forth over Berthoud Pass between Central City and Grand Lake, the mules pulled the wagon loaded with freight, the student, and his books. On his last trip, when a forest fire prevented access to Berthoud Pass, Irving drove over Rollins Pass which had been practically abandoned as a wagon road. Although he had no time to study on that trip, he passed the exams for the U.S. Military Academy and graduated at the head of his class.

Because of his brilliant leadership in commanding the Colorado troops in the Philippines during the Spanish-American War, General Irving Hale came home a hero. A bronze bas-relief of him is now at the head of the south steps of the Colorado Capitol, and Hale Boulevard in Denver commemorates him.

When General Hale was an old man, felled by a stroke, Ellsworth Bethel proposed that a mountain should be named in his honor. Harriet Vaille, in a letter dated June 1, 1915, thanked R. B. Marshall of the Geological Survey for making an exception to the rule that mountains should not bear the names of living persons. She said that General Hale, told of this honor, was, in spite of his loss of the full power of speech, able to convey his special delight at the proximity of his peak to Hell Canyon.

Isabelle Glacier INDIAN PEAKS

Isabelle was the wife of Fred Fair of Boulder. Her glacier clings to the northeastern cliffs of Apache Peak just over the Divide from his Fair Glacier. Both were named by Junius Henderson of the science faculty of the University of Colorado.

Isabelle, Lake INDIAN PEAKS

Hazel Schmoll of Ward remembers when this was called Timberline Lake. It now takes its name from Isabelle Glacier which sends water to it from the ultimate head of South St. Vrain Creek.

Island Lake INDIAN PEAKS

At least four islands lie in this timber-surrounded lake.

Isolation Peak 13,118′ GRAND LAKE, WILD BASIN

This summit on the Continental Divide is definitely isolated; even the trails from East Inlet and Wild Basin do not attempt to climb its formidable cliffs. This may have been the mountain Ellsworth Bethel wanted to call Sioux Peak, a name not countenanced by the U.S. Board

105

on Geographic Names. It remained nameless until 1942 when Colonel Allen S. Peck, supervisor of the Arapaho National Forest, proposed Isolation Peak to the Board of The Colorado Mountain Club. The staff of the Rocky Mountain National Park approved the name, preferring it to the proposed Jewell Peak, after Edward S. Jewell of the Omaha Walking Club. (See Jewel Lake.)

J

Jackstraw Mtn. 11,704' NEVER SUMMER

The child's game of jackstraws consists of tossing many slivers of wood in a heap, then delicately trying to remove one without disturbing the others. This mountain looks like a giant game of jackstraws, with dead trees standing upright or crazily jumbled as they were left by a fire in 1872. The mountain had no name, needed none because it was so seldom seen until 1920 when the automobile road going west from Poudre Lakes afforded a good view of it. Roger Toll named it in 1924.

Whenever a forest fire started in the early West, it usually burned until rain or snow put it out, like the one in 1871 in North Park; Hague reported that this fire kept the King Survey men from doing any topographical work until an October snow brought on sparkling weather. Fires were, and are, often started by lightning. The earliest recorded fire set by a careless white camper was in 1820, when Dr. Edwin James returned after a two-day climb of Pikes Peak to find his food and extra clothing burned at his campsite. Indians deliberately set fires in the mountains as well as on the prairies to drive out game or to frighten white settlers. In 1875 Colorow, the obese Ute, never docile under white rule, set fires designed to burn the settlers' homes on the eastern slope of the northern Front Range. The story is that the wind changed, blowing the fire to the timbered hills in Middle Park where the Utes lived.

One has but to read accounts of early visitors to Denver who could not see the mountains for days at a time because of forest fire smoke (not city smaze) to be grateful for modern fire-fighting methods.

Jacob Spring ESTES PARK

This spring was not named for Jacob's Well in the Bible, nor for "a Mr. Jacobs" who, according to Enos Mills, paid Michael Hollenbeck $250 for the Joel Estes claims in the 1860's, but for Art Jacob who has lived on Fish Creek near the spring since about 1936. He and his brother Ralph, a more recent resident, are expert lumbermen. The

106

Jacob property was homesteaded by Nettie Spalding McFadden at the turn of the century—President McKinley signed the deed—then bought by Will Porter of Denver who sold to Art Jacob. About 1958, when the U.S. surveyors were mapping the area, Art Jacob saved them time by leading them directly to the corner posts of properties on Fish Creek, and the survey men named the spring for him.

Jewel Lake
GLACIER GORGE

On July 14, 1923, the Omaha Walking Club requested that Washington name this lake in honor of Edwin S. Jewell, organizer of their club and a member of the Prairie Club of Chicago. When Washington asked Roger Toll, he approved, providing the word be spelled with one *l*—Jewel—to de-personalize it. Former names for Jewel Lake seem to have been Still Lake, Petite Lake, and Laguna Verde.

Jims Grove
GLACIER GORGE

Rocky Mountain Jim Nugent lived in Muggins Gulch from the late 1860's until his murder in 1874. He claimed to be a Canadian who had wandered the West, in Colorado since 1854. One side of his face had been clawed by a bear; the other side was handsome. He made his living hunting, fishing, and guiding. He wore his hair in 16 long tawny curls, recited poetry of his own composition, and was a madman when he was drunk, which was often. Isabella Bird, the genteel English woman who spent the autumn of 1873 in Estes Park, fell in love with Jim in his civilized moods. She wrote her sister that he was "a man any woman could love, but no sane woman would marry." Isabella claimed that Jim's ghost, complete with 16 curls, appeared to her in Switzerland immediately after it left his body in Colorado in 1874.

In October 1873 no premonition of tragedy marred the Indian summer idyll when Jim Nugent guided Isabella Bird to the top of Longs Peak or, as she herself wrote, dragged the lady "like a bale of goods." They spent two nights in what has since been known as Jims Grove, but Isabella called it "A Lady's Bower." They were chaperoned not only by Jim's dog Ring but by two young lawyers straight out of Columbia University. Isabella was more impressed with Ring's discipline than with the manners of the young men.

We know of her impressions on climbing Longs Peak because she wrote a book—the classic of Estes Park and the best publicity the area ever had. *A Lady's Life in the Rocky Mountains* was published in London in December 1879, then went into six more editions. Translated into French it was published in Paris in 1888. In America it sold eight editions up to 1912, then in 1960 the University of Oklahoma Press reprinted it, earning the gratitude of all Estes Park enthusiasts.

In October 1873, as the party on Longs Peak approached the camp spot the first night out, Miss Bird described Jims Grove:

The pines grew smaller and more sparse as we ascended, and the last stragglers wore a tortured, warring look. The timber line was passed, but yet a little higher a slope of mountain meadow dipped to the south-west towards a bright stream trickling under ice and icicles, and there a grove of the beautiful silver spruce marked our camping ground. The trees were in miniature, but so exquisitely arranged that one might well ask what artist's hand had planted them, scattering them here, clumping them there, and training their slim spires towards heaven. . . . A group of small silver spruces away from the fire was my sleeping place . . . affording a shelter from the wind and a most agreeable privacy. . . . It was exciting to lie there, with no better shelter than a bower of pines, on a mountain 11,000 feet high, in the very heart of the Rocky Range, under twelve degrees of frost, hearing sounds of wolves, with shivering stars looking through the fragrant canopy, with arrowy pines for bed-posts, and for a night lamp the red flames of a camp-fire.

After Jim was shot by Griff Evans in 1874, everyone in Estes Park gave different versions of the circumstances of the shooting as well as different reasons for this deed. Fundamentally it was the fault of the Earl of Dunraven. Griff Evans was the Earl's man, but Rocky Mountain Jim decidedly was not. Living in Muggins Gulch at the entrance to Estes Park, Jim could and did make trouble for British visitors intent on using the Park as their own hunting preserve. Despite two bullets festering in his brain, Jim lived from mid-June to September. From jail (the man who shot him was not jailed) Jim wrote a letter to the Fort Collins paper stating that British gold had done him in. Rocky Mountain Jim may yet take his place in history as the rugged American hero of Estes Park.

Joe Mills Mtn. 11,078'   FOREST CANYON, GLACIER GORGE
Joe Mills, brother of Enos, came to Estes on a bicycle in 1898. While Joe helped his brother run Longs Peak Inn, he and Ethel, his wife, started to homestead near Cabin Rock. After the brothers parted company, Joe and Ethel ran the Crags Hotel at the south edge of Estes village. Joe was a vital force in creating Rocky Mountain National Park. After his death, his wife and the Park rangers agreed that a mountain should bear his name. Many points were considered, and in March 1949 this prominent mountain across from the Little Matterhorn was chosen to bear the name of Joe Mills.

Joe Wright Creek   NEVER SUMMER
The site of Joe Wright's homestead cabin is not far from Cameron

108

Pass. Norman Fry, old-timer on the upper Poudre, reported that Joe Wright Creek was originally the headwaters of the Laramie River.

Chambers Lake was supposedly at one time a canyon of the Laramie River. At some point in the past, a part of the mountain just north of the Lake slipped into the Laramie River which caused a dam and made the small Lake of Chambers. . . . The water from the lake started to flow eastward, and so the early day headwaters of the Laramie River became "Joe Wright" creek.

Julian Lake; Julian, Mt. 12,928' FOREST CANYON

Julian Hayden was born in Chicago in 1886. He first visited Estes Park in 1901. Later, as a civil engineer with a degree from the Armour Institute of Technology, he worked for B. D. Sanborn who, with F. O. Stanley, bought the Dunraven land holdings. Julian Hayden surveyed and built the Estes Park Power Plant, and operated it for a year.

Julian, his brother Al, and Bob Larimer from Chicago hung out their engineering shingle in Estes Park village in 1906. The Haydens were also closely connected with real estate in the area, and stepped into Estes Park genealogy when Al married Louise Reed, daughter of the Reeds who ran the Brinwood Hotel and granddaughter of Horace Ferguson who homesteaded near Marys Lake. After Al's death, Louise married his brother Julian, who died in 1964.

One day the Hayden brothers and Abner Sprague made a trip to a faraway creek that runs into the Big Thompson between the Gorge Lakes and Spruce Creek. They found the canyon rough but the fishing good. Sprague noted two prominent points on the mountain that flanks the creek to the north. One he named Mt. Julian and the other, the great rock that stands at the head of the creek, Hayden Spire. Perhaps the Hayden brothers reciprocated by naming Sprague Mountain which stands just south of Hayden Spire—thus commemorating a notable fishing trip to Hayden Creek.

Junco Lake WILD BASIN

This lake lies about 12,000 feet above sea level. Juncos seldom straggle above timberline, but when W. S. Cooper named this and other lakes in Wild Basin after birds he did not necessarily mean that he had seen that particular bird at that special lake.

The nesting junco of the Rocky Mountains is a gray-headed junco. About the size of a sparrow, gray with a reddish brown back, it flashes white feathers on the sides of its tail when it flies. Basically a ground-loving bird, it nests under small plants in forest glades. Bird lovers say the nests are on the east side of the plants to catch the first rays of the morning sun.

K

Kamloop Cove   LAKE GRANBY

Many of the coves of Lake Granby are named for varieties of
fish. The Kamloop trout gets its name from the Kamloop district
of British Columbia. This trout grows extra large—a regular lunker!
One of the officials of the Colorado Game and Fish Department
explained that a Kamloop was a rainbow trout with an overdeveloped
thyroid.

Kawuneeche Valley (pronounced Ka wu nee' che)   GRAND LAKE

This valley has had at least three names. Its workaday name was
and is the North Fork Valley. Then came the Colorado Geographic
Board with its bagful of Arapaho Indian words. It recommended
Haquihana Valley, meaning valley of the wolves. Haquihana was also
the name of an extinct tribe who lived with the Northern Arapahos.
R. B. Marshall, confident that the name would be accepted, printed
it on his map published in 1915 by the Denver Chamber of Commerce
as the "first and authentic map of the New Park."

But the Colorado Geographic Board changed its mind; with no
explanation in the minutes, it recommended Kawuneeche "as being
somewhat pronounceable." In the report of the 1914 Arapahos this
word is spelled Cawoonache, and defined as meaning coyote.

Keplinger Lake   WILD BASIN

Jack Moomaw preferred Timberline Pond for this lake, but
Roger Toll proposed Keplinger which was approved by the staff of the
Rocky Mountain National Park in 1942. Mountain climbers agree
with Toll that L. W. Keplinger should be commemorated in the
Park. He was one of the college students who accompanied Major
John Wesley Powell on the first ascent of Longs Peak. In fact, young
Keplinger was actually the first on top at 10 a.m. August 23, 1868.
Perhaps this was because of his eagerness, but it might have been an
honor granted the youth by Major Powell because Keplinger the eve-
ning before had scouted the route, almost making a solo climb to the
summit rocks. (See The Notch.)

Keyboard of the Winds   GLACIER GORGE, WILD BASIN

This is a series of jagged cliffs on which the wind, howling
around Longs Peak, plays mournful tunes.

Keyhole, The   GLACIER GORGE

A rock jutting from the northern ridge of Longs Peak has been called The Keyhole ever since climbers first started to ascend the Peak. The hole is shaped like an oval open at the top. At the foot of the Keyhole rocks stands the Agnes Vaille Shelter House.

Kiowa Peak 13,276' INDIAN PEAKS

The name, meaning "principal people," was suggested by Bethel in 1914. Fearless and cruel, the Kiowas were a turbulent element on the plains, fiercely defending their rights against the encroaching whites. The U. S. Government tried to confine them to Oklahoma in 1867. (See also Satanta Peak.)

Knight Ridge LAKE GRANBY

An annual guest at the Lehman Resort on the South Fork of the Colorado River was Harry Knight of St. Louis, with his family, his children's nurses and governess, and assorted servants. Because the Lehmans' was not a working ranch, the Knights repaired en masse to the Killie Ranch (on the south slope of present Knight Ridge) to watch the de-horning and branding of the calves, offspring of the Killies' original herd of 112 Herefords. Knight became fascinated with western life. He proved up, in 1922, on 160 acres southeast of the Lehmans', and acquired most of the patented land along the South Fork, including the Killie and Lehman ranches and the meadows which he later used as a landing strip. In the 1920's a young man named Charles Augustus Lindbergh landed his plane on these meadows when he visited the Knights. Harry Knight was one of the St. Louis men who financed "The Spirit of St. Louis" and its pilot on the first air crossing of the Atlantic. (See Lone Eagle Peak.)

Knobtop Mtn. 12,331' FOREST CANYON, GLACIER GORGE

Named by Roger Toll on September 1, 1924, to harmonize with Flattop and Notchtop.

Kokanee Cove LAKE GRANBY

Kokanee salmon were introduced into Colorado waters in 1951, chiefly because they thrive in reservoirs. Unlike insect-eating fish, they eat plankton—small plants and animals that float on still water. Kokanee, like their cousins the red salmon of the West Coast, usually spawn in the autumn of their fourth year, then die. Kokanee is an Alaskan Indian name meaning little redfish, and comes from the brilliant red color the fish turn when spawning. Lake fishermen catch them by trolling or using small spinners. They do not fight, but are good eating.

Krueger Rock 9335' ESTES PARK

The Kruegers, who celebrated their fiftieth wedding anniversary in 1964, have long ranched in the valley of the Big Thompson.

L

La Poudre Pass, La Poudre Pass Creek　　　　　NEVER SUMMER
When the Grand Ditch first crossed the Divide in the late 1880's, this pass was called Mountain Meadows Pass.

Lady Creek　　　　　NEVER SUMMER
Archie E. Gifford of La Porte, Colorado, an employee of the Grand Ditch Company, was reminded of a lady when he saw the lacy falls on this creek.

Lady Washington, Mt. 13,281′　　　　　GLACIER GORGE
Anna Dickinson is said to have climbed Mt. Washington in New Hampshire 26 times. Perhaps the name of that peak was proposed by her, as she sat with the Hayden Survey men by the camp fire after they had climbed Longs Peak, and the "Lady" may have been inserted by Ralph Meeker as a compliment to the fair climber. The name dates from this climb, September 1873. (See Mt. Dickinson.)

Lake of Glass—See Glass Lake

Lake of Many Winds　　　　　WILD BASIN

Lake of the Clouds　　　　　NEVER SUMMER
This lake lies at the bottom of the cirque on Mt. Cirrus, one of the peaks named for cloud formations. No date has been established for the naming of the lake, but it was after J. G. Rogers christened the Cloud Peaks.

Lambs Slide　　　　　GLACIER GORGE, WILD BASIN
Elkanah Lamb (1832-1915) spent a pleasant childhood on a farm in Indiana. After he became interested in religion, the United Brethren sent him to the St. Vrain District as missionary to preach in the towns at the foot of the mountains. He was a powerful preacher, all six feet four of him, and a man of tremendous energy. After riding from the plains to Estes Park, 35 miles in one day, he was distressed and surprised when he went to the stable the next morning to find his pony dead.

Lamb was twice married, rearing both his children and stepchildren. For this he needed more money than the unlucrative mission field afforded, so he homesteaded 160 acres of land east of Longs Peak. Here he installed his family in 1875. His wife ran a dairy and kept Longs Peak House, Lamb helping between sermons in the South Platte towns. Gradually he forsook his ministerial work. He and his son guided parties to the top of Longs Peak at $5 a trip. "If they would not pay for spiritual guidance," Parson Lamb wrote, "I compelled them to pay for material elevation." As guides, in 1902 they made the ascent easier for their clients by building a trail to the "Bowlderfield," which the son maintained long after their lodge was sold to Enos Mills.

Before Lamb settled for life in Estes Park he made a trip from the plains expressly to climb Longs Peak. In his memoirs he described this August 1871 climb and his descent of what became known as Lambs Slide. He tells that one by one each of the eight people who started the climb fell by the wayside.

Brother Ross would not leave his wife, and the maternal instincts of the mother of the young lady who had fainted would not permit her to leave; another had such a headache; another was frightened. . . . I went forward on my lonely way, . . . humorously remarking that we must climb higher than this if we ever get to heaven. Something over a thousand feet higher brought me to the summit of this historic pile of granite and quartz, a huge monster nearly three miles above sea level, ten miles around its base. The sight is magnificent. . . .

After one hour's feasting of my mental and spiritual and somewhat poetical nature on these sights and scenes, I concluded to go down the eastern face of the mountain, where man had never gone before. Some old roads, rules, grooves, and conventional codes are gray with honor, but to be tied and governed by anything because of the virtue of age is an absurdity, not to be tolerated by intelligent minds. . . .

After getting down more than a thousand feet from the summit, I began to realize the rashness of the undertaking. Having already passed dangerous points, perpendicular places, ice patches, and frowning walls, worse dangers confronted me. I concluded to go back, if possible, and go down the old way; but like thousands in life's downward trend, I soon realized the fact that I had already passed dangerous points and sloping icy places that were almost impossible to round or ascend. I then turned my course to face the music, trying to concentrate all the courage of my normal condition, both occult and physical. Regrets and repentance for rash recklessness are bitter consolations for deviations and perilous ventures, but the most unpleasant medicine must be taken by the transgressor. I hope the reader will remember this.

In my further descent, I came to a place that seemed to say, "Thus far shalt thou go, but not farther." The mountain wall was not only perpendicular, but projected with a frowning incline some degrees over my icy pathway. This miniature glacier was perhaps five rods wide, descending down

113

to a crater lake thousands of feet below, standing at an angle of forty or fifty degrees. This projecting wall was only three or four rods in swing, then receded gradually back. Well, the inevitable in my case was to go forward. With finger holds in meager niches of the wall and my feet pressing the edge of the ice, I started across this dangerous section. Quicker than I can tell it, my hands failed to hold, my feet slipped, and down I went with almost an arrow's rapidity. An eternity of thought, of life, death, wife, and home, concentrated in my mind in those two seconds. . . .

Fortunately for me, I threw my right arm around a projecting bowlder, which stood above the icy plain some two or three feet. This sudden stopping of my acrobatic performance brought my long walking appendages around with a musical swash, turning my overcoat skirts nearly over my head, and spilling all the specimens I had gathered on the summit, which went sliding and jumping downward, seemingly glad of their release from captivity. Here I was swinging with my right arm around this bowlder, at least five feet from the body of the mountain. The conical shape of the bowlder precluded my standing upon it for a jump to safety. Getting my knife out of my pocket, I opened it with my teeth, then reached half-way to the rocks of safety and began digging a niche in the ice for a toe hold, when my knife broke in two. This left me stranded and stopped further progress in digging. My nervous system was very much unstrung by this sliding, swinging experience, but I was compelled to decide—quickly, too. So putting the tip of my left foot in the shallow niche I had cut, (knowing that if my foot slipped I was a lost Lamb,) then working my arm to the top of the rock, I gave a huge lunge, just managing to reach the foot of the mountain. Drawing myself out of this perilous situation, I was plainly impressed that my salvation was a divine and direct providence. I immediately fell upon my knees and thanked God for my deliverance. . . .

Then, on I went, finally coming to a perpendicular granite wall. Grooves were worn into its face by the action of water in streams and drippings for untold ages. My situation was fearful to contemplate. The mountain was perpendicular on the south over the lake; to the north, utterly inaccessible. The only alternative was to go down one of these grooves in the granite wall. Selecting one with projecting rocks sufficient for foot and hand holds, I let myself down this perilous incline. It almost makes my hair stand erect to remember this trying time of thirty-four years ago. This descent brought me to Crater Lake, nestling close to Long's Peak range. . . . Working around the lake's steep margin, I finally reached our camp, and threw myself prone upon the ground.

Lark Pond   WILD BASIN
The greatly-beloved western meadowlark is a blackbird, and the lark bunting, the Colorado state bird, is a finch; the horned lark is the only native American lark. Found throughout the United States, always in open country, in Colorado it nests on the plains and on the alpine tundra, never in between. A sparrow-sized brownish ground bird, its face is patterned in black and yellow surmounted by two small feather horns. Its tinkly bubble of a song resembles not at all the music of Shelley's English skylark. Lark Pond was called Bluebird Lake on the Cooper-Babcock map of 1911.

Larkspur Creek   GLACIER GORGE
The brief course of Larkspur Creek runs entirely above 10,000 feet. There, in the short summer of the Subalpine Zone, where melting snow leaves hillsides spongy, the Barbey larkspur grows waist high and higher. Climbers push their way through its luxuriant green with the short crowded spikes of deep blue flowers, varied once in a while with a pink one.

This is one of the three varieties of larkspur that grow in Rocky Mountain National Park. An even taller variety, the mountain larkspur, blooms in August in the aspen groves of the Montane Zone. In the same zone around the Fourth of July, sometimes among ponderosa pines, sometimes among sagebrush, sometimes in spectacular fields of purplish-blue on open hillsides, Nelson's larkspur blooms.

The shape of the upper sepal gives the plant its name. Long and pointed, it forms a spur like that on the foot of a bird. Larkspur is the same plant as the garden delphinium. Ranch wives have been known to buy plants of highly cultivated delphinium for their flower gardens only to have their irate husbands root out the plants as soon as the characteristic leaves show, because larkspur is poisonous to cattle. In early spring as many as 100 head of cattle have been killed in one area in a few days by feasting on its pleasantly acid leaves. In the Park, even a rancher can enjoy the flowers unreservedly since no cattle now range there.

Lawn Lake 10,987'   MUMMY RANGE
Abner Sprague accompanied some English hunters to this lake in 1871. Because the surface of the water was smooth and green while they were there, he compared it to a plot of mown lawn. Or did the Britishers tell him it looked like the green lawns of England? In the

late 1880's, Hallett's less imaginative name for the lake was Forest Lake. Whatever its name, fishermen early beat a trail up the banks of Roaring River to the lake.

About 1910, Willard H. Ashton of Horseshoe Inn built a shelter cabin at Lawn Lake. He hired two college boys to stay at the cabin, do the chores, cook, and act as guides for flatlanders who wanted to climb Mummy Mountain or Hagues Peak or go over The Saddle to Rowe Glacier. The last permit secured for this shelter was dated 1920. Another shelter cabin was maintained here by the Park for a number of years, but the building was razed in 1964.

In 1911 Hugh Ramsey of Pingree Park built a dam to enlarge Lawn Lake; the water is now used on the plains by the Farmers Ditch Company. Perhaps it was Ramsey, perhaps Ashton, who enlarged the trail to a wagon road, though it really was too steep for horse-drawn vehicles.

Lead Mtn. 12,537' NEVER SUMMER

This name dates back at least to 1879 when prospectors around Lulu City recorded their claims as located in the Lead Mountain Mining District.

Lead ore proved a heavy nuisance to prospectors seeking metals in this district; the owners of the Wolverine Mine found that freight charges ate up their profits. Also, there are tales of pure lead. Trappers told Abner Sprague they had picked up lead nuggets on the Poudre River which they used, unworked, as bullets.

Lehman Ditch GRAND LAKE, LAKE GRANBY

The Lehman family lived on the South Fork of the Grand River. They ran a summer resort, with cottages around their large house. Mrs. Lehman was noted for her feather-beds and her hospitality. When she had not given a dance for a long time, the editor of the Grand Lake paper reminded her in print that the local residents were open to an invitation. The Lehmans had four daughters and a son. The oldest girl married a man named King; their place was about a quarter of a mile from the main road between Granby and Grand Lake. When any mail was destined for Monarch Lake or the ranches on the South Fork, the stagecoach detoured to the King's place. The Lehman Ranch became part of the Knight Ranch. Before Lake Granby covered the South Fork valley, the Lehman ranch house was moved to Murray Camp, half a mile east of the old town of Monarch.

Lily Lake ESTES PARK

"Fittingly called the Lake of the Lilies," is what Isabella Bird wrote in 1873, and in 1888 Chapin and his botanist wife admired the water lilies blooming in Lily Lake.

The yellow pond lily is the common water lily of high mountain

116

lakes, blooming from July to frost. The broad leaves keep the water cool enough for trout, but warn fishermen that the shallow ponds have become too deep for hipboots. Children eat water lily seeds; muskrats eat the rootstocks, as did Indians if they were desperately hungry. (See Nymph Lake.)

Lily Mtn. 9786'   Estes Park

Anyone interested in the evolution of geographic names should trace the name Lily on various maps of the Park area. It has been spelled Lillie, Lilly, Lilie, and Lily; and has been applied to present Twin Sisters, Gianttrack and Lily Mountains. According to Enos Mills, an engineer named Lillie settled very early in the Park. The Hayden atlases, 1877 and 1882, label Twin Sisters as Lillie's Mt., and an 1897 map designates the same summit as Lilie's Peak. Chapin in 1888 wrote of a mountain with stupendous cliffs hanging over the valley which from the west was called Lily Mountain, from the east Twin Sisters.

Present Lily Mountain and Lily Lake are labeled Lilly on Enos Mills' 1905 map and the 1910 Burlington map. Perhaps it was W. S. Cooper's interest in botany that led him to simplify the name to Lily Mountain on his 1911 map. The issue was further confused by the statement by Enos Mills that Lilly Mountain had two wells sunk in solid granite, which are on today's Gianttrack Mountain.

The Colorado Geographic Board attacked the muddle of orthography and geography, and fastened names securely on Twin Sisters, Gianttrack, and Lily Mountain, to the satisfaction of everyone except the ghost of Mr. Lillie, pioneer.

Lion Lake No. 1 and No. 2   Wild Basin

Roger Toll considered the name of Lynes Reservoir No. 2, sometimes spelled Lyons Reservoir, and found it inappropriate. In 1923 he changed the names of these lakes to Lion.

The mountain lion, biggest of the American cats, has been seen in Wild Basin by a few people and usually from a distance. The animal may inhabit low rugged canyons, like those around Devils Gulch, and cruise into the Park during its 100-mile tours in search of game.

Little Matterhorn   Forest Canyon, Glacier Gorge

This was named either by Dr. W. J. Workman of Fern Lake Lodge, or Frank Byerly, a later owner of the Lodge. In 1914 Byerly took his hand-colored stereoscopic pictures of scenic beauties, like Longs Peak, Grand Lake, and the Little Matterhorn above Odessa Lake, to Washington, to show to Congress as part of The Colorado Mountain Club's campaign for the proposed Estes National Park. Arrangements for this pictorial lobbying were made by Morrison Shafroth, son of Senator John F. Shafroth of Denver and an enthusiastic member of the Club.

117

Little Pawnee Peak— (East of Pawnee Peak)

The altitude of the highest point on the ridge that runs east of Pawnee Peak is 12,466 feet. In 1965, Evilio Echevarría, a mountain climber from Chile living in Boulder, proposed that this point be named Little Pawnee Peak. The name was accepted by the U.S. Board on Geographic Names too late to be printed on the Indian Peaks map in this dictionary. (See also Shoshoni Peak.)

Little Yellowstone   NEVER SUMMER

"Winnie" Winston of Kelly, Wyoming, later athletic director of the University of Illinois, was a ranger in the Park. He named this section because of the eroded yellow rocks.

Livingston Lake   NEVER SUMMER

When Julian Livingston came from his large bakery business in Chicago to summer in Estes, he built a vacation home and dammed Black Canyon Creek to make himself a fish pond now called Livingston Lake. For many summers he was an interested and generous citizen of the community. His son, Louis, also in the bakery business in Chicago, now operates a dude ranch on the Devils Gulch road.

Loch Vale and The Loch   GLACIER GORGE

A Mr. Locke, banker from Kansas City who died in 1909, was a guest at the hotel of Abner Sprague. One day he and his host were lost—temporarily of course—on a hill near this lake. Sprague, who was rarely lost, commemorated the trip by naming the lake and the vale after his guest, changing the spelling of Locke to the Scotch word Loch, meaning Lake.

Lochleven Cove   LAKE GRANBY

Brown trout, imported from Europe to America in 1883, are sometimes called Lochleven. They thrive in slightly muddy and warmish waters, and are doing well in the impounded waters of Lake Granby.

Loft, The   GLACIER GORGE, WILD BASIN

In his *Mountaineering in the Rocky Mountain National Park*, published in 1919, Roger Toll wrote about "a perfectly level platform called the Loft, a name strongly suggested both by form and location of the place, and by the mode of access to it." The name was probably in use for years before this by Longs Peak climbers. Has any climber identified what Isabella Bird called The Dog's Lift?

Lone Eagle Peak 11,920′   INDIAN PEAKS

The story of Lone Eagle Peak starts with Fred Fair who lived in Boulder but preferred to spend his time in the mountains. He knew the area around Apache Peak, on both sides of the Divide, as only a surveyor (he was official surveyor for Boulder County) and mountaineer could. In 1908 he discovered the Crater Lake country and sang its praises until his friends called it Fred Fair's Hell Hole.

Fair spent years promoting roads (and transportation companies to carry tourists over the roads) into the glacier country west of his home town. (See Arapaho Glacier.) In 1923 as part of a national publicity campaign financed chiefly by the Denver & Interurban Railway, Fair announced $1000 would be paid to the aviator who would land his plane on the slopes of the St. Vrain Glacier, the smoothest in the vicinity. Such a stunt would certainly create public interest.

No aviator was tempted by this cash award until the day a barnstormer, landing his plane near Boulder, sent word to Fred Fair that he would like to see him. Fair went out to meet a quiet young man from Wisconsin who had some scheme that needed financing; Slim Lindbergh said he would land his crate on a glacier or anywhere else for $1000. Fair looked at the crate held together by baling wire. Thinking to himself that an accident on the glacier would produce the wrong kind of publicity, Fair told the young flyer that the plane would be wrecked. Slim observed that the offer said nothing about a return trip—he was not planning to fly out. But Mr. Fair turned him down.

Four years later, in May 1927, Charles A. Lindbergh flew from New York to Paris in a plane powered by a single engine with nine cylinders. During his subsequent tour of America to promote aeronautics, Fred Fair asked him if he remembered the incident of the glacier flight that was not made. Colonel Lindbergh said he did indeed.

Whenever a national hero emerges, someone in Colorado wants to name a mountain for him. *The Denver Post* proposed that a Colorado peak be named after the daring aviator. Fair's mind flashed back to the glacier country. He remembered a certain sharp rock. "Towering above the ice-gouged abyss of Hell Hole stands a granite shaft that points a solitary finger skyward," wrote a reporter after he had interviewed Fair.

Organizations took up the campaign. In September 1927 Mrs. Clara De Nio of the Federated Women's Clubs of Colorado consulted Colonel Allen Peck of the U.S. Forest Service, who doubted that the peak was prominent enough. By the next August Colonel Peck, having made a trip to see it, had changed his mind. "I was astonished," he wrote, "at the impressiveness of the scenery, to put it mildly; in fact, I have seen nothing of its kind to equal it. . . . There is no question in my mind but that the peak is sufficiently impressive to justify its being named after Lindbergh and also that Lindbergh merits a peak named for him."

Early in June 1929 a promotional organization named the Colorado Association dispatched two members of The Colorado Mountain Club to see if the peak could be climbed. Carl Blaurock and William

F. Ervin first scouted an eastern approach. Between Apache and Navajo Peaks they were blocked by snow and night. On June 20 they tried the western approach. Walking nine miles from Monarch Lake they arrived at the foot of the peak too late for a climb that day. Finally, on Labor Day, September 2, 1929, these two climbers and Stephen J. Hart organized a first-class expedition. They even hired pack horses at Monarch Lake to carry supplies for as long a stay as was needed. Camping at Crater Lake, the following day they climbed "the granite shaft that points a solitary finger skyward." They found the ascent not difficult if the vertical face were avoided.

The committee for naming Lindbergh Peak then considered the desirability of making a view of the peak accessible to motorists by building a road either over Pawnee Pass from the east or from Monarch Lake on the west. In June 1930 the decision was that a road from Monarch Lake be built with government aid, with Fred Fair as construction engineer. The road was to be named Evangeline Road for the mother of Charles A. Lindbergh.

At that point some one thought to consult the U.S. Board on Geographic Names. The Board promptly produced its rule against naming geographical features after living persons. Would the Board approve a nickname? The Board would. Whereupon *The Denver Post* publicized another contest. A school child won the contest with Lindy, but the name that seemed more appropriate to the Committee was proposed by a veteran at Fitzsimons Hospital—Lone Eagle. Fred Fair approved and offered to persuade the club women to change. Harry Knight said that his friend Lindbergh would surely approve. Colonel Peck thought the new name would be "undoubtedly more acceptable to Colonel Lindbergh, and I think a little more appropriate because of the opportunities for symbolism in the name."

As of 1966 the road from Monarch Lake has not materialized, nor is Lone Eagle Peak visible from any present highway. Symbolically, perhaps a mountain named for the man who first dared fly across the Atlantic should remain somewhat inaccessible.

Perhaps Ronald L. Ives of The Colorado Mountain Club thought Lone Eagle Peak should have companions when, in 1932, after he climbed the mountain northwest of Crater Lake, he suggested the mountain be named Dwight Morrow Peak, for Lindbergh's father-in-law. Ives also suggested Anne Peak (Lindbergh's wife) for the 12,799 foot point between Peck and Fair Glaciers. Nothing came of these suggestions and Lone Eagle Peak still stands alone in Fred Fair's Hell Hole.

Lone Pine Lake GRAND LAKE

Fred McLaren said this lake named itself. The lone pine grows on a lone island in the middle of the lake.

Lonesome Peak 10,588'. (Less than 2 miles south of Monarch Lake)
The High Lonesome Mine is on the side of this isolated peak and
the High Lonesome Trail runs beside it.

Long Draw, Long Draw Reservoir—See Grand Ditch

Long Meadows   Grand Lake

Longs Peak 14,256'   Glacier Gorge, Wild Basin
That the highest mountain in the Estes Park region (the fifteenth
highest in Colorado) should bear the oldest name seems appropriate.
A hundred and fifty years is a long time in the West, and the date was
1820 when a young army officer, Stephen Harriman Long, led 22 men
on horseback and two dogs (even the dogs rode part of the way before
they died of thirst on the plains of eastern Colorado) from north to
south along the foot of the Front Range of the Colorado Rockies. Dr.
Edwin James, age 23, was the botanist and geologist of the expedition
and the first person on record to climb Pikes Peak. His journal of the
Long expedition, published in 1823, became the textbook for every
literate traveler who planned a journey west. On its map the plains
of northeastern Colorado, now fertile under irrigation, bore the stigma
The Great American Desert. The mountain toward the northwest was
labelled Highest Peak. Naturally, this soon became known by the
name of the man who led the expedition; in 1842, Fremont was pleased
that fur traders were using the name Longs Peak.

Two names were used for this peak before 1820—one by Indians,
one by trappers. The Indians used the two highest peaks in Rocky
Mountain National Park, Longs and Meeker, for a utilitarian purpose. When the natives traveled the piedmont plains and needed a
compass point, there stood The Two Guides. (The French wrote the
Indian word for this as *Nesotaieux*.) French-speaking trappers, aping
Indians in all things in order to survive in the Indian world, used the
peaks in the same way, calling them *Les Deux Oreilles*, The Two Ears.
Camping under the cottonwoods at the mouth of Cherry Creek the
trappers could tell at a glance which direction was northwest, for there
stood The Two Ears (though Mt. Meeker almost hid Longs Peak).
In 1858 William Larimer laid out the streets of downtown Denver
northwest-southeast, to the confusion of subsequent inhabitants. He
could have used the square top of Longs Peak for his surveying point
on Seventeenth Street. "Longs Peak . . . just fills the vista of the principal business street. . . . The people look upon this glorious alpine
view as one of the properties of the town." So wrote Bayard Taylor in
1866, and so it is a hundred years later. Many a harried banker, emerg-

ing from his skyscraper office onto Seventeenth Street, checks on Longs and Meeker before he goes about his business.

Lookout Mtn. 10,715' WILD BASIN

Because of intervening, lower mountains, it is hard to find an eminence from which to view the peaks that form the jagged rim of Wild Basin. W. S. Cooper used this mountain for a triangulation point when he first surveyed Wild Basin. On the Burlington map of 1910 the mountain is called Triangulation Point.

Lookout Springs ESTES PARK

Loomis Lake FOREST CANYON

A Dr. Loomis is reputed to have built the first cabin at Fern Lake, even before Dr. Workman built Fern Lake Lodge. Dr. Loomis found the skeleton of an especially large fish on the shores of this lake. He talked about it, and talked about it so much that the lake was named for him.

Dr. Workman preferred, as usual, to name this lake for a girl—two girls, in fact. Sally Reed (Mrs. Charles Reed of the Brinwood, mother of Mrs. Julian Hayden), and Dora Sprague Stead (Mrs. J. D. Stead of Steads Ranch) were honored. Saldora Lake was the result, but Loomis Lake is the official name.

Lost Brook—FOREST CANYON; **Lost Creek**—NEVER SUMMER; **Lost Lake** —MUMMY RANGE

Lost Falls MUMMY RANGE

Up to 1961, these falls on the North Fork of the Big Thompson were simply called The Falls.

Louise, Lake MUMMY RANGE

In 1941 E. A. Abbott, Chicago, remembered when Shep Husted, long ago, guided him on a trip above Lost Lake on the North Fork of the Big Thompson. They named a lake there after Mrs. Abbott— Lake Louise.

Love Lake FOREST CANYON

This miniature body of water seems to have had no official name before the 1961 map. Whether it is named for an emotion or a man named Love is not clear.

Pettingell Lake was once unofficially named after a man called Jack Love. He was a carpenter in Grand Lake village, and sometimes worked for Fred McLaren, superintendent of the western side of the Park. Fred regularly sent him up to Pettingell Lake with fingerling trout, and Jack was so impressed with the scenery that the Park rangers jocularly called that Love's Lake, though it was never an official name.

Lulu City (site), **Creek; Lulu Mtn.** 12,228'

Miners started a town in the valley of the North Fork of the Grand River in 1879, naming it after a girl. But what girl? In the memories of old-timers two Lulus vie for this honor. The majority claim Lulu, daughter of Benjamin Franklin Burnett, one of the founders of Lulu City. Squeaky Bob Wheeler remembered her as the most beautiful girl he had ever seen, whose lips were red without benefit of lipstick. H. N. Wheeler, first superintendent of the Colorado National Forest, and old-timers of the Poudre country claim the honor for Lulu Stewart, whose father, Samuel B. Stewart, homesteaded at Rustic on the Poudre in 1881 and carried mail to Teller City.

The Colorado Geographic Board recorded both Lulus but declined to make a choice. They did, however, choose to change the name of Lulu Pass to Thunder Pass. Perhaps as compensation to the girl named Lulu, the Forest Service suggested Lulu Mountain which was accepted by the U.S. Board on Geographic Names in October 1929.

Lumpy Ridge 9606'

The 1914 Arapahos described the rocks that project all along this ridge with a word that translated as Little Lumps. The Colorado Geographic Board, recognizing the appropriateness of the name, retained Lumps but discarded Little. They added two other names in common use on either end of Lumpy Ridge: the rather thick Needles on the northwest, the plump Twin Owls to the southeast.

Lyric Falls

Named by Jack Moomaw, ranger.

M

McDonald Cove Lake Granby

This name commemorates one of the fishing resorts now covered by Lake Granby. When I. L. Killie controlled about 1200 acres on the South Fork of the Grand River, his upper and lower ranches, which he owned, were separated by a school section which he leased at some nominal sum like 6¢ an acre per year. Edgar L. McDonald, a business man from Fraser in Middle Park, acquired the lease on part of the school lands, paying more than Killie; and then Miss Margaret Murray, a spinster, acquired part of the school lands to start Murray Camp at the bend of the river. McDonald was a stockholder in the Rocky Mountain Lumber Company. After its box factory burned in 1908, McDonald, for transportation to Granby and to entertain his guests, equipped an automobile with metal wheels and wooden flanges and ran this contraption on the rails of the Rocky Mountain Railroad. (See Monarch Lake.)

McGregor Mtn. 10,486' Estes Park, Mummy Range

Though this was named for a man who spelled his name Mac-Gregor, the U.S. Board on Geographic Names simplified the spelling by dropping the *a*. Alexander Quinter MacGregor, a lawyer from Milwaukee, came to Denver in 1869. Hunting in Estes Park in 1872, he was entranced not only with the scenery but with Maria Clara Heeney, an art student from Wisconsin on a sketching tour. Her mother, Georgiana, chaperon of the group, proved her own feeling for the scenery by buying land in Black Canyon. To this land MacGregor brought his bride, and this land is still ranched by their granddaughter.

Mrs. MacGregor became the first postmistress of Estes Park, using her home as the post office. Mail usually came in once a week, brought by anybody who happened to be coming from Longmont. In 1875 Alexander MacGregor built a toll road from Lyons, but encountered trouble collecting toll from the rugged individualists who settled Estes Park. MacGregor, hunting with his son in June of 1896, was killed by lightning on top of Fall River Pass.

McHenrys Notch; McHenrys Peak 13,327' Glacier Gorge

B. F. McHenry, who taught higher mathematics and science at Union Christian College, Merom, Indiana, spent three summers in the Estes Park region in the early 1890's, camping one summer in Wild Basin with some boys under his charge. Abner Sprague named the mountain after him, calling him "a nice old man."

On September 19, 1898, Professor McHenry wrote a description of his attempt to climb McHenrys Peak to George H. Knifton, president of the Rocky Mountain Club. The letter tells of a conditioning outing of 20 days.

[We went] up Windy Gulch, over that magnificent Rocky Mountain walk to Specimen Mountain; thence down the worst of mountain trails to a branch of the Grand River which was full of trout easy to catch; thence to Grand Lake; thence to Flat Top Mountain, and down over Bierstadt Moraine. . . .

Feeling now prepared for any adventure, we, J. B. Maple, Howard McHenry, my son, and self set out with determination to go to and climb the mountain they have dishonored by my name. We soon found out that following a trail is an easy task compared with the work of going where never a trail was cut. To get our donkey into the great gorge west of Long's Peak or into any of the many wonderful gorges leading to it; or to find a place for camping somewhere south of Flat Top; or coming in by the south of Grand View Hotel and taking advantage of their 7 miles of new trail, and so finding a camping place within less than a half day's walk (and climb) of the unexplored region, all these were undertakings we submitted to ourselves and did our best to achieve. We failed to accomplish what we set out to do, but we did not fail. We were all the while in country grand beyond description. Whoever opens up to students of nature and lovers of the grand and beautiful that "heart of the Rocky Mountains" a little south of west of Longs Peak will be a benefactor not only to that large class of the best of mankind, but through them to the race. I trust your club will succeed in doing what we have failed to do; and further, I trust that the beauty, the grandeur, the sublimity of that region will so pervade the hearts of those you send that they will not rest till they make a way by which others can go and enjoy the best the Rocky Mountains afford.

Mahana Peak 12,632′ (Pronounced Ma' ha na)　　　　WILD BASIN
Although Ellsworth Bethel submitted Comanche as a name for one of the Indian Peaks (probably present Chiefs Head), the U.S. Board on Geographic Names, doubtless noting that a peak 35 miles to the north had borne the name Comanche since the 1876 King Survey, turned down his suggestion. Bethel was irate until he (or more likely Harriet Vaille, who was a gentle person) discovered a compromise. The Taos Indians called the Comanche tribe *Mahana*; thus the Comanches took their place among the Indian tribes of the Front Range.

125

Many Parks Curve ESTES PARK, FOREST CANYON

Spread out below this vantage point are several open tracts or mountain parks rimmed by tree-covered glacial moraines. Visible are Beaver Meadows, Moraine Park, Tuxedo Park, Glacier Basin (Barthoff Park), and others.

Marguerite Falls FOREST CANYON

This is another of the female names Dr. Workman scattered over the Park. Marguerite Turck, a visitor from Denver, was of the Turck family who pioneered in Central City.

Marigold Lake, Pond FOREST CANYON, GLACIER GORGE

The marsh marigold is not gold at all, except its center, but has white many-petaled flowers, bluish on the underside. Its leaves are dark green and rotund. It grows abundantly in wet ground, either in open places among trees or in alpine meadows. Roger Toll must have wet his boots walking through thousands of these and their usual companions, globeflowers, before he named the lake in 1921.

Marmot Point 11,909′ MUMMY RANGE

Roger Toll named this in 1922. Woodchucks (the eastern name for marmots) love high points like this. Climbers say the marmots who inhabit the square summit of Longs Peak fare well on the lunches exhausted hikers cannot eat.

Marmots are medium-sized western woodchucks. Their nickname "whistle-pigs" describes them well, for they whistle high and shrill. They eat enough to get as fat as pigs in order to hibernate; those who live highest hibernate eight months of the year.

Marten Peak 12,041′ INDIAN PEAKS

Enos Mills showed his naturalist interest by naming geographical features for birds, like Ouzel Lake; for weather, like Storm Mountain; and for animals. Marten Peak is said to be one of his names though it stands far from his Longs Peak haunts. However, when Enos Mills was taking snow measurements he covered the whole area, and if he saw a marten or two on this peak, the sight of them is rare enough to warrant the name.

The marten lives in dense forests, spruce and pine (he is sometimes called the pine marten), and will not stay in woods that have been lumbered or burned. He is long like a weasel, has a bushy tail, is agile and vicious; a marten will kill for the sake of killing, and he has no friends. He feeds everywhere, darting under fallen trees for chickarees, snatching baby marmots from their burrows, and seizing ducks from ponds. Mice and rabbits are his staple food, and when the rabbit population is up, so is the marten.

126

Marys Lake 8046'   ESTES PARK

When Mary Jane Roberts, niece of Griff Evans, told Rocky Mountain Jim of her plan to ride by a certain lake with her fiancé on her birthday in May 1874, Jim gallantly declared that the lake thereafter should be known as Marys Lake. This was probably Jim's private joke, since he must have known that the lake had been called Marys Lake since the spring of 1861, in honor of Mary L. Fleming, bride of Milton Estes.

The Irish Lord Dunraven sainted the lake. He wrote, "The water of St. Mary's Lake is strongly impregnated with alkali and leaves a deposit around the edges. Sheep, deer, and cattle come for the salt."

Meadow Mtn. 11,632'   WILD BASIN

W. S. Cooper submitted this name to the U.S. Board on Geographic Names before publishing his map in 1911, saying the mountain was "a rounded hill covered with a most beautiful alpine meadow." When he talked of this meadow in 1965, in Dr. Cooper's memory the wildflowers were obviously blooming again.

Medicine Bow Curve—MUMMY RANGE; **Medicine Bow Mtns.**—NEVER SUMMER

Looking northwest from the parking place on Trail Ridge Road called Medicine Bow Curve, one sees the Medicine Bow Mountains stretching into blue Wyoming. In that state, however, the popular name for the continuation of the range between the North Platte and Laramie Rivers is the Snowy Range, because the 10,000 foot peneplain of the Medicine Bow Mountains is topped by a range made of crystalline quartzite that glitters like snow. The U.S. Geological Survey in Denver has requested Washington for a decision—should these mountains be written on their new maps as Medicine Bow Mountains, or as the Snowy Range? If the decision is for Snowy Range, Wyoming will have the Medicine Bow National Forest, but the only Medicine Bow Mountains will be in Colorado. Perhaps that is a fair exchange, for Colorado used to have a Snowy Range. Most writers of early Denver spoke of the view of the mountains from that town in two parts: to the southwest stretched the Rampart Range, a low, blue barrier named by Major Long in 1820; west of Denver lay what we call Mt. Evans; and northwest stretched other glistening giants, all called the Snowy Range.

No satisfactory explanation has been found for the name Medicine Bow Mountains. It dates back to the Indians, and one explanation is that Indians thought the range was bow-shaped. The mountains are curved on maps, and from the air, but did they seem curved to Indians on the ground?

The more usual explanation goes back to a legend. Each year, the story tells, friendly tribes met in these mountains to fashion bows out of mountain mahogany and to invoke the blessings of the gods on the bows. This was a ceremony to "make medicine."

The legend is strictly legend. No documentation has been found that any Indians held yearly ceremonials in the Medicine Bow Mountains to "make medicine." The Indians probably made bows in these mountains, but not of mountain mahogany, for the tall-growing variety (*Cercocarpus ledifolius*) does not grow in the Medicine Bow Mountains, nor have we record of any Indian bows made from it. The Indians of the Colorado-Wyoming country made their bows of the horns of mountain sheep or buffalo; or of wood—Osage orange (*Bois d'Arc*), ash, hickory, or juniper, perhaps other wood; but none of these, except juniper, grows in the northern mountains. The Indians traded and raided in Kansas and south of the Arkansas River, and brought back not only horses and slaves but materials they could not find in their own territory, like wood for bows. So unless the legend dates from prehistoric times (as does the Indian name for Specimen Mountain) Indians could not have bows of mountain mahogany from the Medicine Bow Mountains.

The name puzzled early travelers, too. In 1856, Francis T. Bryan must have thought the spoken words had a French accent; throughout his lengthy report to Congress he spelled the name Medicine Bon—good medicine. A century ago a writer heard another name for these mountains, and was as puzzled as we are today about why they were sometimes called Medicine Bow. In 1868 W. E. Waters wrote:

> On most popular maps this spur of the Rocky Mountains is styled Meridian Ridge, or the Meridian Bow Range, but on the topographical charts of the army it is put down as I have written it, and is so called by mountaineers who are familiar with the country. Why it is designated Medicine Bow I have not yet learned.

Meeker Ridge—Wild Basin; **Meeker, Mt. 13,911—**Glacier Gorge, Wild Basin

Nathan Meeker, agricultural editor of the *New York Tribune*, came west in 1869 in search of land on which to start a farming community where he could try out his theories of cooperative agriculture. With the help of William Byers, he picked the place where the Poudre empties into the South Platte River. Returning to New York, he found his boss, Horace Greeley, eager to lend to the enterprise not only the columns of his newspaper but his unblemished reputation. When Greeley became the treasurer of the Union Colony, its success was assured. Though Greeley visited the colony only once, his name was chosen for the town the colonists started.

In 1873 Anna Dickinson, lady lecturer, visited the town and was impressed. Perhaps she wondered why Meeker's name had not been used for the town; he worked very hard for a compensation of $160 a month. While she and Ralph Meeker, Nathan's son, and William Byers and the Hayden Survey men sat around the campfire after climbing Longs Peak, they may have talked of this. Why not name a mountain for Meeker? Byers may have suggested the East Peak of Longs. This would insure that Meeker's name would live in Colorado history. Six years later in 1879, Father Meeker unfortunately insured himself a more prominent niche in history by getting himself massacred by the Northern Utes on the White River Reservation.

Mertensia Falls   WILD BASIN

W. S. Cooper named these falls. Many kinds of mertensia grow in Wild Basin. Probably the variety young Cooper noticed were the tall chiming bells, sometimes called languid ladies because they droop clusters of blue and pink flowers over streams.

Michigan Lakes, River   NEVER SUMMER

At the time of the Lulu City boom, a mine and town flourished near the top of Cameron Pass. Probably a homesick miner named the mine for his home state—Michigan. The name progressed from mine to river to lake to ditch. William Rist and John McNabb, later supervisor of the Grand Ditch, built the Michigan Ditch from Lake Agnes across the Divide to the Poudre drainage.

Mill Creek, Mill Creek Basin   FOREST CANYON

Horace Ferguson in 1876 defied the Earl of Dunraven's claims by homesteading near Marys Lake. When he built his Highlands Hotel, he brought lumber from a sawmill on Mill Creek. Perhaps this was his own mill; H. N. Wheeler, superintendent of Colorado National Forest, wrote that Ferguson was operating a mill in 1880, though he failed to specify its location. Wheeler stated that a sawmill on Mill Creek in 1880 had a 12-horsepower engine that sawed lumber worth $8 to $10 per thousand board feet at the mill, $4 more in Loveland. Hallett and MacGregor were also operating sawmills in the area.

Miller Creek   MUMMY RANGE

This name commemorates the first death by accident in the Park district. Charles W. Dennison, a man who had settled in 1868 near Muggins Gulch, accidentally shot Charles D. Miller on May 17, 1871. A monument to Miller stands at the junction of Miller Creek and the Poudre River, on the exact spot where Miller died, with Miller Creek, as Parson Lamb wrote, "murmuring his last requiem."

Mills Glacier, Lake, Moraine   GLACIER GORGE

Enos Mills is fittingly commemorated by features that bear his name on two sides of Longs Peak. On the northwest, Abner Sprague named Mills Lake after him; to the south, Mills Glacier and Mills

Moraine look down to the site of Mills' hotel, famous Longs Peak Inn.

Enos Mills (1870-1922) was a Kansas farm boy who came to Estes Park when he was 15. He immediately started to walk alone over the northern Colorado mountains, in winter as well as summer. He learned the area in winter as snow observer for the Colorado Department of Engineers, whose managers had recently concluded that if they knew exactly how deep the snow was in any given winter they could estimate how much water would flow in the streams that summer. In order to measure the depth of snow, Enos Mills tramped miles on snowshoes, camping where night found him. On his lonely trips, the young man observed birds, animals, trees—especially trees. In after years his most famous lecture was called "Our Friends, the Trees."

In order to make enough money to buy Longs Peak House from Elkanah Lamb, Enos Mills worked many winters in the mines of Butte, Montana. A few years after he bought the hotel it burned. He built Longs Peak Inn in 1906, demonstrating his interest in trees by using fire-killed trunks and branches as screens, spindles for staircases, and porch railings. This rustic architecture was an unfailing conversation piece, Mills always turning the conversation into a nature lesson. Groups of guests that he conducted up Longs Peak he called Nature Schools. He was a born conservationist, and, about 1909, developed the idea of a large national park. His vigorous efforts to preserve the country he loved so other people could enjoy it were most influential in the formation of Rocky Mountain National Park.

When his busy life as hotel host, guide, and lecturer gave him any time to himself, he spent long winter evenings reading the books he had missed in his youth; then, drawing on his own experiences in the wilds, he wrote books that have brought pleasure to generations of young people. Twelve books were published in his lifetime, four posthumously.

Milner Pass 10,758' NEVER SUMMER

Trail Ridge Road crosses the Continental Divide at Milner Pass. Motorists stop to read the sign at Poudre Lake, look northeast down a long green valley to see the little stream start its trip to the Mississippi River, then return to their cars to follow Beaver Creek west to the Colorado River.

T. J. Milner was prominent in railroad circles in Colorado, though no record has been found of where he came from or where he died. He first appears as city engineer for Leadville in 1880, when that town boomed. He then moved to Longmont, where he was one of the organizers of the Denver and Salt Lake Western Railroad Company (not to be confused with Moffat's road that came 20 years later). Milner's road was designed to run from Denver to Fort Collins, thence "through the canons and narrows of the Cache La Poudre" to the

130

head of its south fork (Milner Pass) and west to the Bear (present Yampa) River, with the privilege to extend to Utah. Because Milner surveyed this ambitious route, Willis Lee of the U.S. Geological Survey named Milner Pass.

When this railroad did not materialize Milner became the chief engineer for the Denver Tramway Company. In May 1902 he resigned to survey another railroad route to cross the mountains at Devils Thumb Pass. This, a scheme of David Moffat, was to be an electric interurban, and two short branches were built on the plains, one to Golden, one to the coal fields at Leyden.

Suddenly, David Moffat changed his mind. He would build a broad gauge, steam-powered railroad across the Colorado Rockies. He hired another surveying engineer who laid out the line up South Boulder Canyon, crossing the Divide at Rollins Pass. The only part of Milner's original survey to be retained was the spectacular double curve south of Rocky Flats, still used by the Denver & Rio Grande Western Railroad. In order to gain enough altitude to cross Coal Creek at the entrance to its canyon, the railroad circles the Arena and executes the Big Ten Curve, a portion of the road still called the Milner Line by faithful admirers of T. J. Milner.

Mirror Lake   Indian Peaks

Mirror Lake   Mummy Range
    The way the boundary line of the Rocky Mountain National Park jogs around this lake suggests a story revolving around water rights which predate the establishment of the Park.

Monarch Lake 8340'   Lake Granby
    When Frank H. Wolcott, long the comptroller of the University of Colorado, was a young man, he camped on the South Fork of the Grand River (see Arapaho Creek) near a cabin belonging to a prospector named Tad Danforth whose mining claims, the Copper King and Copper Queen, were at the head of the Roaring Fork. Frank told his brother Charles about these claims, and Charles and the Waltemeyer brothers of Boulder formed a company to acquire the mines in September 1903. They also bought Tad Danforth's homestead which included the present sites of Petes Cove and the Roaring Fork Ranger Station. The Boulder men called the company The Monarch Gold & Copper Mining & Smelting Company. When asked where they got the name Monarch, Wolcott replied, "They picked it out of the sky."
    Soon the Boulder men decided that lumbering the great stands of timber on the slopes of the South Fork held surer promise of riches than copper mining and organized the Rocky Mountain Lumber Company. In the fall of 1904 they brought in enough men, Frank Wolcott supervising, to throw a rock dam across the Roaring Fork and

build a sawmill. Run by hydro-electric power, this turned out enough lumber to construct a company town below the mouth of the Roaring Fork. The town included a three-story boarding house, a store, an office shack, slab cottages, and an assembly hall with hardwood floors on which the neighbors loved to dance. Families of stockholders, current and prospective, flocked from Kansas and Nebraska to spend their vacations in this town named Monarch. One of the sights visitors enjoyed was the Big Tree, sometimes called The Monarch, publicized as the largest tree in the county, the last of many large spruces that had sheltered pioneers from sudden rain storms. So we have two origins for the name Monarch—a spruce tree and a mining company.

The small sawmill of the Rocky Mountain Lumber Company busily cut lumber, enough to build a larger sawmill and then a box factory. Amazing is the tale of how a husky Swede with 12-horse teams brought five large boilers and other machinery for the new mill and factory from Arrow, the railhead of the Moffat railroad, 50 miles away.

Experienced lumberjacks from Michigan soon were cutting logs too fast for horses to snake them to the mills. To solve this problem the ingenious management manufactured a lake. First they bought 160 acres of land from I. L. Killie (his upper meadows) who had bought the land from William H. ("Commodore") Bryant who had acquired it in 1902 through the Timber and Stone Act. Then the Company hired Bulgarian workmen to dam the South Fork a mile and a half above the town of Monarch, creating Monarch Lake. On the lake plied a homemade steamboat with a rear wheel paddle.

To get the logs to the lake, wooden chutes were built in strategic locations on the steep hillsides. The steamboat pushed the logs across the lake. To get the logs out of the lake, the company hired Japanese laborers to dig a canal from Monarch Lake to the mills.

The next problem was to get the boxes and boards to the Moffat railroad, now only 13 miles away at Granby. A private railroad was the solution. The Rocky Mountain Railroad Company built a broad gauge line from Granby to Monarch, with plans to extend to Grand Lake. So confident was the company of its expansion that tickets and waybills were printed with the names of both destinations. The 13 miles of rails that were actually laid and used ran from the town of Monarch through the upper meadows of I. L. Killie's ranch, through a section of school land, through Killie's lower ranch, and then across the Lehman hay meadows. The rails crossed the Grand River about where the present spillway of Lake Granby stands. Then the railroad ran on the west side of the river through a short gorge, crossed over to the east side of the river above the present Camp Chief Ouray, and took a big curve into Granby.

Starting in January 1907, the little Mogul-type engine nicknamed "Old Huldah" pulled out of Monarch whenever a load was ready. One stop was always made, at the west property line of the Killie Ranch. Here the engineer had to stop the train, jump from the cab, let down three wooden bars of a gate, and put them back after he had run the train through. The railroad officials complained because the landowner would not let them build a cattle guard; the landowner, according to his daughter, Mabel Killie Hamlin in 1966, agreed to let the railroad build a cattle guard when the company paid for its right-of-way.

In the fall of 1908 the South Fork was a noisy place. Logs bumped down the chutes and splashed into the lake, the steamboat whistled as it pushed them across the lake to the mouth of the canal, saws in the mills whined, box factory machinery clanked to keep pace with the conveyor belt, and "Old Huldah" occasionally let off steam. Overnight, a night luminous with the flames of the burning box factory, the noise stopped. After the fire the company dissolved. Buildings not burned were sold and moved to Murray Camp, half a mile east of the old town of Monarch, and ex-stockholder Edgar L. McDonald ran a "Galloping Goose" over the rails from Granby to his resort near the site of old Monarch.

Moomaw Glacier—(West of Frigid Lake in Wild Basin)

A snow-ice field clings to the side of the Continental Divide and drips its milky waters into Frigid Lake. The Moomaw children, five girls and four boys, who knew Wild Basin from childhood, called it the Dresden China Glacier because the stones that dotted it resembled flowers on Dresden china. One of the boys, Jack, became a National Park ranger especially interested in Wild Basin. The U.S. Geological surveyors named Moomaw Glacier for him on the 1958 Isolation Peak quad map, though it was not copied on the 1961 Rocky Mountain National Park map.

Jack Moomaw was born in Nebraska before 1893 when the family moved to a farm near Lyons but spent much of their time in the Estes Park mountains. When Jack wanted to see the world he joined the Navy. Disliking the service intensely, after two years he came home to his mountains. He took various jobs in the Estes Park area, guiding on Longs Peak before he became a National Park ranger. He has seen superintendents of the National Park come and go, capably serving each in turn, on horseback in summer, on skis in winter. As guide to world-famous scientists, Jack acquired an education, especially in archaeology. From Thunder Lake to Table Mountain, his trained eye can pick up flint chips wherever the Indians fashioned arrowheads.

Jack married Lila Weese and they had one daughter. Their home was in Horseshoe Park. Now retired, Jack lives on the bank of the St. Vrain River. He has written two books, and satisfies his curiosity in extensive travel, but always comes home to his mountains.

133

Moraine Park   Estes Park

Because glaciers carved its valleys, the Rocky Mountain National Park is studded with moraines—accumulations of rocks and earth piled up by the grinding movement of glacial ice. A glacier leaves at its side lateral moraines; at its lower end a terminal moraine; and as a rear-guard action during its retreat other terminal moraines called recessional moraines. Marking the north and south boundaries of Moraine Park are two lateral moraines; the South Lateral Moraine especially presents a graphic remnant of glacial action. Abner Sprague said his father named Moraine Park when father and son homesteaded 380 acres on the northern slopes of the South Lateral Moraine.

Mosquito Creek   Never Summer

Until the 1961 map this appeared as Lost Creek. Who decided to memorialize the insect so prevalent in early summer in the mountains is not known. Though insect repellent has alleviated human suffering from these pests, cattle still suffer, and horses seek the smoke of camp-fires, sometimes so close as to burn themselves. One old-timer of the Park wrote a nature note about a local mosquito that successfully fought an eagle.

Muggins Gulch— (East of Estes Park)

Although it lies east of Estes Park, Muggins Gulch is intimately connected with local history. Here lived Rocky Mountain Jim Nugent and his dog Ring and his white mule (Jim's spring is below the present buildings of the Meadowdale Ranch) ; here lived Israel Rowe, mighty hunter, in his nine-room house; here lived Charles Dennison, Estes Park's first (unintentional) man-killer. Each successive road starting up the North St. Vrain through the foothills, from Joel Estes' first cart track to the latest paved highway, converged at the foot of Muggins Gulch, then climbed up the nine-mile slope and came to Park View.

The name has been spelled different ways: Isabella Bird wrote McGinn's Gulch; Elkanah Lamb used Mulgins Gulch. Lord Dunraven did not approve of the name. He wrote: "I do not know who Muggins was—no doubt an honest citizen; but he should have changed his name before bestowing it upon such a pretty spot."

Actually it is a nickname. (The word "muggins," according to the dictionary, is sometimes used as an affectionate diminutive and means simpleton.) Milton Estes wrote:

> Muggins Gulch was named for George Hearst, whose nickname was Muggins. He was given the name by Dan Gant, who, with a man named Sowers, had some cattle in the Park, and Muggins was their herder. Muggins built a cabin at the

head of the gulch, so he could watch the cattle, lest any should
try to leave and go back down the valley.

Mummy Pass, Mummy Pass Creek, Mummy Range;
Mummy Mtn. 13,125' MUMMY RANGE
This spectacular range was called White Owls by the 1914 Arapahos because the snow lying on Chiquita, Ypsilon, and Fairchild seemed
whiter than other snowfields. Perhaps the artist Bierstadt named
the range when he came to Estes Park in 1876 with the Earl of Dunraven; perhaps William Hallett, cattleman, used his imagination to
name it. Authorities give both men the credit.

Presumably, the range resembles an Egyptian mummy lying on its
back. You may use Mummy Mountain or Hagues Peak for the head,
with Fairchild representing the drawn up knees, Ypsilon the feet, Chapin and Chiquita the footstools. Or you may make up your own sil-
houette as you chant the names of the mountains in the Mummy
Range—Chapin, Chiquita, Ypsilon, Fairchild, Mummy, and Hagues.
The Rowes are not visible from the Estes Park village area, and if
you add Dunraven it spoils the rhythm. (See each of these names.)

Murphy Lake GRAND LAKE
Who was this man Murphy? He had a set of lakes, now known as
Haynach Lakes, named for him, and later this lake.

N

Nakai Peak 12,216' FOREST CANYON, GRAND LAKE
The 1965 Chairman of the Navajo Council is Raymond Nakai,
and one Navajo clan is called Nakai Denih, meaning Spanish people.
This information came from the Public Relations Director of the
Navajo Tribe at Window Rock, Arizona, in July 1965; but he added
in answer to a question about the clan's being descended from a white
woman captured by Indians near Socorro, New Mexico, "We cannot
verify the statement."

This is probably one of the names given by the Colorado Geographic Board, and just as probably one suggested by Harriet Vaille
who produced so many Indian names from her reading. She often
consulted Hodge, the Indian authority. He wrote that Nakai means
"white stranger, i.e. Spanish," and that Nakaydi referred to the Mexi-
can way of walking with the toes turned out. (Any Boy Scout knows
that Indians walk with feet parallel.)

Nanita, Lake (Pronounced Na' ni ta)   GRAND LAKE

Hodge gives two origins for this word: one, that Nanita was the Navajo word for the plains Indians, collectively, meaning aliens, or many tribes; the other, that a tribe of Texas Indians used the name Nanita for Comanches. If this is true, three names in the Park area—Comanche, Mahana, and Nanita—commemorate the Comanches.

Navajo Peak 13,409'   INDIAN PEAKS

This proud peak with its tremendous northwestern face bears the name of a proud people who not only survived their harsh treatment by the conquering white men but have increased on their reservation. The word means very great farmers, and they were known as such by the Spaniards of the seventeenth century. After the Navajos acquired horses they no longer farmed; they raided.

The name followed one of Bethel's suggestions for calling a certain area of the Front Range mountains after Indian tribes.

Needles, The 10,068'   ESTES PARK, MUMMY RANGE

These cliffs, part of the Lumpy Ridge of the 1914 Arapahos, were named either by James of the Elkhorn Lodge or MacGregor of Black Canyon. The Estes Park Needles are fatter than the spires which mountaineers often call needles, or aiguilles.

Neota Creek; Neota, Mt. 11,734'   NEVER SUMMER

The 1914 Arapahos said their word for this mountain—*Hota-neo-tah*—meant mountain sheep's heart. From Thunder Pass the mountain looked like that to Indians, who must have known what a mountain sheep's heart looked like. Does its shape differ from the hearts of other animals?

Neva, Mt. 12,814   INDIAN PEAKS

The prospector who discovered gold near Idaho Springs, George A. Jackson, jotted down in his diary of 1858-59, "Niwot has moved up the South Fork of the St. Vrain. Neva is with him. Gave Neva his dinner and they moved on."

Ellsworth Bethel honored this Neva, an Arapaho, by naming a mountain for him. Evidently Bethel tired of people misinterpreting the name because he wrote a statement saying that Neva was an Arapaho Indian; that the name did not derive from the Latin meaning white; nor from Mt. Neva in Switzerland. Nor, it should be added, is it from nevé (pronounced nevay), a granulated form of snow which compacts under pressure to become ice, as in glaciers.

Never Summer Mountains   NEVER SUMMER

The 1914 Arapahos called this serrated range, which rises over 3000 feet abruptly from the floor of North Fork Valley, *Ni-chebe-chii,* translated as Never-No-Summer. The Colorado Geographic Board considered the word difficult for the American tongue to pronounce, and preferred not to use the double negative in English, so settled on Never Summer Mountains.

Before this name was chosen, the range had been identified as part of the Medicine Bows, or was called the Rabbit Ear Range, often confused with Rabbit Ear Pass, on the far side of North Park. The Never Summer Mountains were added to the Rocky Mountain National Park in 1929.

Nimbus, Mt. 12,706′ NEVER SUMMER

One of the Cloud Peaks named by James Grafton Rogers of the Colorado Geographic Board. Meteorologically, a nimbus is a uniformly gray rain cloud which covers the entire sky. Mythologically, a nimbus means the luminous vapor surrounding a god or goddess when on earth.

Nisa, Mt. 10,788′ GRAND LAKE

Here was another mountain with two almost identical summits. What should the Colorado Geographic Board name it? Not Twin Peaks—not Doublehead! Ellsworth Bethel had been studying Arapaho vocabularies; he produced *Nisi*—two;; *Nisah*—twins. The Board approved his clever substitution.

Niwot Ridge 13,023′ INDIAN PEAKS

At the end of this great ridge that runs east from Navajo Peak stands Niwot Mountain, originally called Bald Mountain. For the 1961 map, the U.S. Geological Survey did not entirely endorse the new name—they compromised, printing Niwot (Bald) Mountain. The Survey surely agreed that too many Bald Mountains dot the map of Colorado—in 1923 the count was 19 Balds and 10 Baldys—but hesitated to replace the old name because so many mining claims specify this Bald Mountain as their reference point.

Niwot (sometimes spelled Nawat) is an Arapaho word meaning left-handed. A picture of Chief Niwot, or Left Hand, indicates that the fingers of his right hand had been cut off between the second and third joints. Goldrushers who arrived at the site of Boulder in 1858 found Niwot and his men camped nearby. By the 1860's, although he was only 23 or 24 years old, he had become an influential leader among the Southern Arapahos. A settler of that time wrote, "Chief Left Hand was the finest looking Indian I have ever seen. He was over six feet tall, of muscular build and much more intelligent than the average Indian. . . . When wearing his war bonnet and full warrior's regalia he looked every inch a chieftain." He had learned to speak English in boyhood, when traveling in the East, and often acted as interpreter for other Indian chiefs.

He was reportedly killed at the Sand Creek Massacre in November

137

1864. Legend even tells how he stood with his arms folded, saying "I will not fight. Whites are my friends." He may very well have been at Sand Creek—he was in that eastern Colorado neighborhood, seeking peace, a few weeks earlier—and he was considered by the whites to be friendly, "a good chief." However, he lived to kill Major Joel Elliott and his band of 19 men four years later in Oklahoma in the battle of Washita, in which fight the Cheyennes and Arapahos were decisively defeated by General G. A. Custer. This was Niwot's last stand. He later said of himself, "All of my time was taken up on the warpath. It was my aim that my name should become great among my people. I had a brave heart." He was principal chief of the Southern Arapahos from 1889 until the early 1900's when he was succeeded by his son, Grant Left Hand (named for President U.S. Grant, the great warrior.)

Converted to Christianity in his closing years, Niwot told of his experience in simple forceful language at a great meeting of the Baptists in Oklahoma City in 1908, although he was old and blind and had to be led. He died in 1911.

An historical confusion resulted when Niwot Mountain was named, because on its east side rises Lefthand Creek. The creek was named not only years before the mountain, but years before Chief Niwot of the Arapahos was known to white men—probably before he was born. Andrew Sublette, fur trader of the 1830's, was a "south paw"; the creek was named for him.

Nokhu Crags 12,485'   NEVER SUMMER

An American name for these rocks was Sawtooth, certainly not a distinctive name, so the Colorado Geographic Board abbreviated the name used by the 1914 Arapahos, *nea ha-noXhu,* (Eagle's nest). Watch for these cliffs to flash into view at one point on Trail Ridge Road.

Nokoni, Lake   GRAND LAKE

One of the leading chiefs of the Comanche tribe was named Nokoni, according to the Colorado Geographic Board who named the lake for him.

North Fork of the Big Thompson River   MUMMY RANGE

The Rowe Glacier gives birth to this fork, once called Cow Creek.

North Fork of the Colorado River   GRAND LAKE, NEVER SUMMER

In the days when the Colorado River was called the Grand, and up to the time of the Colorado-Big Thompson Project, four forks joined together to form the headwaters of the Grand River. Now the Lake Fork is under Shadow Mountain Lake; the East Fork is called Buchanan Creek; the South Fork is under Lake Granby. That leaves only the North Fork, which is smaller than it was before the Grand Ditch caught waters that formerly belonged to it. The North Fork rises east of the Never Summer Mountains in the inverted U made by the Continental Divide, and ends in the southern part of Shadow Mountain Lake.

North Inlet   GRAND LAKE
As early as 1882 Abner Sprague was urging that a trail be built from Flattop down the North Inlet to Grand Lake, a much shorter route than the long-established Big Meadows Trail. Ten years later when Charles Hanington, summer resident of Grand Lake, descended from Flattop via the North Inlet, he noted with regret that the trail had been neither blazed nor cleared but that the canyon had plenty of thick timber, fallen logs, and steep and slippery slopes.

In 1901 Franklin I. Huntington, the same engineer who helped survey the Fall River Road, and Fred Sprague blazed a trail down the North Inlet. They managed to get themselves and their pack horse from Bear Lake to Grand Lake in four days. Today a 17-mile trail, one of the Park Service's best, connects the two points, but even this wide path has a long history of disasters and near-disasters during blizzards or sudden summer storms.

North Ridge   WILD BASIN
This appeared first on W. S. Cooper's 1911 map, "as the most prominent feature of the north wall of Wild Basin."

North St. Vrain Creek—See St. Vrain Creek

Notch, The   GLACIER GORGE, WILD BASIN
The Notch cuts into the ridge south of the East Face of Longs Peak. The name dates back at least to 1868. L. W. Keplinger, first man on the summit of Longs Peak with the Powell party of August 23, 1868, wrote in 1919 of his attempt to make a solo climb the evening before.

> Wouldn't it be a bully thing to go ahead and get a scoop on the other boys? I went ahead, into and through the Notch; the distance is only a few yards, not to exceed twenty-five, as I now remember. At the northerly edge of the Notch, Estes Park was before me for the first time. . . . I started up on the Estes Park side, using hands and feet. All was well until I paused and looked down. . . . A lonesome feeling came over me. I started back. . . . Finally I got where I could let go without slipping over, and dropped a short distance onto an ice formation in the northwest corner of the floor of the Notch. I feel quite sure that ice has not melted yet.

Notchtop Mtn. 12,129′   FOREST CANYON, GLACIER GORGE
This name was suggested by Dr. W. J. Workman who built the Fern Lake cabins.

Dr. C. C. Parry found the type specimen of the yellow pond lily on a tarn, which he called Osborns Lake, near Gold Hill, west of Boulder, in 1864. Botanists called it *Nymphae polysepala,* and R. A. Small used the first part of the name for this Nymph Lake. Later botanists substituted *Nuphar* for *Nymphae,* but the lake retains its name and its lilies. Nymph Lake formerly had more mundane names—Lily Pad Lake and Grant Lake.

In mythology a nymph was a divine and beauteous maiden who dwelt in forests. The Rocky Mountain National Park actually had one of these—at least she was a beauteous maiden who ran around in a leopard skin, appearing occasionally to unwary tourists. As to her divinity, *The Denver Post* merely claimed she was "a modern Eve."

If L. C. Way, the second superintendent of the Rocky Mountain National Park, really did think up this publicity stunt to advertise the beauties of the Park, he certainly went to the right man to manage it. Al Birch, an old-timer in Estes Park, was the promotion manager of *The Denver Post,* and the campaign he waged for the Modern Eve is a sample of his expertise.

The July 29, 1917, *Post* spreads pictures of Agnes Lowe all over the front page. She, a Michigan coed whose family has a summer cottage near Estes Park, wants to prove that the modern girl can live in the wilds. July 30—a picture shows her standing lonely by a tree waving farewell to her mother. She is wearing a leopard skin, ample according to 1966 standards, daring in 1917. The next day she is back in the *Post* because she had sought shelter from the pouring rain at a cottage. (Most unusual weather, said Superintendent Way.) August 6—more pictures. Front page. Leopard skin. She is going back to the wilds. More than 2000 people see her off! (Quite a crowd for the Park in 1917. The publicity was working.)

The *Post* does not mention the Modern Eve for four days. Perhaps it was during this time that Ranger Dixie McCracken, under orders from the Superintendent, delivered her to an inn where she rested for a day or two, then returned her to Wild Basin dressed in a dry-cleaned leopard skin.

August 10—Enos Mills and Superintendent Way have lunch with her. She serves nature's food. Menu: pine bark soup, mountain trout, mushrooms, chipmunk peas, wild honey, chokecherries. "Every one of these articles, of course, had been obtained in the wilderness about the lake." On August 13, Agnes Lowe, the Modern Eve, triumphantly returns to Longs Peak Inn after a week in the wilds near Thunder Lake. Movies of her will be shown at Denver theaters.

A month later *The Denver Post* runs the first of a three-part serial written by the Modern Eve herself. Double-page spread in the Magazine Section. With pictures. The last installment tells of her terror as she flees from a pursuing Adam. The Park rangers rescue her from a fate worse than death. A picture of this Adam, known to the rangers as the Crazy Greek, shows a sheepish youth in a bearskin.

O

Odessa Gorge, Lake   FOREST CANYON, GLACIER GORGE
On the shore of Odessa Lake, W. J. Workman, who ran Fern Lake Lodge, built a cabin for his daughter, his second child by his second wife. The daughter said her real name was Dessa, but "guessed her father used the longer name because he thought it more poetic." (She herself used the full name in the Denver Directory of 1904 when she was teaching school in that city.)

Ogalalla Peak 13,138'   WILD BASIN, GRAND LAKE
One of Bethel's tribal names for the Indian Peaks. The Oglala (the name has a variety of spellings) were the principal division of the Teton Sioux, producing such leaders as Sitting Bull and Crazy Horse. The tribe now lives at the Pine River Agency in South Dakota.

Oldman Mountain 8310'   ESTES PARK
The rock that squats west of the village of Estes Park resembles the profile of a sitting man, which is the direct translation of the name used for it by the 1914 Arapahos. The name Oldman predates 1914 by decades; the first settlers used it. The U.S. Board on Geographic Names, at the suggestion of the National Park Service, sanctioned the name on February 9, 1965.

At the foot of this rock sits Elkhorn Lodge, for many years run by the James family. Their guests used this rock as an evening climb, but did not remain on top for days, fasting, as did the Arapahos.

Olive Lake, Ridge   WILD BASIN
The Olive Mining and Milling Company, organized by a group of men from Omaha, sank a shaft 120 feet deep on this ridge. It was not deep enough to find gold. By 1906 the Olive corporation was defunct and the shaft house demolished. The lake, spring-fed, is still there except when it dries up in long hot summers.

Opposite Olive Ridge, west of the highway, the Clara Belle Mine operated at about the same time. With local stockholders, its annual meetings were held at Allenspark. In 1903 it was building a 2000-foot flume to carry water for power from the North St. Vrain River, the mill was just about completed, the tramway finished, and both day and night shifts worked the main lead of the Clara Belle. It had no more success than the Olive operation, and folded about the same time.

Olympus, Mt. 8808'— (East of Estes Park village)

The 1914 Arapahos called this mountain and two adjacent hills by words which translate as Faces to the Wind.

By naming Mt. Olympus, Fernando C. Willett is given credit for bringing Greek mythology to the Park area. Willett was a school teacher who had served with great success as the principal of the high school in Evansville, Indiana, from 1866 to the spring of 1870. He resigned because of ill health. After staying in Denver, he came to Estes Park in May 1873, where he tutored the Griff Evans' children and lived with his cousins, Mr. and Mrs. John Hubbell, in a two-story house over a mile from Evans' cabins. In Estes Park that summer of 1873 were other educated people—two geological survey parties whose leaders were Ivy League graduates, titled British sportsmen, Miss Anna Dickinson of the lecture circuit, Miss Isabella Bird, world traveler, and Rocky Mountain Jim Nugent. Surely Fernando Willett's classical allusion to Mt. Olympus, the home of the gods, was not only applauded but comprehended.

Both John Hubbell and Fernando Willett had hoped to find health in the mountains. Mr. Hubbell's seven months' stay did him no good; he died the following January. Willett recovered sufficiently to become secretary of the American legation in Mexico City, where he died somewhat later.

Onahu Creek (First and last syllables accented)   Grand Lake

The 1914 Arapahos used this name for Fish Creek, a tributary of the North Fork of the Colorado River. It means "warms himself," and refers to one of the Indian race horses who on cold evenings came up to the fire to warm himself. This horse died on Fish Creek, whose undistinctive name the Colorado Geographic Board changed to Onahu.

Opposition Creek   Never Summer

Some old-timers think the 1961 map misplaced this creek. They claim that Opposition Creek runs in what is called Red Gulch on the 1961 map. Others say the map correctly places it in Hells Hip Pocket, and the reason the Grand Ditch ended here for so many years is that an especially obdurate boulder opposed its strength to that of the ditchdiggers, stopping the ditch and naming the creek.

Orton, Mt. 11,724'   Wild Basin

Professor Edward Orton, Jr., of the Chemistry Department of Ohio State University, conducted a survey of Mills Moraine and the Longs Peak area one summer in the early 1900's. Dean Babcock, a summer resident, who joined Orton's Ohio students, remembers that they wanted to name a peak in honor of their leader. Professor Orton declined the honor, but offered his father, Edward Orton, Sr., as a worthy candidate. Orton, Sr., was president, first of Antioch College, then of Ohio State University (1873-1881) and was state geologist for 20 years. Babcock saw to it that Mt. Orton appeared on the Cooper-Babcock map of 1911. The younger Orton commissioned Dean Babcock to paint a portrait of the mountain and presented the painting to Ohio State University as a memorial to his father.

Otis Peak 12,486' GLACIER GORGE, GRAND LAKE

Edward Osgood Otis, M.D., was born in New Hampshire in 1848, attended Phillips Exeter and Harvard, and received his degree from the Harvard School of Medicine in 1877. He became a prominent physician in Boston. In the 1880's he climbed with Chapin in the Estes Park region, and Chapin named the mountain south of Hallett Peak after him. Dr. Otis wrote in 1915, "under what circumstances my name was given to the peak I do not remember."

Ouzel Creek, Falls, Lake; Ouzel Peak 12,716' GRAND LAKE, WILD BASIN
(Pronounced oo z'l)

The water ouzel, a chunky gray bird, is sometimes called a dipper. He bobs up and down on water-washed rocks, then plunges headlong into the swift stream to catch his insect bill of fare.

In the early 1900's when young William Cooper came to climb in Wild Basin, he saw a great peak towering above a certain lake. He knew that Enos Mills had named Ouzel Lake so, by association, he called the mountain Ouzel Lake Peak. Enos Mills probably had first named Ouzel Creek and then, by association, Ouzel Lake, for Mills was a naturalist who knew that water ouzels frequent swift water, not still lakes.

The Colorado Geographic Board wanted to change the name of Ouzel Lake Peak to Tawawa Peak, though it left no record of the meaning of the name. R. B. Marshall used Tawawa on his map of the newly-created National Park, but Washington decided on Ouzel Peak.

143

P

Pagoda Mtn. 13,497'   GLACIER GORGE, WILD BASIN

The name first appears on the Cooper-Babcock map of 1911, and Dean Babcock wrote in 1965 that he gave the name because to him the mountain looked like a pagoda. Few people have known the Rocky Mountain National Park as well as Dean Babcock, artist. Born in Canton, Illinois, in 1888, where he grew up, he started summering in the Park area when he was 15. With his cousin, Louis Levings, he took an extended walking trip from Boulder to Boulder by way of Estes Park, Grand Lake, and the Arapaho Peaks country. (See Spectacle Lakes.) By 1908 he had won two scholarships at the New York Art Institute and had traveled in Spain, but he returned to the Park in 1908 when he was with Edward Orton in Wild Basin, and helped Cooper survey that area the same summer. That fall Babcock's mother bought 80 acres of land under the Stone and Timber Act and they started their mountain home—The Ledges—in 1910. That was the first winter he spent in Estes Park. From 1918 to 1921 Babcock was a ranger-naturalist for the Park Service. Babcock's ability as an artist is shown in the maps he drew of the Estes region, but more especially in his paintings, his water colors of aspens being particularly pleasing.

Paiute Peak 13,088'   INDIAN PEAKS

The Board on Geographic Names refused to let Bethel use Ute for any point in the Indian Peaks because many other mountains in Colorado bear that name. This upset Bethel—the Utes were the most important tribe in the Colorado Rockies—but he compromised by using Paiute, the common name for several tribes related to the Utes. The word means either Water (pah) or True (pai) Ute.

Paradise Creek, Park   GRAND LAKE, LAKE GRANBY

Without even a trail crossing its wilderness, Paradise Park (once misnamed Hell Canyon) shows no marks of man. Ecologists think that the Engelmann spruce and alpine fir here form the climax of a forest which has developed without disturbance since the last glaciation. This means that when the last glacier melted, leaving the valley covered with bare boulders, the natural succession of plant life began, from rock to soil to forest. First lichens and mosses gained footholds; they gave way to plants, then shrubs, then to aspen and lodgepole pine; finally the climax growth of spruce and fir took over. Evidence of the undisturbed growth is the uniformity of the stand of spruce and fir, and the regularity of the forest floor, covered only with blueberries. A welter of fallen timber and rotting logs makes it virtually impassable. No elk and few deer venture through this jumble. Hikers traverse the

144

park through soggy subalpine meadows and sphagnum bogs which, like the forest, represent a succession uninterrupted since the Ice Age.

Park Hill— (East of Estes Park, head of Muggins Gulch)

When the motorist on the North St. Vrain highway drives up Muggins Gulch to the crest of the hill, he suddenly sees Estes Park lying at the foot of the Mummy Range. Today this is "a grand sight and a great surprise," just as it was in October 1859 when Milton Estes and his father Joel first saw it. An old pine tree used to stand south of the old road at the crest of Park Hill. Every traveler, on horseback, in carriage, or in classic car, had his photograph taken here with the Mummy Range as a backdrop. Today the Highway Department provides ample parking space from which to see the Park.

Patterson, Mt. 11,424'   GRAND LAKE

In January 1915 the Colorado Geographic Board asked that the name Mt. Senator be substituted for Bald Mountain. "Bald Mountain is not well established locally, is objectionable, and Mt. Senator has been used somewhat in the Grand Lake country as a memorial to Senator Patterson, who was influential in establishing the National Park and is now seventy years old." The U.S. Board on Geographic Names agreed that Bald Mountain was a poor name, but chose Patterson instead of Senator.

Thomas M. Patterson (1847-1916) was a power in Democratic politics from the time he arrived in Denver in 1872, when almost immediately he became city attorney. He was Territorial delegate to Congress when Colorado became a state in 1876, returning to Washington the next year as representative. Proof of his political influence lies in his return to Congress as senator in 1901, a quarter century later. In 1890 he bought the *Rocky Mountain News*. Through it, he fought for what he believed were people's rights, too long abused by corrupt politicians and untouchable corporations. Specifically he fought Bonfils of *The Denver Post*; Robert Speer, mayor of Denver; and the Colorado Supreme Court. He was instrumental in making Denver an independent county, freed from the control of the State Legislature.

Tom Patterson's log cottage still overlooks Grand Lake on Campbells Point, which was named for the Senator's son-in-law and business manager of his newspaper, Richard Crawford Campbell.

Pawnee Lake; Pawnee Pass 12,541'   INDIAN PEAKS

A Forest Service trail from Brainard Lake to Monarch Lake crosses Pawnee Pass. Topping the Divide south of this pass, another and earlier trail bears an interesting name—Breadline Trail. In 1882 engineers for the Union Pacific, ubiquitous in their search for possible railroad routes across the Rockies, surveyed a line west, planning a tunnel above Lake Isabelle to pierce the Continental Divide. Like the newly built Georgetown Loop on which the Colorado Central Railroad crossed above its own tracks by means of a high trestle, the proposed Union Pacific line was to gain the needed altitude by two double loops.

Canadian Indians, hired by the Union Pacific, carried supplies to the engineers working on the Western Slope. The supplies included bread—hence the Breadline Trail. The Indians walked from Brainard Lake past Long Lake and Lake Isabelle, then left the present route over Pawnee Pass to cross the Divide at the next saddle south. Thence they found a way down the only passable gulch in the steep cliffs east of Crater Lake. Members of the Boulder Group of The Colorado Mountain Club still use the Breadline Trail occasionally, but it is unmarked and hard to find, and sometimes they miss the western gulch. Then they climb back up, using ropes and pitons, knapsacks heavier at every step, to regain the regular Pawnee Pass trail which is longer but easy to follow.

Pawnee Peak 12,943'   Indian Peaks

In this name Ellsworth Bethel commemorated the Pawnees, an Indian tribe which roamed between the Platte and Arkansas Rivers in eastern Colorado. They now live in Oklahoma. This name derives from *parika,* meaning a horn, because the Pawnees stiffened their scalp lock with paint and grease to make it stand up like a horn, daring their enemies to remove it.

Peacock Pool   Glacier Gorge

Pear Reservoir 10,582'   Wild Basin

Joe Mills, as a boy camping alone in Wild Basin, amused himself by naming lakes according to their shapes. "This one that bulged out at one end was surely a plump 'Pear'." Pear is one of the Arbuckle reservoirs filed on in 1902. (See Bluebird Lake.) The 1906 amended filing for Pear (Arbuckle #4) specifies a lake depth of 15 feet and a dam 11 feet high, at an estimated cost of $400. (When the city of Longmont bought Pear Reservoir along with Bluebird and Sandbeach Lakes in 1933, during the economic depression, it paid $92,000 for the three—down from an asking price of $200,000.) Today the dam at Pear Reservoir, badly deteriorated, holds no appreciable amount of water and the pond has reverted to its original shape—a plump pear.

Peck Glacier   Indian Peaks

A group of photographers, led through the Crater Lake country by Fred Fair in 1922, decided to name the glacier southwest of Lone Eagle Peak after the supervisor of the U.S. Forest Service in Denver.

Allen Steele Peck (1880-1951) graduated in forestry from the University of Michigan. After World War I, in which he earned the rank of lieutenant colonel, he came to Denver as chief of the regional

146

Forest Service, where he served 24 productive years. His many activities connected with the enjoyment and preservation of the outdoors included a directorship in The Colorado Mountain Club.

Pennock Creek MUMMY RANGE
Charles Pennock of Bellvue was a pioneer fruit-grower in the Cache la Poudre Valley. He planted the first orchard in 1889, and his homestead was a mecca for horticulturists because of his successful experiments.

Petes Cove LAKE GRANBY
Pete Youngblood served for many years as caretaker, alone in the winter, for various buildings around Monarch Lake.

Pettingell Lake GRAND LAKE
In 1942 the Rocky Mountain National Park staff officially recommended for this lake the name local people had long used—the name of Judge J. N. Pettingell. Originally from Boston, he settled at Hot Sulphur Springs in the 1880's. During a long and useful life he held several public offices in Grand County, including that of County Judge. (See Love Lake.)

Phantom Creek NEVER SUMMER
Years before Lester Scott bought Squeaky Bob Wheeler's ranch, he rode one evening at twilight downstream from the ghost town of Lulu City; both he and his horse seemed to sense the phantoms of Indians, trappers, surveyors, Chinese coolies, fishermen, and miners who once had peopled the North Fork Valley. He thought at that time that if he owned Squeaky Bob's camp he knew what he would call it. When he and his partner bought Bob's place in 1926 he remembered his ride and changed the name to Phantom Valley Ranch.

Scott had three partners in succession; the last one, an attractive young Easterner, Milton Statler, was the son of the tycoon of the Statler Hotel chain. Scott and Statler planned expansion for the ranch, but Statler was killed in an automobile accident in Arizona before the plans materialized. The ranch was sold to Irwin Beattie in 1941. In the early 1960's the National Park Service bought the establishment and tore it down in order to recreate the wilderness—adding to the phantoms of the valley the many guests who had stayed at the ranch. The North Fork owes a debt of gratitude to the person who, by naming Squeak Creek and Phantom Creek, has kept history alive.

Pierson Park ESTES PARK
Pierson was "kind of a prospector or trapper," remembers Emma Moomaw Hutchins, "and his name was already on Pierson Park when we camped there one summer about 1905. Dad was sawmilling, but

147

when we had an earthquake Dad was scared and got out the next day. (It was time for school to open anyway.) "

Pilot Mtn.   WILD BASIN

Pine Ridge   GLACIER GORGE

W. S. Cooper noted the fine stand of lodgepole pines covering this ridge and named it on his 1911 map. Nature, who fashioned these trees thin, with small, easily chopped-off branches, obviously designed them for the use of Indians to prop up their lodges—lodgepole pines. One can recognize the lodgepole by its short needles, about two inches long, which grow in bundles of two, and its solid little cones. These stick to the branches years after they have dropped their seeds.

Along with aspens, these pines often spring up on fire-burns. Perhaps the warmth of the fire helps germinate the pine seeds lying below the charred ground. Thousands of the baby trees will appear in one season, 50 or more to a square yard. In their adolescence they look like perpendicular matchsticks, all practically the same size. The lodgepoles in older forests stand so close together that the sun scarely penetrates to the forest floor. This needle-covered ground provides an ideal nursery for shade-loving spruce and fir seedlings which, in a few decades, crowd out the lodgepoles that sheltered them in their youth. The lodgepoles, without sun, die. On Pine Ridge even now, small stands of spruce and fir mingle with the dominant lodgepoles, as the story of unrelenting forest succession unfolds. In the year 2000 A.D. accuracy will demand that the name be changed to Spruce-Fir Ridge. Later, perhaps, a fire will come, and aspens and lodgepoles will start all over again.

Around Grand Lake today the lodgepoles are being killed by dwarf mistletoe. No chemical is available to control its spread, but hope is held that such will be found soon. The Forest Service recommends speeding up the natural succession by planting spruce among the dying trees so that the shores of Grand Lake will not be bare when the lodgepoles die.

Two other kinds of pine trees grow in the Park—limber pines above the zone where the lodgepoles flourish, and ponderosa in lower altitudes. Limber pines also have short needles but with five in a bundle instead of two. On windswept ridges where weather thwarts their normal growth, the grotesque trees may spread horizontally instead of vertically, and put one inch on their girths while their protected neighbors add ten. Climbers caught in a timberline storm sometimes crawl under the roof made by their matted branches. The thick-trunked limber pines at Emerald and Haiyaha Lakes may be the oldest living things in the Park.

A typical stand of the third pine that grows in the Park surrounds

148

the Beaver Meadows Entrance Station. The ponderosa, or western yellow pine, grows in open forests in lower regions of the east side of the Park. Unlike the lodgepoles, they grow far, far apart, with plenty of room to develop character. These striking red-trunked trees have needles four to six inches long in clusters of twos or threes. Children gather their large open cones for starting fires or making Christmas decorations.

These three—lodgepole, limber, and ponderosa—are real pines, not to be confused with spruce, fir, Douglas-fir, and juniper. When a name is needed to cover all mountain evergreen trees, many people mistakenly say "pine trees." The accurate covering term is conifers, meaning cone-bearers.

Pinnacle Pool NEVER SUMMER
An especially high pinnacle juts above this small pond southeast from Mt. Howard.

Pipit Lake WILD BASIN
This is one of the lakes William Cooper named in Wild Basin. A high mountain lake like this most appropriately bears the name of the water pipit, one of four birds that nest above timberline. (The others, all of which are commemorated by lake names in the Park, are ptarmigan, horned lark, and rosy finch.) Resembling a slim sparrow, the water pipit is striped brown with inconspicuous white sides on its tail. When standing on the ground it wags its tail; it flutters into the air and sings on the wing. Its song consists of *chwee* repeated seven times.

Pisgah, Mt. 8630'— (East of Estes Park)
In the Bible, Mt. Pisgah was the name of the mountain east of the Dead Sea from whose summit Moses looked down on the Promised Land just before his death. The name appears on various heights all over the West, a pathetic symbol of the high hopes of many early settlers.

Placid Lake ESTES PARK

Pole Creek GRAND LAKE, LAKE GRANBY
Probably named for trees which were cut along its course by Indians for lodge poles, or by whites for cabins.

Pool, The FOREST CANYON
Of course many pools form in the streams of the Park, and many ponds are called pools, but The Pool is always this one, just as The Saddle refers only to the saddle near Rowe Glacier.

Frederick K. Funston spent the summer of 1889 in Moraine Park with a biological expedition including journalist William Allen White, naturalist Vernon Kellogg, Chancellor Snow of Kansas University, and

149

a group of fun-loving boys. When Funston fell into a pool below Fern Falls, the boys claimed he was frightened by a bear. They dubbed the place Funston Pool. The U.S. Board on Geographic Names in June 1932 shortened this to The Pool.

Funston became famous as a general in the Philippines during the Spanish-American War. He brought order to San Francisco when federal troops were called after the fire and earthquake. Camp Funston in Kansas bore his name during World War I.

Potts Puddle Mummy Range

Ranger Jack Moomaw once dumped about 2000 rainbow fry into this high pond. Three years later Merlin Potts came upon the pond. He was a ranger officially assigned to study mountain sheep but somehow he managed to carry on his survey near fishing holes. When he threw a line into this lake, his excitement about the size and quantity of the fish that rose caused fun-loving Jack Moomaw to name it Potts Puddle. The name appears on the 1961 map. Mr. Potts retired as chief naturalist of Rocky Mountain National Park in 1965.

At one time this lake and another near by were known as Clara and Emma Lakes, names connected with the MacGregor family.

Poudre Lake Never Summer

The old maps specify two lakes here at Milner Pass. Folklore has it that one drained toward the eastern slope, the other toward the west. Whatever happened to the other lake? It is all one lake now, thanks to a bulldozer. In July 1965 the U.S. Board on Geographic Names changed the name from the plural to the singular. (See Cache la Poudre River.)

Powell, Lake Glacier Gorge, Grand Lake, Wild Basin

This, a recent name, is presumably for John Wesley Powell, leader of the first party to climb Longs Peak. In 1868 Powell and his group came from Grand Lake, and, leaving their horses when the going got rough, climbed the peak from the Wild Basin side. Accounts of their trip appear in reports by Powell, Byers, Keplinger, and others, but their specific route is hard to trace. The lake was named for the one-armed leader of the expedition who later became famous as the first navigator of the Colorado River. In 1960, Ranger Ritterbush wanted the lake named for Clarence King, after the campaign to change Copeland Mountain to Mt. Clarence King had failed. (See Copeland Mountain.)

Powell Peak 13,208′ Glacier Gorge, Grand Lake

The February 1961 decision of the Board on Geographic Names states that this name was proposed by the National Park Service because of a nearby feature, meaning, probably, Lake Powell. This

150

mountain should not be confused with Mt. Powell in the Gore Range, climbed by Powell in 1868 after his Longs Peak climb. (See Gore Range Overlook.)

Prospect Canyon   GLACIER GORGE
The name comes from an old tunnel made by a prospector in his unsuccessful search for rich ore.

Prospect Mtn. 8900'   ESTES PARK
The 1914 Arapahos called this The Shirt, because on its northern slope four or five hostile Indians had been killed, one of whom was wearing a shirt. The American name comes, of course, from the splendid view from the top, gained today by riding a cable car, but on August 30, 1873, W. H. Jackson lugged what he called his "traps," meaning the paraphernalia needed to take pictures with glass plates, to the top of Prospect Mountain without benefit of cable car.

Prospect Mtn. Tunnel   ESTES PARK
The third, and last, tunnel of the Colorado-Big Thompson Project pierces Prospect Mountain.

Ptarmigan Creek, Lake, Pass; Ptarmigan Point 12,363'   GRAND LAKE
The ptarmigan, probably the best-known, certainly the best-publicized bird of the tundra country, is an alpine grouse. It changes color with the season; snow-white in winter, only its black eyes and bill betray its presence; in summer its mottled brown blends with the rocks. Trusting in its camouflage, it usually lets intruders approach quite close; a little too close and it walks away, still believing it is invisible.

The abundance of ptarmigan on the Flattop peneplain gave the name to the pass. Roger Toll proposed the name Ptarmigan Point in 1924 because of its proximity to the pass; the name also attaches itself by association to the creek that drains the area, and to its lake.

Ptarmigan Mtn. 12,324'   GRAND LAKE
Arapaho National Forest files show that this mountain was named as early as 1860 because of the numerous ptarmigan on its slopes. Although the Forest Service had officially ceded jurisdiction of this territory east of Grand Lake to the Park Service, in 1916 it recommended retaining the name in order not to confuse "innumerable land-office records," since the mountain had long served as a tying point for mineral rights.

R

Rainbow Bay LAKE GRANBY

Rainbow trout bear a brilliant reddish "rainbow" streak on their sides. Introduced from the West Coast years ago, these sporty fish now make up more than half the trout caught in Colorado.

Rainbow Curve FOREST CANYON, MUMMY RANGE

When the clouds are right, this parking place makes a splendid viewpoint for rainbows, often double.

Rainbow Islands GRAND LAKE, LAKE GRANBY

Rainbow Lake FOREST CANYON, GRAND LAKE

The north edge of this lake shines through the water like a rainbow. Until the 1961 map, this and Irene Lake together were known as the Rainbow Lakes.

Rams Horn Mtn. 9314' ESTES PARK

Early settlers called this Sheep Mountain, for the same reason others called it Rams Horn Mountain. The authorities, in an effort to avoid the commonplace Sheep Mountain, approved Rams Horn. A note in the Arapaho National Forest files states that this name was given either because bighorn sheep are seen on this hill every year, or because a great quantity of their horns were found here. Mountain sheep do not lose their horns every year; then why so many on one mountain? Was this a slaughter house like Milton Estes' Sheep Rock?

In his memoirs, Milton Estes wrote a description of what pioneers did when they saw sheep on Sheep Rock:

> There was a rocky mound which we called "Sheep Rock" about 150 feet high. There was a crevice or seam running from the bottom to the top, on the north side of the rock, by which the sheep could climb to the top of the rock, single file. On the top of Sheep Rock there was a large basin which filled with water when it rained. In winter or during the hunting season, there was not much water in the basin. The sheep used the rock for a place of safety; after feeding they would climb to the top of the rock and lie down to rest. But we always knew when a flock was on the rock, by seeing one lone sheep standing guard on top, on the rim of the rock. He would be looking out for danger while the sheep were in the basin. That was the way father [Joel Estes] first discovered that the rock was a retreat for sheep; so he named it "Sheep Rock." From that time, the rock has been called "Sheep Rock." [Not on 1961 map.]

152

When the sheep were in the basin, you could not see them
from the ground, but they would walk up to the brow or edge
of the rock, to look at us; and we would pick them off. When
they fell outward, which they often did, the fall mashed them
to a jelly. On the west side, where they nearly always fell, the
rock was perpendicular. That rock was the cause of the
mountain sheep, except a few stragglers, being exterminated
in the Park. When we saw a flock of sheep within a mile or
two of the Sheep Rock, we had a trained dog that we set on
them, and they would strike straight for the Sheep Rock, then
we would get the whole flock.

Rams Horn Tunnel   ESTES PARK
The second tunnel of the Colorado-Big Thompson Project was
bored through Rams Horn Mountain.

Ramsey Peak 11,582'   MUMMY RANGE
This peak was named for Hugh B. Ramsey by his son-in-law,
Frank R. Koenig, one of the first National Park rangers. In answer to
inquiries about Hugh Ramsey, his daughter Hazel B. Koenig, wrote a
letter on August 11, 1965, saying:

> Yes, Ramsey Peak was named for my father. He was born
> in Cass County, Nebraska, Dec. 17, 1862, and moved from
> there to Loveland, Colorado, where he built a brick plant and
> built the first brick houses in Loveland. He also played his
> violin for dances in Loveland.
>
> Mr. Ramsey came to Pingree Park to homestead a ranch
> in 1890. There were no roads at that time, only a trail. He
> built the first road from the Ranger Station (which in those
> days was the Mac Hammond place), over the Pennock Pass to
> Twin Lakes, then down to Pingree Park. [Pingree was the
> name of an early trapper.]
>
> He built two sawmills in Pingree Park. The first one was
> with a steam engine, the second run by the power of water
> brought down off the hill from Fall Creek by a pipe line. He
> sold the lumber in Loveland. He built Lawn Lake in Estes
> Park, and after moving to Pingree Park, he built Hour Glass
> Lake and Twin Lakes.
>
> I can remember my father speaking the Arapaho Indian
> language when I was a little girl. He had a young Arapaho
> Indian friend and this is perhaps where he learned their lan-
> guage. [Hugh Ramsey helped the Nomenclature Committee
> of The Colorado Mountain Club with the 1914 Arapaho
> words.]

Ranger Creek   GRAND LAKE

Raspberry Park
FOREST CANYON

The tasty wild raspberry grows on sunny rocky slopes up to 10,000 feet. In 1864 Byers noted "inexhaustible" fields of raspberries on his way to Longs Peak but he reckoned without the population explosion. Housewives intent on raspberry shortcake try to time their berry-picking expeditions when the berries are ripe but before the bears have eaten them.

Red Gulch; Red Mtn. 11,605'
NEVER SUMMER

Old-timers told Arapaho National Forest men that Indians used earth from this mountain for war paint.

Ribbon Falls
GLACIER GORGE

The Park records state that the name was suggested by Roger Toll in 1922, although until the publication of the 1961 map these falls were known to Park personnel as "The Silver Slide."

Richthofen, Mt. 12,940'
NEVER SUMMER

Here follows the case of Ferdinand vs. Walter, both Barons von Richthofen from Silesia in eastern Germany, but not close kin. (They were descended from two brothers who lived in 1660.) The question is—which baron left his name on handsome Mt. Richthofen in the Never Summer Mountains?

Counsel for Ferdinand rises first and calls to the witness stand the ghost of Henry Gannett, chief topographer of the U.S. Geological Survey, and president of the National Geographic Society. Gannett is shown a book called *The Origin of Certain Place Names in the United States,* published in 1902. He admits he wrote it, and reads from the book a flat statement: "Richthofen, a mountain in Colorado named for the geologist." Counsel enters this book as Exhibit A.

Counsel asks the witness what geologist he had in mind. The answer is Ferdinand Paul Wilhelm, Freiherr von Richthofen (1833-1905). This man worked from 1862 to 1868 as a volunteer with the Whitney Survey in California where Gannett knew him. Baron Ferdinand developed theories about volcanic rock, recorded in his treatises on the Comstock lode. Later the Baron penetrated into central China where he made the first map of its mountains. He was encouraged by Josiah Dwight Whitney, who had become interested in the young German in California. Their friendship lasted a lifetime, the Baron writing Whitney in 1895, "I never forget what you have been to me in California," signing himself, "I remain in ever grateful memory."

Counsel for Ferdinand continues the examination of the witness, Henry Gannett. Q. Did Josiah Whitney name Mt. Richthofen? A. No, Whitney was not in Colorado with the King Survey. Q. What was the King Survey? A. The Survey of the 40th Parallel under the direction of Clarence King. They worked the Estes Park region in the early

154

1870's, and named mountains. Q. Was Baron von Richthofen with them? A. No, he was in China, but surveyors had a habit of naming mountains after fellow scientists. I cite the highest mountains in four western states: Mt. Whitney in California, Wheeler Peak in New Mexico, King Peak in Utah, and Gannett Peak in Wyoming.

Counsel then hands Gannett a copy of the *Atlas* of the King Survey. Gannett opens it and points to two mountains—Hagues Peak named for Arnold Hague who was in Estes Park with the King Survey; Mt. Richthofen, named, Gannett maintains, for the geologist who was in China. Counsel for Baron Ferdinand von Richthofen enters the *Atlas* as Exhibit B and rests his case.

Opposing counsel intends to prove that Walter, Baron von Richthofen, was an important man in Denver and therefore commemorated by the Colorado mountain. He calls various witnesses to the stand, living and dead, who knew this red-bearded Junker, 27 years old when he arrived in Denver in 1877. Their testimony proves that Baron Walter used his tremendous energy to promote south and east Denver. Near Exposition Avenue and South Broadway he built Sans Souci, a beer garden where ladies were served strawberries and cream. He had stock in the Denver Circle Railroad that ran to present Overland Park where he raced his blooded horses. Tiring of south Denver, he turned east to the little town of Montclair. Here he built a lonely castle for his second wife whom he had met at the horse races, and a Molkerie where health-seeking consumptives sat on porches drinking milk furnished by imported cows stabled on the ground floor of the milk parlor. Both of these buildings still stand. The Baron planned to create a German Spa on the high plains, piping water—"ginger champagne," he called it—about 20 miles from a well near Barr Lake to the site of the present headquarters building of Lowry Air Force Base.

Before this scheme materialized, the Baron died, in 1898, two weeks after he personally had presented a bouquet to each of 1200 soldiers as they marched down Seventeenth Street en route to the Spanish-American War. How proud this military-minded man would have been of his nephew, Manfred von Richthofen, the ace aviator of World War I, known as the Red Knight of Germany!

The last witness for Baron Walter is Edward Ring, teller of Colorado tales. He testifies that Richthofen was president of the Corkscrew Club of Denver to which the Earl of Dunraven belonged but cannot prove that the Baron was ever with the Earl in Estes Park.

Baron Walter's counsel submits two exhibits to prove the superior claim of his client: *Cattle Raising on the Plains of North America,* a book written by his client; and a street-sign from east Denver reading "Richthofen Place."

Counsel for Baron Ferdinand, in rebuttal, introduces a new exhibit: a newspaper obituary of Baron Walter von Richthofen. He points to the date Baron Walter arrived in Denver—1877. Then he flips open his Exhibit B, the King Atlas, first to the map showing Mt. Richthofen; then to the date of publication—1876.

With this conclusive evidence against the red-bearded promoter, counsel for Ferdinand moves for a directed verdict. The judge grants the motion and directs the jury to bring in a verdict in favor of the geologist, Ferdinand von Richthofen, who knew well the Chinese mountains but never saw his Colorado Rocky.

Roaring Fork (of Arapaho Creek) —Lake Granby; **Roaring Fork** (of Cabin Creek) —Glacier Gorge; **Roaring River** (tributary to Fall River) —Mummy Range

What a noisy place the Park must be! Roaring is used in mountain nomenclature almost as much as Fork.

Rock Creek   Wild Basin

Rock Cut   Estes Park, Mummy Range

When Edmund Rogers, as superintendent of Rocky Mountain National Park, was closely supervising the building of Trail Ridge Road, he arranged to blast the route through this spectacular cliff.

Rock Lake, Little Rock Lake   Forest Canyon

Rock Lake was formerly Big Rock Lake; Little Rock Lake was called Primrose Pool by Dr. Workman.

Rocky Mountain National Park

Herbert N. Wheeler was the first superintendent of the Colorado National Forest. According to his memoirs he moved his headquarters from Estes Park to Fort Collins in June 1908, but before he left he talked to the Estes Park Improvement Association. "If you want to draw tourists," said he, "you should establish a game refuge where tourists can see the wild life," and he produced a map of four townships stretching northwest toward North Park, which the Forest Service could probably control as a game refuge.

Many people—too many to mention by name—took up the idea. For example, according to Wheeler, Gifford Pinchot of the U.S. Forest Service hired Enos Mills at a salary of $1,600 a year and travel expenses to make a lecture tour advertising the beauties of the region to women's clubs.

Gradually the idea of a game refuge administered by the Forest Service under the Department of Agriculture changed to the thought of a national park administered by the newly created National Park Service under the Department of the Interior. As the idea grew, so did

Joseph L. Wescott
came to Grand Lake in June 1867.
Trapper, poet, and raconteur, Judge
Wescott lived on the southwestern
shore of Grand Lake for almost 50
years. Mt. Wescott bears his name.
Photo—Edith Hanington Ward

Eng⁴ by G.E.Perine & CᵒN.Y.

Anna Dickinson
was the first woman to stand on top
of Longs Peak. In September 1873
the Hayden survey men invited this
glamorous lady lecturer to climb
the peak with them. Mt. Dickinson
is named for her.
Photo—Denver Public Library
Western Collection

William L. Hallett
with his four sons at the summer
home (still standing) he built in 1881
at Marys Lake. Cattleman and engineer by vocation, he was one of
Colorado's first mountaineers, in
1896 Chairman of Explorations of
the Rocky Mountain Club. Hallett
Peak bears his name, as did Hallett
Glacier until 1924 when the name
was changed to Rowe Glacier.
Photo—State Historical Society of Colorado

Photo—George Barnard, from
Colorado Mountain Club L

Members of The Colorado Mountain Club load into Stanley Steamers at Longs Peak Inn, 191:

**Dedication of
Rocky Mountain
National Park
September 4, 1915**

Among those who celebrated
result of their efforts that
were Robert Sterling Yard of
National Park Service,
named Sky Pond; Enos Mill
Longs Peak Inn, who na
Storm Peak; F. O. Stanley,
ventor of the Stanley Steamer.
whom Stanley Park was nan
Congressman Ed Taylor,
managed to change Grand
er's name to Colorado River;
Mrs. John D. Sherman, presi
of the National Federation
Women's Clubs.

Photo—Denver Public Library Western Collection

Arapaho Indian trip in Estes Park, July 1914

In the picture the man on the left is Shep Husted, Estes Park guide and wrangler, who conducted the party on a two week trip. The Arapahos called him "Sage-Brush-Dude," though he was an outstanding mountain man. Next to Husted is Gun Griswold, dignified patriarch, 73 years old. Old Man Gun's only luggage was an eagle-feather fan. Although the tired old man asked to be left to die on Flattop Mountain, he was returned to the Reservation. Sherman Sage, aged 63, wears the important uniform of Chief-of-Police of the Northern Arapahos. He and Shep Husted enjoyed a humorous camaraderie. Next stands Tom Crispin, fluent interpreter, a 38-year-old Arapaho. On the right is young Oliver W. Toll, "The Tall One," chosen by his cousin Harriet Vaille to lead the party and record the information gleaned from the Indians. David Hawkins, "The Short One," seated, was an Eastern dude brought along by Shep Husted.

This chart shows pioneer cabins and resorts

built prior to 1878. The present day roads

are shown in order to orient the visitor.

Although not classed as resorts, many of

the private homes took in guests in the

early days.

(1) Joel Estes original cabin built
in 1859.

(2) The second Estes cabin built in
1860, which in 1867 was owned by Griff
Evans and was important for keeping
guests.

(3) Cabin of Rocky Mountain Jim
built in Muggins Gulch in 1868.

(4) A. Q. MacGregor's cabin which
entertained guests in the early days.
Post Office in 1875.

(5) Sprague's, built in 1875, began
taking guests in 1877 and became Steads
in 1904.

(6) John Hupp settled in Beaver
Meadows in 1875.

(7) W.E. James cabin built in 1875.

Rev.

nes

④
acGregor

Devils Gulch Road

Big Thompson Road

⑬ odge

⑨ Henry Farrar

Joel Estes
①

Chas. Dennison
⑫

Joel Estes ②

⑪ Israel Rowe

⑭ Estes Park Hotel

Marys Lake ⑩

son

Creek Road

No. St. Vrain Road

Muggins Gulch

Rocky Mountain Jim ③

Fish

St. Vrain Road

Twin Sisters Mt.

⑮

(8) Rev. E. J. Lamb settled in Tahosa Valley in 1875.

(9) Henry Farrar built a cabin on the present site of the Presbyterian Church in 1875.

(10) H. W. Ferguson settled near Marys Lake in 1875. This later became "The Highlands" Hotel.

(11) Israel Rowe built a cabin in 1876 on the site of the present Crocker Ranch.

(12) Charles Dennison built a cabin in 1868 midway between the cabins of Rowe and Evans.

(13) W. E. James moved from site No. 7 and established Elkhorn Lodge in 1877.

(14) The Estes Park Hotel (also known as the Dunraven or English Hotel) was built and opened in 1877.

(15) Ruins of cabin said to have been built by Kit Carson about 1841.

BASED on UNDATED MAP made by staff of

ROCKY MOUNTAIN NATIONAL PARK.

James Grafton Rogers
First President of the Colorado
Mountain Club, Chairman of the
Colorado Geographic Board, pro-
moter of Rocky Mountain National
Park. He named the Cloud Peaks in
the Never Summer Mountains.
Photo—The Colorado Mountain Club Library

Harriet Vaille
Chairman of the Nomenclature
Committee of the Colorado Moun-
tain Club, Secretary to the Colorado
Geographic Board, organizer of the
1914 Arapaho Indian trip to Estes
Park. Her influence is felt in many
of the Indian names in the area.
Photo—Polly Bouck

Ellsworth Bethel
Most active member of the Colo-
rado Geographic Board. He chris-
tened the mountains north of the
Arapaho Peaks with the names of
Indian tribes. Mt. Bethel near Love-
land Pass bears his name.
Photo—State Historical Society of Colorado

George Barnard

eader of Colorado Mountain
 trips into the northern Front
ge, member of committee of the
rado Geographic Board to sug-
names for the 1915 U.S. Geo-
al Survey map of Rocky Moun-
National Park. He named Dream
 and Shadow Mountain, and
 his mountaineering call came
name on Terra Tomah Moun-
The picture shows him at the
 Fern Lake winter outing.
—The Colorado Mountain Club Library

WINTER OUTINGS
AT FERN LAKE

he trail to Odessa Lake, 1915

e trip from Fern Lake to Odes-
ake, with Notchtop towering
the quiet trail, was the high-
of the annual winter outings
by The Colorado Mountain
at Fern Lake Lodge.
—The Colorado Mountain Club Library

Photo—Denver Public Library Western Collection

Lulu City
July 28, 1889

The 10-year-old town was already disintegrating.

ON THE NORTH FORK OF THE COLORADO RIVER

Both the town of Lulu and the dude ranch are gone, but their names remain on three creeks — Lulu Creek, Squeak Creek, and Phantom Creek.

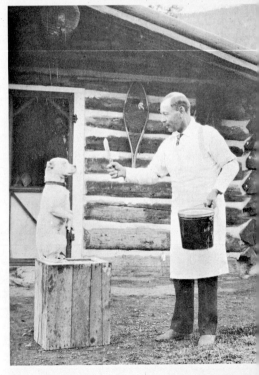

Photo—George Harvey from The Colorado Mountain Club

Squeaky Bob Wheeler (shown with his dog Jack) ran a hunting lodge on the North Fork. The next owner called it Phantom Valley Ranch.

the boundary lines of the proposed Estes National Park. The first bill presented to Congress designated Rollins Pass as the south boundary line. The final bill (all the bills were drafted by members of The Colorado Mountain Club) that passed January 26, 1915, had moved the line up to the Middle St. Vrain, but Robert Sterling Yard of the National Park Service in Washington continued to have a larger vision. He wrote:

> My dream is to see it [the Park] eventually in three sections, with general headquarters in Denver; the Longs Peak section enlarged to include the Arapahoe Peaks; the Mount Evans section, to add which there is already [in 1919] a bill before Congress; and the Pikes Peak section.

To cover such a dream, obviously the original name—Estes National Park—had to be replaced. R. B. Marshall of the U.S. Geological Survey suggested in his report on the proposed National Park that

> it should bear a name of broader significance and it is certainly fitting that this striking park section of the Rocky Mountains —the backbone of the country—should be honored in the naming of this proposed park . . . it should be called the "Rocky Mountain National Park."

In 1915, Rocky Mountain National Park became the tenth national park. The revolutionary National Park idea, a concept described by Freeman Tilden as "successfully impractical," is preservation. Americans since Pilgrim days have fought to tame the wilderness; the National Parks preserve it. The Parks are designed to remain in their natural state in order to perpetuate America's natural heritage.

Man disturbs the Park as little as possible. No commercial enterprises which consume resources operate within its boundaries—no logging, grazing, farming, or mining, nor hunting and trapping. (The Forest Service, operating on the principles of multiple use, accepts these uses as well as recreation, and tries to conserve in spite of the uses.) But the Park Service confines the works of man to the minimal necessary to handle human visitors: campgrounds, a few ranger stations and back-country shelters, museums in Moraine Park and on Fall River Pass, and roads to Bear Lake and over Trail Ridge. Ghost towns, irrigation ditches and dams, and two or three resorts now in the Park boundaries were there before the creation of the Park. Other resorts, like Steads Ranch and Phantom Valley Ranch, have been bought by the Park Service and razed. The National Park Service itself has interfered with naturalness by fighting blights and forest fires, an action questioned by some naturalists. If they stop forest fires, will they doom to extinction the after-fire succession of raspberry bushes, spindly lodgepole pines, and autumn-spectacular aspens?

Rocky Point   LAKE GRANBY

Roosevelt National Forest   INDIAN PEAKS, WILD BASIN
Most of the land within the boundaries of the Roosevelt National
Forest was withdrawn from settlement from 1902 to 1905. On May 17,
1905, it was added to the Medicine Bow Forest Reserve. On July 1,
1910, the name was changed to Colorado National Forest. On March
28, 1932, President Herbert Hoover announced that the name was
changed to Roosevelt National Forest in honor of President Theodore
Roosevelt, the champion of forestry and conservation who first established the Forest.

The Roosevelt National Forest is adjacent to the Rocky Mountain
National Park on the north, east, and southeast. The eastern slope of
the Indian Peaks is under its jurisdiction.

Round Pond   FOREST CANYON

Routt National Forest (Rhymes with shout.)   NEVER SUMMER
On June 12, 1905, President Theodore Roosevelt established the
Park Range Forest Reserve. In 1908 the name was changed to honor a
governor of Colorado, John L. Routt. He was appointed by President
U. S. Grant as Territorial Governor in 1875. The next year, when
Colorado became a state, Routt was voted into the office of governor,
serving until 1879. From 1891 to 1893 he was again governor, having
served as mayor of Denver in the interim (1883-85). In 1877 the
western part of Grand County was made into a separate county, called
Routt. Later Routt helped develop the rich coal mines of the county
that bears his name.

Rowe Glacier, Peak; Mtn. 13,184' (Rhymes with how.)
                                                        MUMMY RANGE
In the fall of 1875, Israel Rowe came to Estes Park to work on
MacGregor's toll road, his wife cooking for the road gang over an
open fire. He eventually built a nine-room house on land which later
became the Crocker Ranch. Rowe discovered Gem Lake, but his
discovery of Rowe Glacier should really be credited to dead grasshoppers and black bears. In 1880 grasshoppers flew over the Rockies
in great clouds, myriads of them dying on the high snowbanks of the
peaks. (Thawed, they smell like long-dead whales.) Bears consider
grasshoppers a delicacy worth climbing high to secure, and Israel Rowe
liked to hunt bears. Hunting, he came upon what he thought was the
largest snowfield in the Rockies.

Rowe took two other hunters to see this marvel, and also told
William Hallett about it. In 1884 Hallett investigated, alone. He fell
into a fissure two feet wide and 30 feet deep, its bottom filled with
water and its sides made of clear, crystalline ice. He extracted himself

by the grace of God and extreme exertion. Convinced that such a crevasse could occur only on a true glacier, Hallett told Professor G. M. Stone of Colorado College about his experience. Stone, through scientific channels, publicized the discovery of a glacier so far south in the Rockies. Thereupon glacialists from east and west swarmed to measure and admire Hallett Glacier.

Hallett Glacier was its name from 1888 until Abner Sprague tired of explaining to his guests that Hallett Peak was south of Flattop, above Tyndall Glacier, whereas Hallett Glacier was across the Park, nowhere near Hallett Peak, but in the Mummy Range. Sprague suggested in 1924 that Hallett Glacier be renamed Rowe Glacier. Many people objected. Charles Hanington, friend of Hallett in the Rocky Mountain Club, wrote a letter of protest to The Colorado Mountain Club. Finally Roger Toll, noted for his ability as a peacemaker, suggested that the glacier keep the name of Hallett but that a certain mountain, hitherto unnamed, be called Rowe Mountain. The suggestion backfired. In June 1932 the U.S. Board on Geographic Names not only changed the name of the glacier to Rowe but also pinned the name on two mountains. Now we have Rowe Glacier (formerly Hallett Glacier), Rowe Peak just to the north of it, and Rowe Mountain north of Rowe Peak. The latter pair is the only duplication of peak names in the Park area. Perhaps correspondence explaining this may someday be found in the files of the U.S. Board on Geographic Names. One hopes that either Rowe Peak or Rowe Mountain commemorates Mrs. Israel Rowe who camped, took care of two small children, and cooked for a road gang over an open fire.

167

S

Saddle, The
MUMMY RANGE

Any low place between two mountains may be called a saddle, but this is The Saddle, a name in use by 1913. Willard H. Ashton of Horseshoe Park Lodge used to send his guests to Lawn Lake where he had built a shelter cabin, then across The Saddle, and on north until the western side of Hagues Peak flattened out enough for them to describe a U-turn and come south to Rowe Glacier. (See Lawn Lake.)

St. Vrain Creeks, Glaciers; St. Vrain Mtn. 12,162'
INDIAN PEAKS, WILD BASIN

This name dates back to fur-trading days, but the creek had a previous name. On the night of July 3, 1820, Major Long's expedition camped on the South Platte River nearly opposite the mouth of the St. Vrain, which he called

> Potera's Creek, from a Frenchman of that name who is said to have been bewildered upon it, wandering about for 20 days almost without food. He was found by a band of Kiawas, who frequent this part of the country, and restored to his companions, a party of hunters at that time encamped on the Arkansa.

The name of the bewildered Potera gave way to the name of a storekeeper. Since any efficient storekeeper locates his store in a solvent community, successful merchants of the fur trade era, such as the brothers Bent and the brothers St. Vrain, built stores near where their customers, the Indians, could kill buffalo and bring robes to trade for luxuries like looking-glasses or a slice off a sugar loaf. Bent's Fort stood on the Arkansas River; another store financed by Bent and St. Vrain rose about 1837 on the east bank of the South Platte River, one and one-half miles below the mouth of St. Vrain Creek, three miles west of the present town of Gilcrest. This, the heart of the Arapaho country, was frequented also by Sioux, Cheyenne, Shoshoni, Pawnee, and other tribes whose names Ellsworth Bethel tried to affix to the peaks that tower on the skyline to the west. The store, or post, was first called Fort Lookout, then Fort George in honor of one of the Bent brothers, then gradually became Fort St. Vrain; the stream that joined the river near the fort became known as St. Vrain Creek.

Ceran St. Vrain was the capitalist of his family; but his younger brother Marcellin reigned as bourgeois (storekeeper) of the fort. He was a pleasant host with cultivated St. Louis manners and a Sioux wife, who brought trade from the plains Indians. In 1843 John Charles Fremont and William Gilpin celebrated the Fourth of July with

Marcellin St. Vrain, eating fruitcake shipped from St. Louis, and ice cream made with snow from Longs Peak. Gilpin's note on this feast did not explain how the snow was transported without melting.

How appropriate that the three branches of St. Vrain Creek have their origins in the Indian Peaks, since the Indians were the source of the success of St. Vrain's store!

Sandbeach Creek, Lake 10,283' WILD BASIN

Dr. Cooper remembers that this lake was named by Enos Mills. The sandy beach was covered up when the dam was built which turned the natural lake into a reservoir. The Supply Reservoir Company, in its filing in 1902, called the lake Supply Reservoir #1, and called the creek on which it lies Big Cascade Creek, but these names never became general. By 1916 the road to the lake had deteriorated into a trail. (See Bluebird Lake.)

Satanta Peak 11,979' INDIAN PEAKS

Another way of spelling this name of a Kiowa warrior is *Set-T'ain-te* (White Bear). Satanta (1830?-1878), known as the Orator of the Plains, lives in the memory of his people as one of the irreconcilables who strewed the path of white conquest with as much cactus as he could. Despite his hostility, he was a favorite with U. S. Army officers— in war, an able antagonist; between wars, a man of humor. When they visited his camp, he spread factory-made carpets on the ground and served them meals on tables of painted boards 20 inches wide by three feet long, ornamented around the edges with bright brass tacks (an early version of TV tables). To announce dinner, Satanta blew vigorously on a trumpet.

Kit Carson captured Satanta, holding him hostage in a vain attempt to subdue the Kiowas. Two years later the Indian brave left Fort Sill, but the prison cell had drained the gaiety from his heart and filled it with hatred for the white conquerors. Henceforth, the only times he played his trumpet was to confuse the U. S. Cavalry; when their bugler sounded "Charge," Satanta played "Retreat."

On a friendly visit to General Sherman, Satanta boasted of a recent murder of white settlers. General Sherman had him seized. An eyewitness described this six-foot Kiowa as he arrived at the Huntsville, Texas, jail, his feet lashed together under the belly of a small pony: "His muscles stood out on his gigantic frame like knots of whipcord, and his form, proud, erect in the saddle, his perfectly immobile face, and his motionless body, gave him the appearance of polished mahogany."

Three years in the Texas prison were enough for this vigorous man. One day he chanted the Kiowa death song, folded his arms, and plunged to death on the stone pavement three stories below the prison hospital windows.

Sawmill Creek NEVER SUMMER

A sawmill built on this stream provided lumber for the construction of the Grand Ditch.

Sawtooth Mtn. 12,304' INDIAN PEAKS

As seen from the Boulder Turnpike this mountain stands against the sky between Mt. Audubon to the south and Ogalalla Peak to the north, both much higher. The precipitous south face of the ripsaw tooth of this mountain makes it easy to recognize from the plains. Sawtooth has the distinction of marking the extreme eastern point reached by the Continental Divide in the United States.

Seven Utes Mtn. 11,458'—(Four miles west of Nokhu Crags)

This is the only mountain in the Park region that bears the name of the Ute Indians who inhabited the western mountains of Colorado, and this name was given to the mountain not to commemorate the independent Ute nation but to mark the place where the Utes suffered a tragedy. The 1914 Arapahos had a long name for this mountain which meant Where-the-Arapahos-killed-seven-Utes. The Colorado Geographic Board struggled with the original Arapaho words, hoping to use them or part of them for this mountain, but decided to use "the translation of an unpronounceable word from the 1914 Arapaho trip meaning Seven Utes."

Shadow Mtn. 10,155' GRAND LAKE

The 1914 Arapahos knew this mountain as Pine Ridge. When George Barnard and Jim Rogers asked local people what they called it, everyone gave a different answer. Some called it Lookout Mountain but, according to Charles Hanington, no true Grand Lake resident ever used that name. They preferred Wooded Mountain, except those who used Echo Mountain. In the summer of 1915 James Cairns pointed to this mountain opposite his store window and told Harriet Vaille it had three names, a middle and two sides. The central part was Cornstalk Mountain because of fire-killed timber sticking up like stubble in a cornfield. To the west the ridge was Echo Mountain; to the east the ridge was the Lady of the Lake.

Official approval by the Colorado Geographic Board of any one of these would inevitably antagonize someone. Lawyer Rogers, chairman of the Board, formulated a policy for such contingencies: In case of altercation, all old names should be replaced with an entirely new one, and he noted, "Old names replaced were in no case undisputed names." But what name should replace Lookout-Wooded-Echo-Cornstalk, and Lady of the Lake? George Barnard suggested Shadow Mountain because the ridge cast its shadow on Grand Lake.

Shadow Mtn. Lake 8367'   GRAND LAKE

George Barnard could not have dreamed that Shadow Mountain would someday also cast its shadow on a man-made lake that covers the sagebrush flats through which the Colorado River once meandered and children hunted Indian arrowheads among the gentians. Made by damming the river below the confluence of the Lake Fork and the North Fork of the Colorado River, Shadow Mountain Lake is part of the Colorado-Big Thompson Project. Water pumped by electricity from Lake Granby, also man-made, to Shadow Mountain Lake flows to Grand Lake; thence, via the 17-mile Alva B. Adams Tunnel to the Eastern Slope. Here the fall of water creates electricity which is carried back by power lines across the Divide to the pumps at Lake Granby, a system which approaches perpetual motion.

In an effort to preserve the especially attractive shoreline of Grand Lake, the U.S. Bureau of Reclamation agreed with the Grand Lake community that the water should rise no higher than its natural level when the big project was completed. The levels of Grand Lake and Shadow Mountain Lake are quite constant, while Lake Granby rises and falls with the runoff and with irrigation demands.

Shadow Mtn. Lookout 9923'   GRAND LAKE

Although this lookout is over 200 feet lower than the top of Shadow Mountain, the view is ample. In the Forest Service lookout building, well protected against lightning, the summer firewarden watches for forest fires, augmenting the modern air patrol. The warden's job is eagerly sought and often held by honeymooners, whose only contact with the world below is by telephone, except for Forest Service men on horseback who bring them supplies, and for hikers.

Shadow Mountain Recreation Area   GRAND LAKE, LAKE GRANBY

Lake Granby and Shadow Mountain Lake, man-made reservoirs linked by channel to Grand Lake, Colorado's largest natural body of water, comprise the "Great Lakes" of Colorado. The recreational potential of the area, recognized as one of the greatest in the United States, is being developed by the National Park Service through agreement with the Bureaus of Reclamation and Land Management, U.S. Department of the Interior.

So reads the official folder of this area. Boating, water skiing, and lake fishing on a lake as large as Lake Granby, about eight miles long, are unusual for a state full of what easterners call ponds, but few states can supplement the boating with a mountain view such as that of the Indian Peaks on the Continental Divide seen from Lake Granby.

Sharkstooth, The 12,630'   GLACIER GORGE

171

Sheep Lakes ESTES PARK, MUMMY RANGE

Mountain sheep often come to these lakes today as they did in 1917 when Willis T. Lee wrote, "This lake has long been a favorite resort for the bighorns. . . . They come down to Sheep Lake nearly every day for water. A supply of salt placed here has tempted them to frequent the spot." (See Bighorn Mtn., Rams Horn Mtn.)

Sheep Mtn. MUMMY RANGE

Sheep Rock NEVER SUMMER

Surprisingly often, bighorn sheep look down from this rock at the motorists who have stopped at Milner Pass to read the Poudre Lake sign. Look up to them!

Shelf Creek, Lake GLACIER GORGE

This lake in Glacier Gorge is an example of the ice-action that leaves lakes—hanging lakes—perched on shelves above the valleys.

Shelter House GLACIER GORGE, WILD BASIN

There is good reason for a mountain shelter-house to be marked on a map; it can mean survival. The shelter at Chasm Lake marks the end of the horse trail. Climbers often spend the night there before attempting the ascent of the East Face; and it houses the Park Service rescue equipment—litters, ropes, bandages, emergency food.

At the Keyhole on Longs Peak is another, smaller shelter, erected by her family near the spot where Agnes Vaille died on January 12, 1925. This structure was designed by Arthur A. Fisher, Denver architect, along lines suggested by some ancient dwellings in Apulia, southern Italy. The heavy walls, the floor, the bench, even the bee-hive roof are stone.

On the Boulder Field stood for many years still another shelter-house, run by Robert Collier and his wife Dorothy—at 12,500 feet, the highest tourist hotel in Colorado! Though built on rock, it proved to have a precarious foundation. The alternate freezing and thawing of water below caused the huge boulders to shift their positions slightly; the walls cracked and finally fell.

Shelter Island GRAND LAKE, LAKE GRANBY

On Lake Granby, shelter from eccentric winds and forceful white-caps can be as important to the boatman as shelter on a mountain is to a climber.

Shipler Park; Shipler Mtn. 11,317′ NEVER SUMMER

Joseph L. Shipler, a Civil War veteran, built a cabin in Shipler Park in 1876, the first cabin in the valley of the North Fork. Shipler was a forerunner of the mine rush, one of the discoverers of the Wolverine Mine on Bowen Mountain. In December 1882 he located the

Collins Lode in the Lead Mountain Mining District; its enormous mine dump on Shipler Mountain is conspicuous from Shipler Park.

Mr. Shipler was still living in his cabin when The Colorado Mountain Club camped in his park in August 1914. One of the 30 members of the Prairie Club of Chicago who came on this outing wrote an account of his cabin, reached at the end of a long walk from Grand Lake. Her report of the lonely walk on a dirt road contrasts with motor travel on today's paved highways:

The walk of 16 to 18 miles to our Shipler Park camp, which was 1000 feet higher than Grand Lake, was one of the finest trips of the whole outing. A wagon road leads from Grand Lake to Shipler Park, and we followed it all the way, through seas of flowers of every hue imaginable. The fringed blue gentians grew so thick that one swoop of the hand would have secured a large bunch, and they formed pools of blue, first on one side and then on the other side of the road. . . . We also found quantities of wild strawberries, and you know how sweet they were. . . . The only people we saw that day were two Forest Rangers, for we were in the Arapahoe Forest Reserve; Squeaky Bob, who kept a fishing resort a mile and a half below our camp, and a Prairie Schooner drawn to one side of the road. . . . by 3:30 we arrived at Squeaky Bob's Camp which he called the Hotel de Hard Scrabble. It is a pleasant looking log cabin resort surrounded by tents, and much frequented by trout fishing enthusiasts, as the trout fishing in Grand River is very good. [The next day, George Barnard, leader of The Colorado Mountain Club outing, caught 127 brook trout for the group's breakfast.] Squeaky Bob is considerable of a character, having been everything from a cow puncher, horse thief, and guide, to a resort keeper, and he got his name from his voice which is high pitched and has a falsetto note in it. . . . I was anxious to see the camp so I pushed on, and I was well rewarded. It was really the most beautiful camp of the whole trip . . . this park was adorned by the finest grove of Engelmann Spruce and Fir Balsam trees I have ever seen, and bounded on the one side by the Grand River and the other by a swift running mountain brook.

The only person up there was an old miner, Mr. Shipler, who had several claims in that region, and from whom the Park as well as a mountain looking down upon it, got their name. Mr. Shipler proved to be the soul of hospitality, and when the wagons and provisions did not arrive, gave us all the coffee he had, so we secured a hot drink at least. Then

173

hearing that one of the girls was sick, he fixed up the other bed in his cabin and came out to offer it to her, as it began to look as though we would have to spend the night outdoors. The sick girl, however, had already been sent down to Squeaky Bob's, so Mrs. Pettengill who was beginning to feel cold, made a dicker with Mr. Shipler whereby she and I obtained the much coveted bed, and it was quite an experience I can assure you.

The bed was made from four wide slabs of rough wood put together to form a square box into which spring and mattress had been placed, and this bed with another of similiar make occupied one side of the cabin, the only other furniture being a kitchen table, small stove and two chairs. Tiny windows high up on either side, together with a glass pane set into the upper half of the one door, let in the light of day, and we could peer out through chinks from which the clay had fallen as well. The inscription on the door was the best part of the cabin though, as it read as follows: "Everybody welcome here, except a low down cur of a thief who belongs in the Penitentiary, and I have his name and number and will get him. G. Shipler."

Ships Prow   GLACIER GORGE, WILD BASIN

Shoshoni Peak 12,967′   INDIAN PEAKS

In 1965 a young man from Chile named Evilio Echevarría, a teacher at the University of Colorado, and a mountaineer, proposed that an unnamed peak on the Continental Divide between Apache Peak and Pawnee Peak, 12,967 feet high with a precipitous southeast face, be named Shoshoni Peak. The U.S. Board on Geographic Names sent out inquiries concerning it in January 1966 and accepted it in July. How pleased the spirit of Ellsworth Bethel must be that the Shoshoni tribe has taken its place among the Indian Peaks, 50 years after he heatedly tried to have Mt. Alice changed to Shoshone Peak.

Of the many western Indian tribes belonging to the Shoshonean linguistic stock, including Ute, Comanche, and Bannock, the Shoshoni tribe was the farthest north. Today about 1,600 Shoshonis live on the Wind River Reservation in Wyoming with headquarters at Fort Washakie, named for the wise and famous chief.

Signal Mtn. 11,262′; South Signal Mtn.   MUMMY RANGE

White pioneers who watched smoke rise in spurts from the top of Signal Mountain wondered what the redmen's signals meant, and later told their children of seeing the smoke. The 1914 Arapahos did not remember signaling from the mountain; they called the two mountains Wolf Ridge.

Skeleton Gulch   Never Summer

Two men caught in a snowslide were carried far down this gulch where their skeletons were found in the late spring.

Skull Point 12,026′   Mummy Range

On August 9, 1927, Charles R. Hughes of Denver found a human skull in rocks near the summit of this point. Roger Toll and others, investigating, found animal bones there, and concluded that mountain lions had denned on this point long, long ago. Toll proposed the name on September 15, 1927.

Sky Pond   Glacier Gorge

By eastern standards, Sky Pond is just a small pond; by western mountain standards, Sky Pond is big enough to be called a lake. It was named by an easterner, Robert Sterling Yard, who fully appreciated the spectacular scenery when Abner Sprague guided him to the head of Loch Vale. Yard was investigating the area in order to prepare the first official pamphlet for tourists about the newly created Rocky Mountain National Park.

Robert Sterling Yard (1861-1945), after securing a B.A. from Princeton in 1883, was connected with both Scribners and Century magazines. From the inception of the National Park Service in 1914 to 1919 he was chief of the educational section. In 1919 he organized the National Park Association, and in 1935 helped establish the Wilderness Society. It is pleasant to think of Sky Pond and Lake of Glass, probably Icy Brook, as names given by this dedicated conservationist.

Snow Lake   Never Summer

Snowbank Lake   Wild Basin

Snowdrift Lake   Grand Lake

The sizable cirque enclosing this lake shelters a snowdrift; Ferril Atkins, Park ranger-naturalist, "suspects a glacierette." Before this lake had a distinct name all its own, it and Murphy Lake to the north of Snowdrift Peak were called Murphy Lakes.

Snowdrift Peak 12,274′   Grand Lake

This was labeled Mt. Fisher by R. B. Marshall on the map he drew for the Denver Chamber of Commerce about 1915, but the Colorado Geographic Board "could find no local authority whatever for the name and it seemed meaningless." (One wonders if they thought of Arthur Fisher, a government surveyor for the original Longs Peak quadrangle map and a companion of R. B. Marshall on his official tour of the proposed Park area in 1913. This Fisher was no relation to Redwood Fisher, prominent rancher near Grand Lake.) Because of a snowdrift conspicuous from the Flattop Trail, the Colorado Geographic Board asked to have Fisher Peak renamed Snowdrift Peak in February 1915, the U.S. Board on Geographic Names making the change official in 1932.

Soda Creek, Spring   LAKE GRANBY

Solitude Lake—GLACIER GORGE; **Solitude, Lake**—GRAND LAKE

South Fork of the Colorado River—See Arapaho Creek.

South Lateral Moraine—See Moraine.

South St. Vrain Creek—See St. Vrain Creek.

Spearhead, The 12,575′   GLACIER GORGE, WILD BASIN
Dean Babcock knew this name in 1922, and Roger Toll recorded it officially in July 1923 after he and a group of Colorado Mountain Club members had climbed it. "This sharp wedge-shaped spur running north from Chiefs Head is a prominent feature of Glacier Gorge," Toll wrote. Superintendent Toll fancied balanced names like Arrowhead and Spearhead, Knobtop and Notchtop.

Specimen Creek   NEVER SUMMER
Before the 1961 map, this was called Volcano Creek.

Specimen Mtn. 12,489′   NEVER SUMMER
The 1914 Arapahos, with no hint from Oliver Toll or Shep Husted that the area was of volcanic origin, said they knew this mountain as Mountain Smokes. One of the Indians, Sherman Sage, told a legend, illustrating it by arranging eight stones on the ground, each representing a generation of his ancestors. As he placed the last stone he said, "This man, when he was a boy, saw smoke coming out of the mountain."

Geologically speaking, Sherman Sage should have spent all day heaping up stones to represent the generations of man that have lived and died since smoke came out of Specimen Mountain; but smoke it did, once. Its appearance today, so entirely different from that of other mountains in the Park, testifies to its volcanic origin. Specimen Mountain is formed in layers laid down by eruptions—volcanic, glass, ash, lava, mud-flows, breccia, and pumice. The cone probably once stood thousands of feet higher than the present summit of the mountain, and what is called The Crater on its southwest side is not a crater. The name Specimen Mountain appears on an 1882 township map. The specimens are gemstones, like opal, agate, chalcedony, and black obsidian. All these and more may be observed on the mountain, especially in The Crater. Observed, but NOT collected. Collecting is prohibited in national parks.

Frank Byers, son of William Byers who climbed Longs Peak in

1868, remembered that when he was a boy at his father's ranch at Hot Sulphur Springs this mountain was called Geode Mountain. A geode is an ordinary looking stone with a crystal center. Young Frank doubtless spent happy hours breaking open stones with the hope of finding beauty within.

Spectacle Lakes MUMMY RANGE

Named by Roger Toll in 1922, not for their spectacular appearance at the foot of Ypsilon's cliffs, but for their shape, which resembles a pair of eye-glasses.

Above the lakes is the grave of a 21-year old youth who was killed on August 2, 1905. Louis Raymond Levings and his two cousins, George Black and Dean Babcock, had climbed Fairchild Mountain that day. Dean returned to camp but the other two youths wanted a picture of one of the snow cornices that protrude over the arms of the Y on Ypsilon Mountain. About 600 feet down, Louis fell when a rock he was using as a hand hold gave way. His body was left on the mountain, cement being poured over the grave. By 1929, when the cement started to disintegrate, iron plates for a coffin were packed up the trail, then bolted together, and he was reburied about 700 feet above and to the north of Spectacle Lakes.

Spirit Lake GRAND LAKE

This was the Ute name for Grand Lake. (See Grand Lake.) The name Spirit Lake was ignored by white settlers. Fortunately someone saved the Ute name from oblivion by moving it upstream on the East Inlet of Grand Lake.

Sprague Glacier, Pass; Sprague Mtn. 12,713′—FOREST CANYON, GRAND LAKE; **Sprague Lake**—ESTES PARK

Before he died in 1942, Abner Sprague was the patriarch of Estes Park. His two manuscripts on the Park's history are gold mines.

Abner Sprague had come in 1864 by covered wagon from the Middle West with his family to settle on a farm near Loveland. In 1875 young Abner braved the animosity of Dunraven's overseer to squat on land in Moraine Park. Later Sprague found that the Earl, in grabbing his huge hunting preserve, had filed on the South Lateral Moraine, but had neglected to claim the valley floor of Moraine Park. There Abner and his father pre-empted two quarter-sections of land. His wife soon was cooking for hunters and fishermen who appeared at the only door within miles to ask for food and shelter, and the Spragues found themselves in the hotel business. About 1900 Jim Stead, Abner's brother-in-law, bought the place, thereafter known as Steads Ranch.

After a sojourn away from dude ranching, Abner Sprague acquired land in Glacier Basin. Here the Spragues built another hotel, provided a lake for the aesthetic and fishing pleasure of their guests, and Abner returned to his expert guide service. Sprague's nephew took over this hotel in 1943. By 1960 both this and Steads Ranch had been bought by the National Park, the hotels razed and the land returned to nature, but Abner Sprague's name still rests on Sprague Lake.

Abner Sprague delighted in taking discriminating guests to the Continental Divide at the head of Spruce Canyon. He probably knew this terrain as well as any man will ever know it. Enos Mills acknowledged this when his 1905 map appeared with Sprague's name on the glacier that feeds Spruce Creek. Whoever applied Sprague's name to the adjacent mountain and pass, on the 1961 map, paid a little of the debt the Park owes Abner Sprague.

Sprague himself made maps. He ran lines for railroads and private property-owners, and, for three years around 1890, was official surveyor for Larimer County. In trying to map the Estes Park area, he found his sketch a confusion of hachures denoting many nameless mountains between Longs and Hagues, between Richthofen and Mt. Olympus. Because a map without names lacks character, Sprague set about naming the natural features of the land he loved. He honored old-timers, neighbors, and guests at his hotel whom he had guided across the mountains, reserving a beautiful waterfall for his wife, Alberta.

Spruce Canyon, Creek FOREST CANYON

These features originally were called Willow. Abner Sprague changed the name to Spruce because of the splendid Douglas spruce that grew in the canyon upstream from The Pool. It was not his fault that dendrologists later changed the name of the tree to Douglas-fir. The name of the canyon, however, need not be switched to Fir, as Engelmann spruce do grow at the head of the canyon. Douglas-fir is really neither a spruce nor a fir. David Douglas, a Scottish botanist who went to Oregon in 1823 as a collector to the Royal Horticultural Society, admired the enormous conifers, collected specimens, and found the tree popularly identified by his name. Its Latin name for many years was *Pseudotsuga taxifolia* (literal translation—pseudo, Greek word for false; tsugo, Japanese word for hemlock; taxi, from *taxus,* Latin word for yew; folia, from Latin word for leaf. This means the tree is a false hemlock with leaves like a yew.) However, Douglas was not the first man to identify the Douglas-fir. Another Scottish botanist named Archibald Menzies (pronounced in Scotland, Mee nus) had collected the type specimen from Vancouver Island in 1791. In an effort to give credit where credit is due, dendrologists have recently changed the Latin name of the Douglas-fir to *Pseudotsuga menziesii.*

What is the amateur botanist to do among this confusion of spruce, fir, hemlock, yew, Greek, Japanese, Latin, and two Scots? He can call the Douglas-fir a Christmas tree, and identify it by its soft, flat needles and hanging cones with three-pronged tongues protruding between the scales.

Spruce Lake

Besides the Douglas-fir, which is neither spruce nor fir, real spruce and real fir grow in the Park. One way to tell them apart is to feel the needles. The spruce needle is sharp and four-sided; the fir needle soft and flat. The Boy Scouts remember this by four words: spruce—square; fir—flat.

Two kinds of spruce grow in the Park. The Engelmann spruce dominates the subalpine zone, and the Colorado blue spruce groups along streams in the lower mountains. The Engelmann spruce was named for the same St. Louis botanist for whom the mountain with the great cirque, south of Berthoud Pass, was named.

The blue spruce is the official state tree of Colorado. This tree emigrated from Colorado to the Middle West in the 1860's, carried by the turn-backs of the Pikes Peak Gold Rush who loaded small silver-blue spruce instead of gold nuggets into their empty prairie schooners before turning their backs on the Rocky Mountains. The gardens of Iowa, Missouri, Illinois have been ornamented by Colorado blue spruce for a hundred years.

Spruce Lake was named by Cliff Higby in 1914, probably because it lies in Spruce Canyon. Cliff Higby and his brother Reed were first boys and then businessmen in Estes Park, enthusiastic about all aspects of the mountains. After serving in Europe during World War I, Cliff refused to come home until he had climbed the Matterhorn. In Colorado he not only climbed with The Colorado Mountain Club but was instrumental in forming the Club's Estes Park group (now incorporated by chapters in Boulder and Fort Collins). Later Higby homesteaded in North Park near the Wyoming border, running a guest ranch called the Skyland Ranch.

Before 1914 Dr. Workman had named Spruce Lake for Fred Dille, naturalist, for whom Ed Andrews assiduously collected bird eggs. At the age of 19 Fred Dille was the second school teacher in the Estes Park school. His reminiscences are in the library of the Rocky Mountain National Park. On June 30, 1932, the U.S. Board on Geographic Names recognized Spruce Lake, "Not: Dilly."

Squeak Creek

Robert Wheeler (1865-1946) arrived at his brother's ranch in North Park in 1885 in a silk hat, striped coat, and kid gloves. To acquire this correct traveling outfit young Bob had saved for months. He soon learned how to dress and how to hold his own in a world of men, despite his short stature and high-pitched voice. During the Spanish-American War he had charge of the horses for a troop of

Rough Riders who never got out of Florida. He worked in mines at Encampment, Wyoming, and at Lulu City, then in 1907 homesteaded 160 acres on the North Fork of the Grand River. Here he built a tenthouse resort. It went by three names: formally it was Camp Wheeler; its owner always referred to it as Hotel de Hardscrabble; and to sportsmen it was Squeaky Bob's place. The last was inevitable because in excitement Robert Wheeler's high, thin voice rose to a falsetto squeak.

His guests took for granted the first-class hunting and fishing, but never Squeaky Bob's tales interlaced with wit and inventive profanity. Though he had housekeepers, Bob usually did the cooking himself, for what did a woman know about cooking wild game? Bob married the last of his housekeepers, and in 1924 sold his camp for a life in the lowlands. The new owner, Lester Scott, changed the name to Phantom Valley Ranch and tore down the tent houses, but among the new buildings he erected was a cabin where Squeaky Bob and his wife might spend the summer. (See Phantom Creek.)

Stanley Park   Estes Park

Freelan O. Stanley (1849-1940) and his twin brother were inventors. Among their varied products were the Stanley Dry Plate for cameras (later Eastman Kodak bought the patent) and a horseless carriage powered by a steam engine—the Stanley Steamer. When his doctors gave him only one summer to live, F. O. Stanley came west for his health. Summering in Estes Park and wintering in Massachusetts, he died 37 years later, age 91.

He came to Colorado in June of 1903 and drove his Stanley Steamer up to Estes Park. Tradition in Estes has it that his was the first horseless carriage to arrive in that mountain fastness. But tradition has forgotten the first gasoline buggy, which, on May 7, 1903, chugged up the wagon road from Lyons in eight hours, 40 minutes—only four hours longer than the time required by the regular four-horse stage. The Burlington Railroad had sent the automobile touring car out from Chicago especially to attempt the trip. The Burlington envisioned transferring its Estes Park tourists from the end of the railroad at Lyons to its own modern automotive stages. Besides the chaffeur, T. A. Brady of The Chicago Motor Vehicle Company, and a stand-by chauffeur from Denver, the 12-passenger, 30-horsepower car carried nine men. The Lyons paper reported:

> The machine worked first class with the exception of where it encountered mud holes on heavy upgrades . . . the machine going into the mud up to its axle in numerous places, but not once did it refuse to act or a single break occur. And the 20 and 25 percent grades were easily ascended where the roads were in good condition. [Because no gasoline

was in Estes Park, the automobile had to wait until a new supply could be brought from Lyons. Impatient passengers] could not wait so they had the pleasure ? of seeing the scenery on the return trip from afoot.

Stanley's trip went faster but no smoother. Not waiting for the young man who was to help him in the heavy work of carrying water for the engine, he left Denver at noon, missed the road to Longmont, and sundown caught him somewhere north of Boulder. Getting directions from a farmer, he arrived that night at Welch's resort, four miles above Lyons on the North St. Vrain. (The Copper Kettle Tea Room now marks the site.) Billy Welch, having no confidence in the Stanley Steamer, next morning refused to sacrifice a man to it, but the car's inventor knew what it could do and again started out alone. An hour and 50 minutes later he telephoned Welch from Sam Service's store in Estes village, but Welch refused to believe that the steamer was really there until that volatile Irishman, Service—himself—got on the line.

The troubles Stanley encountered decided him to reroute and improve the road. Except for the State's contribution of $2,500, he raised the money himself—some say $50,000, some $16,000, and some $9,000— and secured the rights of way. In late August of 1907 he notified the County Road Commissioner that the road was ready for acceptance.

Stanley planned a fleet of four automobiles, each to be equipped with a telephone which could be attached at any point to the telephone line. This would be valuable in case of breakdown. He guaranteed a trip of no more than an hour and a half from Lyons to Estes Park. The next summer, and many summers thereafter, his 12-passenger stages hissed up the new road with ease. Nothing more was recorded about the emergency telephones.

Freelan O. Stanley had a singular quirk for a man who had invented an automobile; he refused to drive backwards. To avoid it he installed a turntable in the garage of his Estes Park home.

On acreage he acquired from the Dunraven holdings he built a hotel, which he was going to name the Dunraven Hotel. *The Mountaineer* protested the name all the summer of 1908. Stanley offered a prize of $10 for a better name, but finally, acquiescing to popular demand, called it the Stanley Hotel. There he played his home-made violin with its professionally sweet tone, and described the sunsets over Longs Peak to his wife, who was blind.

The power plant Stanley built supplied electricity not only to his hotel but to the village of Estes Park until it was bought by the Public Service Company in 1926. Through his efforts the village acquired a water system; through his generosity land for its sewage disposal plant. Stanley helped pick up the tab for transporting elk from Yellowstone

181

to repopulate the big game herds of the Park region, and deeded to the village the seven acres of land now known as Stanley Park.

Static Peak   Never Summer

In 1942 the Rocky Mountain National Park staff suggested that, since Thunder Mountain stood east of Thunder Pass, Lightning Peak should stand to the west. Why the authorities refused this suggestion is not recorded, but Static was substituted—a good name, as any mountain climber will testify. Caught in a lightning storm above timberline, he compacts himself into as small a bundle as possible, while his hair rises, his fingers tingle, and his ears buzz until lightning discharges the static, which soon starts the demonstration all over again.

Steep Mtn.   Estes Park

This hill had an Indian name with the same connotation as steep. The name translates into Where-the-Buffalo-Was-Chased. Old Gun Griswold of the 1914 Arapahos could even date the year it was thus named—1860. That summer he was camped with many other Arapahos in Tuxedo Park. Boys herding the camp's horses chased a buffalo part way up the mountain, noteworthy because the mountain was steep.

Abner Sprague thought that the name came from a map of a subdivision of Estes Park on which a surveyor had noted "a steep mountain." The name appears on the 1874 township map.

Stillwater Creek   Lake Granby

Placid Stillwater Creek runs into Lake Granby, which has inundated the old Stillwater Ranch, once a landmark on the stage road to Grand Lake.

Stone Lake   Indian Peaks

Stone Man Pass   Glacier Gorge, Wild Basin

Dean Babcock, on September 8, 1922, wrote a letter to Roger Toll telling of a rock 40 feet high which he had seen from Glacier Gorge. It looked like the upper part of a man's figure—hat, face, and coat. The next month Roger Toll climbed McHenrys Peak and agreed that the rock looked like a man "when seen from Flattop Pass, like an old woman of the Dutch Cleanser form when seen from Frozen Lake, and at other times it looks like anything you please."

Stones Peak 12,922'   Forest Canyon

This is a puzzler. No record has been found stating that this mountain was named for Mr. So-and-So by Mr. So-and-So. It puzzled both Abner Sprague and William Hallett, who both thought it might have been named by the King Survey. But the name is not on the King Atlas of 1876 nor the Hayden Atlas published the following year, nor was any likely candidate named Stone found in the literature of the early surveys or in any other printed matter until the 1880's. In 1887 a man named G. M. Stone climbed with Frederick Chapin in the Estes Park region. Chapin named many peaks for his climbing companions, even those not members of the Appalachian Mountain Club. Perhaps he named Stones Peak for this man.

G. M. Stone (1841-1917) was a professor of geology and natural history at Colorado College from 1881 to 1888, and acting curator of the botanical collection. He once worked with a geological survey party and invented surveying instruments. He also invented devices to aid helpless invalids. During the summer vacation of 1886 Stone stayed at Ferguson's hotel near Marys Lake where Hallett had his summer home. Hallett reported his discovery of a glacier to Professor Stone. (See Rowe Glacier.)

The 1914 Arahapos called Mt. Julian and Stones Peak the Bear Paws. These mountains were a favorite habitat of bears.

Storm Pass; Storm Peak 13,326′ GLACIER GORGE

Enos Mills, observer of nature, knew where the clouds gathered when the elements prepared to battle. He named both Battle Mountain and Storm Peak.

An earlier name for Storm Peak was Velies Peak. Jacob W. Velie (1829-1908), at one time curator of the Chicago Natural History Museum, in 1864 came from Rock Island to explore with Dr. C. C. Parry, tireless botanist of the Front Range. In August they joined William Byers and George Nichols in Byers' first attempt to climb Longs Peak. Byers called Velie "an ornithological sportsman." After climbing part way up the mountain together, the four men parted, Byers and Nichols to climb Mt. Meeker. Parry and Velie, according to Parry's account of the climb, "winding around the western face toward the south, came upon a rugged ridge that connects Long's Peak with the main range. On one of the highest points of this ridge, named (after one of the party) Velie's Peak, the barometer was set up." Besides estimating the altitude, the men closely observed the water courses of Longs Peak and decided that the mountain was definitely east of the Continental Divide.

Stormy Peaks Pass; Stormy Peaks 12,148′ MUMMY RANGE

Lester Scott, Rocky Mountain Park ranger and later owner of Phantom Valley ranch, named these peaks.

Stratus, Mt. NEVER SUMMER

After Roger Toll led climbers up this mountain on August 4, 1921, he proposed this name to conform to its neighbors, Mts. Nimbus, Cumulus, and Cirrus. Stratus is a cloud-form characterized by its horizontal extension and low altitude.

Strawberry Bench, Lake   LAKE GRANBY

On the steep mountain slopes in the Monarch Lake area the walker can pick quantities of wild strawberries without bending down.

Sugarloaf Mtn.   MUMMY RANGE

Have you ever puzzled over the shape of the many mountains named Sugarloaf in eastern America, western America, or Rio de Janeiro? They do not resemble the shape of our lump sugar, cube sugar, domino sugar, or any other angular shape of modern pressed sugar. Most Sugarloaf Mountains are cone-shaped.

This leads us back to the days before granulated sugar was sold in bulk. Loaf sugar was a fully refined crystallized sugar which, while hot and in liquid form, was run into molds of terra cotta or iron, and allowed to cool and solidify. The syrup either dripped out of a hole in the bottom of the mold, or was sucked out by vacuum. A favorite size was conical in shape, five and one-half inches in diameter at the bottom, three inches at the top, 13 inches high. It weighed slightly over seven pounds. This was called cone or loaf sugar. It was wrapped in heavy paper—usually blue paper to counteract any yellow tinge in the sugar that was supposed to look like a piece of white marble.

The sugar brought west in prairie schooners was loaf sugar, and was a luxury, which accounts for so many Sugarloaf Mountains being named by men who craved sweets.

Summerland Park   GRAND LAKE

Ezra Kauffman homesteaded this land on the North Inlet of Grand Lake. He later built the Kauffman House at Grand Lake. When his widow sold the homestead for the Summerland Park development, she retained two lots, but the National Park bought them from her.

Sundance Creek; Sundance Mtn. 12,466′ FOREST CANYON, MUMMY RANGE

Bill Currance used to watch the early-morning play of sunlight on this mountain so he named it Sundance. Currance's cabin and prospect holes were two miles above Chasm Falls on Fall River, and there he lived until his death, paying no attention to the claims of the Rocky Mountain National Park to his land, nor to the people who called him "Miner Bill" or "Crazy Bill." On one of the summits of Sundance Mountain is the Toll Memorial with its mountain indicator.

Sunset Point   LAKE GRANBY

Surprise Beach   LAKE GRANBY

T

Table Mtn. 8830′   LAKE GRANBY

Spaniards call them mesas, these flat topped mountains with steep sides; Americans call them tables. On the top of this Table Mountain, Indians sat in the sun to fashion arrowheads and axheads, scattering so many scraps of rock that archaeologists consider this one of the more important Indian factories in northern Colorado.

The 1914 Arapahos used a more distinctive name than Table— *Haa konon*—but even less poetic; translated it means The Lungs. According to Oliver Toll, the Arapahos thought the color of jasper and agate found on this mountain resembled the color of animal lungs freshly drawn from a carcass. Chalcedony and petrified wood are also found here. Remember—neither rocks nor artifacts may be collected. Table Mountain is in the Shadow Mountain Recreation Area where the rule holds that specimens may be admired but must be left.

Tahosa Creek   WILD BASIN

This creek that runs through Tahosa Valley was known as Cow Creek until the U.S. Board on Geographic Names changed it to the poetic Tahosa Creek in March 1961.

Tahosa Valley   WILD BASIN

The Colorado Geographic Board had nothing but trouble naming this valley. Five names they considered. The first was Longs Peak Valley, an early name for the strip of land east of the great peak. The second was Glacier Valley, used by Enos Mills on his 1905 map. A surveyor suggested Meridian Valley, noting that the land lay on a north-south line. None of these names seemed distinctive. Then a certain faction in the community produced Elkanah Valley as a name, which upset the easily upset Enos Mills.

In the Bible, Samuel's father was called Elkanah (El kay' nah). The name means Whom God Possessed. It was the Christian name of the tall preacher-climber, the first guide on Longs Peak, the first owner of Longs Peak House—Parson Elkanah Lamb. One evening the Bitners of Columbine Lodge gave a party which was attended by the elderly minister and other members of the Front Range Settlers League. One of the Hewes brothers, of Hewes-Kirkwood Inn, suggested that Lamb's first name be given to the area he had homesteaded. Many of the neighbors approved the name; by 1913 Clatworthy had inscribed it on his map; in 1914 Charles Edwin Hewes published a poem called " 'Tis Evening in the Valley of Elkanah."

Enos Mills objected, militantly. (Basically, the fight was not over a name for the valley, but was one of the skirmishes in the long war waged between Enos Mills and the Front Range Settlers League over the establishment of a national park in the area—National Park vs. Forest Service.) Enos Mills spoke to Harriet Vaille, secretary of the Colorado Geographic Board. She dutifully reported to the Board that "Mr. Mills, for personal reasons, very much resented the name Elkanah, saying that the name had no particular connection with the valley." Though the minutes of the Board report nothing further, surely Miss Vaille must have pointed out that Mills well knew Lamb's first name. They had traveled together in Europe, and Mills not only had bought Longs Peak House from Elkanah Lamb, but in 1905 had written an introduction to Parson Lamb's memoirs. Elkanah no connection with the valley, indeed!

Seeking peace, the Colorado Geographic Board, as was its wont in intramural wars, produced an entirely new name—Tahosa (Ta ho' sa), meaning Dwellers of the Mountain Tops. The name, once seriously considered by Congress for the territory admitted to the Union under the name Colorado, was probably of Kiowan origin, since a Kiowa had signed a treaty in 1837 as "Tahosa, the Top of the Mountains."

Believing in democratic processes, the Board canvassed families in the Longs Peak vicinity, tallying votes for Elkanah or Tahosa. The count was about even, so the Board still had to decide. Not wishing to offend Enos Mills who was working for the establishment of the National Park, and fancying the appropriateness of a name that meant Dwellers of the Mountain Tops for this high valley, the Colorado Board recommended Tahosa to the U.S. Board on Geographic Names.

But peace did not spread over the valley. A member of the Front Range Settlers League, Burns Will, who was county commissioner and owner of Copeland Lake Lodge, wrote the Colorado Geographic Board in March 1915, denouncing Tahosa in particular and Indian names in general. He wrote that these were "due to the efforts of Miss Harriet Vaille, a very sentimental young lady of Denver who does not know the country in question." Following up the letter, Burns Will headed a three-man delegation that waited on the Board to complain about Tahosa. Chairman Rogers opened the meeting by reading a letter from the U.S. Geological Survey stating that the Longs Peak quad of 1915 had gone to press with the name Tahosa Valley on it. Because of this *fait accompli*, Rogers observed that any discussion of the matter would be academic. Whereupon the delegation discussed the matter all evening, with the Chairman murmuring every now and then that the map had gone to press. The meeting finally broke up after the Board agreed to spread the whole matter over the minutes, where it could be consulted before the next printing of the map.

The U.S. Board on Geographic Names in March 1916 decided for Tahosa Valley, a decision that has not changed.

Tanima Peak 12,420′ (Pronounced Ta ni′ ma)   Wild Basin
The name was proposed to the Colorado Geographic Board by Roger Toll, who said it was the name of a Comanche chief. It was also the name of a tribe. The Tanima tribe (the name means liver-eaters) was one of the 13 recognized tribes of Comanches when white men first came west, but by 1892 only one old man survived.

Tanima Peak had at least one previous name—Kirkwood. When the Hewes brothers and their mother, Mrs. Kirkwood, ran the Hewes-Kirkwood Inn, Charley Hewes went into Wild Basin with W. S. Cooper, and the young men had fun putting family names on unnamed peaks. Kirkwood appeared on Cooper's 1911 map for what is now Tanima, and Hewes for a mountain to the south, either the present Isolation or Mahana.

Taylor Glacier; Taylor Peak 13,153′   Glacier Gorge, Grand Lake
Albert Reynolds Taylor, president of Kansas State Normal School in Emporia, with his family spent the summer of 1895 in Colorado. "He does not grow weary," reported the school's monthly magazine that September, "of telling of thrilling scenes, of crossing rivers on logs, mountain climbings and tumbles, broncho rides, and trout fishing." Evidently Sprague gave his guest much attention that summer, and liked him well enough to name a peak for him.

The name is also applied to the glacier on its southeast face. Taylor Glacier is a true, living glacier, the others in the Park being Andrews, Rowe, Sprague, and Tyndall; lying to the south of the Park are the St. Vrain Glaciers; Peck, Fair, and Isabelle Glaciers; and the Arapaho Glaciers, the southernmost remnant of the ice age in the Front Range of the Rockies.

Before the arrival of white men, the 1914 Arapahos called Taylor Peak by a word that means The Bangs. They had killed a man, probably a Pawnee, near the summit on the south side. What made this memorable was that the foe wore his hair cut straight across his forehead, like a girl!

Teddys Teeth   Estes Park
A mountain topped with granite cliffs stands east of the Y.M.C.A. Camp. The boys at the camp called it Teddys Teeth because of the protruding rocks. The name dates from Theodore Roosevelt's presidency, 1901 to 1909, when cartoonists pictured him with his face full of teeth. Flippant, the authorities found this name, and not appropriate for a great green mountain, but when they gave the ridge the name of Rams Horn Mountain, they kept Teddys Teeth as a name for the rocks.

Ten Lake Park   Grand Lake, Lake Granby

187

Tepee Mtn.

Named by Frank Wright, a wrangler at the Phantom Valley Ranch who was interested in Indian lore.

Terra Tomah Mtn. 12,718'

In the summer of 1914, George Barnard topped a rise in the rough country of the Gorge Lakes and exclaimed, "Oh, there's the lake they told us about!" Turning toward his friends who followed him, members of the Third Annual Outing of The Colorado Mountain Club, he sang out his usual expression of delight—"He ne Terratoma, ne terratoma," and the others answered with an echo.

Since this lake had no name, James Grafton Rogers, president of the Club and chairman of the Colorado Geographic Board, assigned the name Terra Tomah to it. He printed the name on the advance sheet of the U.S.G.S. map. "Evidently we didn't write very plainly," remarked Jim Rogers in 1965, recalling the episode, "because, when the map came back from Washington with the approved names added, Terra Tomah was on a mountain, not the lake." (The lake later became known as Doughnut Lake.) Since the name Terra Tomah had an Indian flavor, the Board let it remain on the mountain.

The history of the name concerns the Cohuila Indians who lived on the slopes of the San Jacinto mountains in southern California. The remnant of their band—by 1902 only 159 members survived—in 1892 held their last fiesta. Two youths from Pomona College, near Los Angeles, spent their vacation with these Indians and one night, from a hiding place, listened to a war chant accompanied by tom-toms and the low moaning of women around the fire.

The young men, David P. Barrows and E. P. Brackett, took the haunting melody back to Pomona College. There, in 1894, George Barnard, later of Denver, and climber-extraordinary, was a student. He heard Barrows lecture on the Cohuila Indians and chant the war song. The students took it up as a college yell. In 1902, A. D. Bissell incorporated the chant into a song called the Ghost Dance. Singing it, the Pomona Glee Club won national awards, so many that the judges of at least one convention ruled out the song as unfair competition. The Ghost Dance is still Pomona's college song.

Refrain: He ne Ter - ra - to - ma, ne ter - ra - to - ma.

What do the words *He ne Terratoma, ne terratoma* mean? Dr. Barrows asked some Cohuila Indians. "We do not know," they replied, "The words are archaic." Dr. Barrows surmised in 1936 that "this may have been so, or they may not have wished to tell me, or the ones I

188

asked to interpret the lines may not have known."

Today, old-timers of The Colorado Mountain Club still chant "He ne Terratoma, ne terratoma" across high valleys, and listen for the echo.

Thatchtop 12,668′ GLACIER GORGE

Brinton W. Woodward, chancellor of the University of Kansas, who spent many summers at Spragues Hotel, arranged one autumn to stay until the aspens turned yellow and the tundra changed to orange, red, and brown. He was especially impressed with the ground-cover on the roof-shaped mountain west of Glacier Gorge, noting that as it turned from green to brown it matted down like a thatched roof. Sprague adopted this name for Thatchtop.

The 1914 Arapahos called this mountain The Buffalo Climb, in memory of the year many buffalo were caught by a storm on its top, enabling the Indians to kill them with ease.

Thousand Falls FOREST CANYON, MUMMY RANGE

Thunder Falls, Lake WILD BASIN

Charles Edwin Hewes, in his book of poems with historical notes called *Songs of the Rockies,* states that this lake in the upper end of Wild Basin was "named by Harry Cole, an early settler, on account of the deep reverberations of thunder which roll grandly from Kirkwood's [Tanima's] mighty slopes and boom tempestuously across the lake." Eleanor James Hondius bought her first horse from this Harry Cole, who had a ranch south of Longs Peak Inn. Mr. Cole put on a skirt in in order to break the pony to side-saddle. He was evidently a cattleman with a ranch on the plains as well as one in the mountains, since the *Lyons Recorder* of May 21, 1903, states that he had driven his cattle through Lyons to his mountain ranch.

Archaeologists find indications that the shores of Thunder Lake held Indian camps, one of at least six such sites in Wild Basin. On its shores in 1917 the Modern Eve spent part of an idyllic week. (See Nymph Lake.) The National Park has a patrol station at the lake, used often by Jack Moomaw who knows the Boulder-Grand Pass country so well. St. Pat's Cathedral is his unofficial name for the rocks that tower above Thunder Lake.

Thunder Mtn., Pass NEVER SUMMER

The pioneers called the pass Lulu Pass. (See Lulu City.) The Arapaho words for Thunder Pass were *bohah ah ah* (thunder) *netheson* (pass). Although their word for thunder, pronounced explosively enough, is positively onomatopoetic, the Colorado Geographic Board chose the English translation. "The Arapahos said that there was always a black cloud over it," reported Oliver Toll. A non-official story about the name tells that by the time the two older Indians of the 1914 Arapaho party got to Squeaky Bob's ranch they were exhausted and tired of answering questions. After Squeaky administered to their needs with a little "red-eye," they were willing to answer questions but had no interest in historical accuracy. Noting a thunder cloud over Lulu Pass, they stated that their people always called it Thunder Pass.

Thunderbolt Peak 11,938'   INDIAN PEAKS

Surveyor Jenkins named this peak Electric Peak because he had seen lightning strike it. The Colorado Geographic Board considered this name in February 1915. Noting several Electric Peaks in Colorado, they thought "Thunderbolt Peak more graceful and would still satisfy his idea." The next month an Arapaho National Forest man agreed: "I think it is perfectly satisfactory to everyone concerned to rename Electric Peak—Thunderbolt Peak."

Tileston, Mt. 11,254'   MUMMY RANGE

This name came from the Colorado Geographic Board, proposed by Ellsworth Bethel at the suggestion of Enos Mills. So far, information about this man Tileston has come in shattered bits. Name—Merrill Tileston, or Henry Merrill Tileston; profession—"a noted preacher or author," according to a note in the Park files; summer residence—"cottage at James', now Elkhorn Lodge;" hobby—"he made cinder glasses;" publication—*Chiquita, The Romance of a Ute Chief's Daughter;* date—1902; publisher—Merrill of Chicago.

Amplification of these facts is sought. Where was he noted as a preacher? No references to him can be found at the library of the Denver Iliff School of Theology, nor in the historical societies of Colorado, Kansas, or Illinois. Who published his book? The Rocky Mountain National Park staff wrote to Merrill of Chicago and Bobbs-Merrill of Indiana, both of whom denied any responsibility. And what are cinder glasses? Optical or receptacle? Since the name of two mountains stem from this man and his novel, more information is desired.

Timber Creek   NEVER SUMMER

This name obviously must date back to pre-National Park days when lumbermen delighted in the board feet of fine timber available on the Western Slope of the Continental Divide.

Timberline Falls   GLACIER GORGE

Named by Robert Sterling Yard, author of the earliest information brochure on Rocky Mountain National Park. He was a good publicity man who knew that timberline is an interesting phenomenon of mountain scenery. Timberline marks the level on mountains above which trees cannot grow. The height of this treeline depends on the climate, timberline in Mexico being thousands of feet higher than timberline in Alaska. In northern Colorado it usually runs along the 11,500-foot contour, give or take a few yards depending on exposure.

Timberline Pass 11,484'   Forest Canyon

At the head of Windy Gulch, this pass leads to Tombstone Ridge. Roger Toll named it in 1914, noting it as the only pass on the Ute Trail that is not above timberline.

Toll Memorial 12,310'   Mummy Range

A mountain indicator was erected in 1941 on Sundance Mountain in memory of Roger Wolcott Toll, superintendent of Rocky Mountain National Park from 1921 to 1929, who was killed in an automobile accident in 1936. The 360-degree view from the memorial includes many mountains, most of which he had climbed, many of which he had named.

Roger Toll (1883-1936) and his three brothers, Charles, Henry, and Oliver, spent their childhood summers at Tolland, their winters in a home east of Cheesman Park in Denver. For this house the architect had been instructed to make three bays, one facing Longs Peak, one Mount Evans, and one Pikes Peak. After Roger was graduated from Columbia University he and his brother Charles made a round-the-world tour, stopping longest for climbs in Switzerland. In 1908 Roger worked with the Coast and Geodetic Survey at Cook Inlet, Alaska; then came home to be chief engineer of the Denver Tramway Company.

With mountains in his blood, Roger was of course interested in The Colorado Mountain Club. In 1915 he invented for the Club a cast bronze container to hold a pencil and registration book for climbers to record their achievement of reaching the summit of a mountain. This was a lightning- and water-proof container (as are the plastic ones used since 1960), and much neater than scribbles on scraps of paper enclosed in bottles or beer cans. Roger put the first of these registers on top of Mt. Blaine, near Kenosha Pass, in 1915. Since then, he and other members of The Colorado Mountain Club have inserted the containers in the rocks of summit cairns on all the highest peaks of Colorado, leaving fresh books when needed, and bringing the old records to file in the Club rooms. Rangers carry registers to the summits of Rocky Mountain National Park and retain the old files from Longs Peak.

The Colorado Mountain Club also keeps records of mountain climbs that describe routes and the time consumed. Roger Toll compiled from these records, many of them his own climbs, a guide called *Mountaineering in the Rocky Mountain National Park*. Edited by Robert Sterling Yard, chief of the Education Division of the Department of the Interior, it was published in 1919, after Major Roger Toll returned from World War I. In that year Toll climbed in Hawaii, and Stephen Mather, director of National Parks, was also in the Islands. One day Mather was driving along a road when he caught sight of Roger Toll. Mather stopped the car. When he drove on Roger Toll was the new superintendent of Rainier National Park.

Both Toll and Colorado were delighted in 1921 when he was transferred to Rocky Mountain National Park as its third superintendent following C. R. Trowbridge and L. C. Way. The new superintendent inherited a quarrel over the Rocky Mountain Transportation Company's monopoly of Park roads. Roger Toll had a gift for making peace, but this dispute ended in the U.S. Supreme Court.

The Colorado Mountain Club published a list of mountain peaks in Colorado with their altitudes, compiled by Roger Toll in 1923. Although some of the names have been changed and a few added, and although the altitudes have grown or shrunk with each new survey, this is still a unique reference tool.

One of Roger Toll's dreams was to enlarge the Rocky Mountain National Park. To the west he was instrumental in adding the Never Summer Mountains in 1929, but was unable to acquire the Indian Peaks south of Wild Basin for the Park.

Roger Toll's final contribution to the Park came in 1929 before he was transferred to Yellowstone. He persuaded Edmund Rogers, a born outdoorsman then working in a Denver bank, to accept the position of superintendent of Rocky Mountain National Park. Edmund Rogers, brother of James Grafton Rogers, had served as president of The Colorado Mountain Club and been active in its climbs, and had worked for the U.S. Geological Survey. On all of his experiences he would draw in his new position. Edmund Rogers was superintendent of Rocky Mountain National Park from 1929 to 1936, then succeeded Roger Toll as superintendent of Yellowstone National Park.

Toll, Mt. 12,972' INDIAN PEAKS

Roger Toll and Charles Buckingham of Boulder climbed four of the Indian Peaks in one "much too long a day," wrote Toll in his meticulous log of the trip. They reached the summit of Paiute at 10:10 a.m.; of Ute Horn, which he suggested as a name instead of Paiute Horn, at 1:40 p.m.; of Pawnee Peak at 2:45 p.m.; of Apache Peak at 4:30 p.m. The summit of Apache "gives the impression of a desire to fall, though it will doubtless be there for some time to come," noted Toll. They were back at Brainard Lake, in rain, at 7 p.m.

Roger Toll's familiarity with the Indian Peaks and his attempt to have them included in the Park, led to the naming of one of them in his memory. The Colorado Mountain Club and the U.S. Forest Service suggested changing the name of Paiute Horn to Mt. Toll. The Board

192

on Geographic Names accepted the recommendation on November 14, 1940, four years after Toll's death.

Tombstone Ridge FOREST CANYON

The rocks on Tombstone Ridge reminded some early traveler of gravestones. Of this name the Colorado Geographic Board approved, then searched for a name for the whole stretch of the Ute Trail from Windy Gulch to Milner Pass. J. G. Rogers recommended Tombstone Ridge for the whole. The other members of the Board disagreed, especially since to them the rocks "scarcely looked like tombstones." They voted for Trail Ridge, Chairman Rogers dissenting. He had a flair for drama. If today's highway across Trail Ridge were called Tombstone Ridge Road, the name would be more dramatic though the road might not be so attractive to tourists.

Tonahutu Creek (Pronounced To na hu' tu.) GRAND LAKE

The 1914 Arapahos used this word which means Big Meadows, and the Colorado Geographic Board adopted it.

Tourmaline Gorge, Lake FOREST CANYON

Dr. Workman named this lake, not for a girl, but for the tourmaline, a gem stone usually black.

Trail Ridge—See Tombstone Ridge, Ute Trail.

Trail Ridge Road

One of the many acrimonious fights connected with the early years of the Rocky Mountain National Park was settled in February 1929 when the Colorado State Legislature voted to cede jurisdiction over the roads in the Park to the United States. (When the Park was created, Colorado had retained jurisdiction in order to finish Fall River Road.) The very day Governor William H. Adams signed the bill, the head of the National Park Service announced the government would build a "wonder road" to be called Trail Ridge. Immediately the Bureau of Public Roads advertised for bids on a new road, in two sections: one from Estes Park to Milner Pass, to replace the steep Fall River Road; the other from Milner Pass to the North Fork of the Colorado River, more or less following the old road.

W. A. Colt, a 73-year-old contractor from Las Animas, Colorado, took on the eastern end of the job. Starting in October 1929 at Deer Ridge, he worked into Hidden Valley. Colt's road machinery cut through heavy stands of conifers in a wide U-turn to timberline, then described great curves across the tundra. Contractor Colt completed the eastern part of the road to Milner Pass in 400 instead of the 500 days allowed in his contract.

Meanwhile, another contractor, L. T. Lawler of Butte, Montana,

193

rebuilt the western section of the road. The whole spectacular highway was completed by the fall of 1932.

Trap Creek   NEVER SUMMER

Up to the 1930's when bear trapping was still legal in Colorado, at least six bear traps—the pit type—were dug along this creek. One or two may still be located. Who knows when they were dug? Trap Creek is named on early maps.

Another interpretation of the name is that the water of Trap Creek contained poison, perhaps arsenic, that killed fish and game. Although mining men admit that water flowing from certain mines may carry poisonous material, the shallow prospect holes at the head of Trap Creek on Iron Mountain have produced neither pay dirt nor water, nor has any record been found that cattle grazing in Trap Park have been poisoned.

Triangle Lake   INDIAN PEAKS

Trio Falls   WILD BASIN

Named by Jack Moomaw, Park ranger, in 1921.

Triple Lakes   INDIAN PEAKS

Tundra Curves   MUMMY RANGE

Tundra, a Russian word, designates the treeless land of the Alpine Zone, whether it be in the Colorado Rockies or the Arctic Circle. In both, tundra plants are the same—the forget-me-nots are as blue and smell as sweet on Trail Ridge as in northern Alaska. In a 50-mile-drive from Lyons to the Tundra Curves, the motorist passes through the same vegetation zones as he would in an 8000-mile trip from Colorado to the Arctic Circle. These zones include the semi-arid Foothills Zone; the lush growth of the Montane Zone; the brilliant plants of the Sub-Alpine Zone; and the dwarf growth of the Alpine Zone in the tundra.

Tuxedo Park   ESTES PARK

A sub-tribe of Delaware Indians known as P'tuksit, meaning wolf, lived east of the Hudson River centuries before 1886 when Pierre Lorillard IV founded a millionaires' community about 40 miles northwest of New York City, borrowing the Indian name for his Tuxedo Park. Here commuting Wall Street executives stepped from the Albany Express to carriages waiting to carry them to their 20-room cottages; there they changed to sport clothes for fishing or tennis or ice skating, then expressed their appreciation of the informal life by dining at the Club dressed not in their customary tails but in English dinner jackets. These jackets soon acquired the name Tuxedo. The ladies dressed simply for dinner in last year's Newport gowns, according to Emily Post's 1911 account of Tuxedo Park.

F. O. Stanley transferred the name Tuxedo Park from New York to the Estes Park area. Perhaps he planned some day to create a hunting and fishing preserve for tired executives in the West, like the New York community, but he never got beyond the name.

Twin Creek—LAKE GRANBY; **Twin Lakes**—WILD BASIN

Twin Owls, The   ESTES PARK, MUMMY RANGE

"The two sculptured figures . . . appearing almost exactly like two great owls" were noted by Chapin in 1887. His observation may have established the name, but more probably he heard it from an earlier settler. No such name had been used by the Arapahos.

Twin Peaks 11,957'   LAKE GRANBY

Twin Pines Point   LAKE GRANBY

Twin Sisters Peak 11,428'   ESTES PARK

On March 7, 1907, Ellsworth Bethel wrote the Geographic Board in Washington that the name Twin Sisters Peak was well established. "Not Lillie," he urged. (See Lily Mountain.) Later, in 1915, Bethel changed his mind. He wanted this mountain named Tahosa. "Not Twin Sisters nor Lillie Mountain," he wrote, stating that the peak showed twin tops only from one angle. But this name was rejected, Twin Sisters retained. (See Tahosa Valley.)

Two Rivers Lake   FOREST CANYON, GLACIER GORGE

The "rivers" that theoretically originate in this lake are Fern and Mill Creeks. Although the lake has no visible outlet, its water percolates underground to both creeks.

An undocumented rumor credits Dr. Workman with using the same name for this lake as he used for Lake Helene. A girl named Helen and a girl named Mary, having heard he often named lakes for girls, teased him into naming one for them. He obliged—Helmary Lake.

Tyndall Creek, Glacier, Gorge   GLACIER GORGE

Enos Mills thoroughly educated himself by intensive reading during the long winter evenings he spent alone in his cabin. He read much about John Tyndall (1820-1893), the great English physicist and student of glacial phenomena. Mills wanted to rename the present Copeland Mountain after Tyndall. The Colorado Geographic Board raised the objection that Tyndall had no direct connection with Colorado. After Mills' suggestion for a Tyndall Mountain was rejected, the naming of Tyndall Glacier may have been a compromise, although the name was not adopted by the National Park Service until June 30, 1932.

U

Ute Trail

FOREST CANYON

The 1914 Arapahos spoke of three trails leading from Estes Park toward Grand Lake—the Big Trail (Flattop), the Dog Trail (Fall River), and the Childs Trail. This last went up Windy Gulch to the head of Hidden Valley, then went approximately where Trail Ridge Road goes now, crossing it at various points on the Tundra Curves.

The trail was called the Childs Trail because the Arapahos said it was so steep in places that children had to dismount and walk. Oliver Toll does not state where these places were, and the Indians probably did not tell him. It seems odd that this trail earned a reputation for steepness since it is the gentlest of the three trails. The Arapahos pointed out monuments, about four feet in diameter, that marked the trail, not on the tundra, but on both the east and west ascents. The Indians said they always passed on the same side of a monument and added a stone to it each time they passed by.

How much this trail was used by the Indians is hard to tell. Abner Sprague, who came to the Park in 1875, stated definitely that he saw no trace of an Indian trail across Trail Ridge at that time. In the 1870's, Ferguson and Farrar cut a trail at the mouth of Windy Gulch to bring out the carcasses of three elk they had killed. However, miners headed for Lulu City or Gaskill, and hunters headed for Squeaky Bob's soon wore ruts deep into the tundra across the alpine meadows. They called it variously North Fork Trail, Specimen Mountain Trail, Poudre Lakes Trail, Squeaky Bob's Trail—whatever its name, it was the standard trail from Estes Park to the North Fork of the Colorado River. It may have been named Ute Trail by the Colorado Geographic Board in 1915. Today, the Rocky Mountain National Park officially calls it the Ute Trail, and has marked it by small, neat cairns.

V

Verna, Lake

GRAND LAKE

Five lakes stretch along the East Inlet of Grand Lake—Lone Pine, Verna, Spirit, Fourth, and Fifth Lakes. The five are called the Shoestring Lakes by some Grand Lake old-timers; Charles Hewes knew the three lower lakes as the Trinity Lakes. The longest lake, extending between steep granite walls with hardly enough shoreline for a fisherman to stand on, is Lake Verna, named for the sweetheart of a member of the U.S. Geological Survey. Neither authority for this statement, George Barnard or John King Sherman, state what survey, what member, or what sweetheart.

W

War Dance Falls   GRAND LAKE

Watanga Creek, Lake; Watanga Mtn. 12,375′   LAKE GRANBY
This name was probably proposed by the Colorado Geographic
Board because of its vast interest in Indians. Watanga (Black Coyote)
a Southern Arapaho, lived in Darlington, Oklahoma. E. A. Burbank
painted his portrait with scarlet crosses scattered over his body; these
marked the scars from the day Watanga offered pieces of his own flesh
as sacrifice to the Sun to save his children from death. Watanga, with
one of his wives, signed the Cheyenne-Arapaho Treaty in 1890; he was
captain of Indian police, a delegate to Washington, deputy sheriff of
Canada County, Oklahoma. Artist Burbank stated that Watanga was

> of considerable importance to his tribe and in his own sight.
> . . . Black Coyote once received $800 in cash from the govern-
> ment for some service. He immediately bought a new team
> of horses for his carriage and hired a coachman. . . . It was an
> amusing sight to see Black Coyote with his squaw and children
> step out of the carriage in style and crawl into the tepee,
> after which the carriage rolled on to the barn, where the
> coachman slept with the horses.

Wescott, Mt. 10,421′   GRAND LAKE
Named for Judge Joseph L. Wescott, pioneer of Grand Lake,
called Judge because he was Justice of the Peace. His service with the
Union Cavalry during the Civil War left him crippled with rheumatism.
Somehow he got to Georgetown, Colorado, and arranged to travel
with a group across Berthoud Pass, lying in a hammock slung on poles
between two burros. In Middle Park he soaked in the healing waters
of Hot Sulphur Springs. In the pool he regained his health but almost
lost his life when an Indian shot at him. In June 1867 he settled at
Grand Lake, where he lived in a cabin on the southwestern shore of
the lake until he died in 1914. He wrote a long poem, called "The
Legend of Grand Lake." (See Grand Lake.) He was a good story-teller
—children adored his tales. His speech indicated a good education
and even culture. Patience Stapleton's book, *Kady*, features Wescott
under the name of Judge West.

Some Grand Lake people who appreciated Judge Wescott's unique
character thought the most prominent mountain to the east of the
lake should bear his name. The Colorado Geographic Board disagreed.
They retained Mt. Craig for that mountain and named the mountain
west of it for Judge Wescott.

West Creek   MUMMY RANGE

197

Reverend S. R. Wheeler, who was born in England in 1834 and died in Boulder in 1925, brought his family west and established the Seventh Day Baptist Church in Boulder in 1893. He had three sons and two daughters. One girl married Darwin M. Andrews of the Rockmont Nursery in Boulder. (See Andrews Peak.) The oldest son, H. N. Wheeler, became supervisor of the Colorado National Forest. (See Arapaho Glacier.) The third son, Alfred Truman Wheeler, trapper, prospector, Forest Service worker, and for some years caretaker of the Boulder water supply at Silver Lake, knew every rock in what is now called Wheeler Basin.

He and James C. Bennett first ventured into that area in search of gold in 1903. They built a cabin and then trails—the first trail to Monarch Lake, and a ten-mile trail to Arapaho Pass. This involved 26 bridges and the original switchbacks leading to the Pass. About 1915 Wheeler staked two placer claims in the basin southwest of Arikaree Peak. These gave him control of a deposit of rock flour, or glacial milk, which had a certain amount of radioactivity and was said to have medicinal values. Though the claims have never been patented nor the medicine proved, the Wheeler family in Boulder has kept the claims alive by annual assessment work these 50-odd years.

Wheeler Basin was known as Hell Hole. A. T. Wheeler, maintaining that "the devil owns too much of God's beautiful earth," wanted to rename it the Garden of Pinnacles. Asked for help in this campaign, the Boulder Chamber of Commerce countered by suggesting that it be called Wheeler Basin. Fred Fair, county surveyor, tried unsuccessfully to accomplish this. Largely through the efforts of Robert Woolfolk of the Arapaho Valley Ranch near Monarch Lake, the name Wheeler Basin appeared on the 1958 Monarch quad map.

The U. S. Board on Geographic Names in its 1958 Bulletin confused father and son, recording that Wheeler Basin was named for "A. T. Wheeler, pioneer clergyman, now over 90." The father, whose initials were S. R., was the clergyman. No matter—Wheeler Basin honors a Boulder family especially attached to that certain corner of the earth.

Wild Basin   WILD BASIN

When Joe Mills sat on Longs Peak making a rude sketch of Wild Basin in his notebook, he labeled it "Land of Many Waters," an appropriate name for this lake-dotted country drained by the North St. Vrain Creek. Equally appropriate is the official name Wild Basin, which dates back to early days in the Park—perhaps to Elkanah Lamb. That Wild Basin is today still an appropriate name is due to the wise decision of the National Park Service 50 years ago to preserve the southern part of the Park as wilderness. Except for reservoir dams, constructed before the Park regime and now deteriorating, very little of man is noticeable. Wild Basin's trails are used well and often by the kind of people who go beyond paved roads.

The first person to map Wild Basin in detail and name many of its features was William S. Cooper, now living in Boulder after a distinguished career as head of the Botany Department of the University of Minnesota. Largely because of his study of plant ecology and glaciers in Alaska, Glacier Bay National Monument was created. One of the mountains of the Fairweather Range, the backdrop of the Bay, is scheduled to be named Mt. Cooper.

In June 1965, for *Trail and Timberline,* Dr. Cooper wrote about Wild Basin as he knew it in 1904 to 1908.

In July 1904, a botanist of tender age—the undersigned— along with father and mother, by train from Denver to Lyons, by four-horse stage the rest of the way, arrived in Estes Park. We settled at Elkhorn Lodge, but Longs Peak was the main attraction for me. Enos Mills brought down two horses for a companion and me and we rode up to Longs Peak Inn, most of the way at a gallop, with several stops to open and close gates. A few days later Enos guided us to the summit of Longs Peak by moonlight. . . . For me the Longs Peak region brought love at first sight. The mountains themselves I am sure came first, but science was not completely neglected. On the basis of one month's field work I contributed a brief account of the wildflowers to Mills' *The Story of Estes Park and a Guide Book* published in 1905.

In 1906 I returned to the Longs Peak region, this time without parents. For the most part I stuck closely to my scientific duties, varying these with several climbs of Longs and other peaks. From these studies came my first scientific publication: "Alpine Vegetation in the Vicinity of Long's Peak, Colorado" (*Botanical Gazette,* vol. 45; 319-337, 1908). . . .

In 1908 I again returned, planning to continue my scientific work. But I thought it would be fun, in addition, to make a map of the region centering on Longs Peak, which, except for a limited portion covered by the rough Mills map of 1905, had never been surveyed. So I bought myself a small plane table with a simple alidade, taught myself how to use it, laid out a half-mile baseline near the Inn, and gradually developed a triangulation net. Numerous climbs were made to points of vantage for triangulation and the sketching in of topography, represented by hachures. No attempt was made to measure altitudes. Particular attention was given to Wild Basin, the headwaters of the North St. Vrain river system, because it was the least known part of the region covered.

One trip to this area is particularly memorable: personnel, Charley Hewes, the writer, and Pat, the burro. . . . The time was mid-June; snow lay deep in the higher forests, the streams were raging torrents. Pat did not like either condition. Forcing him to cross belly-deep streams required invention of new engineering methods. . . . On that expedition we climbed Mt. Copeland and Elks Tooth and enjoyed an exciting glissade to the frozen surface of Pipit Lake.

At summer's end my good friend Dean Babcock, a far better topographer than I, was my prospective companion on a final trip to cover the northwest corner of Wild Basin. Our first night's camp was at Sandbeach Lake. After dark, just about bedtime, a distant shot rang out, and shortly Enos Mills appeared, with the news that my father in Detroit was dangerously ill. I made all haste to return, but was too late. [See Cooper Mtn.]

Dean finished the survey, and in 1911 we published our map, which sold for fifteen cents per copy. On it we attached names to various natural features. Some, quite personal, have been rightfully ignored. Eleven were officially accepted, most of them in Wild Basin, and appear on the latest map of Rocky Mountain National Park: Ouzel Peak [Enos Mills had named Ouzel Lake], Meadow Mountain, Mt. Orton, Pine Ridge, Bluebird Lake, Junco Lake, Pipit Lake, Chickadee Pond, Calypso Cascades, Mertensia Falls, Columbine Falls.

Willow Creek—Never Summer; Willow Creek—Wild Basin; Willow Park—Mummy Range

So many willows grow in the area, it is a wonder that no more than two creeks and one park bear their name. Of the many varieties of willows that grow in the Park, three are easily identified: alpine willows by their enormous catkins; mountain willows of the Montane Zone by their yellow twigs; and the whiplash willows of the lower hills by their shining red stems. Willow colors enliven the winter landscape, growing more vivid as spring comes on. The late spring snowstorm of the mountains is often called the willow bender.

Wind River, Wind River Pass · Estes Park

The 1914 Arapahos used a long name for Tahosa Valley, literally translated as "woman-log-it-killed-her." They recalled riding through the gap at the head of the valley—Wind River Pass—when a horse bumped a dead tree which fell on a woman and killed her. Interpreter Tom Crispin slowly dictated the Arapaho words for "woman-log-it-killed-her" to Oliver Toll who meticulously wrote them in his notebook: *issā-bes - di - noX - kah - wah - nāt ȯwah ah-nȧt*, 30 letters divided into 12 syllables. Both the young Coloradan and the interpreter were amused at the end when the Indian remarked, "That makes it short and clear." The Colorado Geographic Board retained the name Wind River Pass.

Windy Gulch, Windy Gulch Cascades FOREST CANYON

Perhaps the name for this gulch is as old as the first men who felt its breezes, but the first trail up Windy Gulch can be dated to the early 1870's, when H. W. Ferguson and Hank "Buckskin" Farrar, two early settlers who refused to be intimidated by Dunraven's minions, went hunting. According to the "50 Years Ago" column in an Estes Park newspaper, they "killed three elk on the south slope of Brinwood Mountain in Moraine Park. The trail they had to cut to get these elk out was the beginning of the Windy Gulch Trail"—the eastern end of the present Ute Trail.

Wuh, Mt. 10,761' FOREST CANYON

This Arapaho word means grizzly bear. The phonetic spelling is *woX*, with the X pronounced as an explosive *h*. It is more often pronounced (and often spelled) Mt. Woo. Not the 1914 Arapahos but Roger Toll in 1923 named the mountain, even though he must have known the Park no longer harbored grizzly bears. Naming Mt. Wuh settled the problem of which was Steep Mountain, a name definitely fixed now on the mountain east of Wuh.

Y

Ypsilon Lake; Ypsilon Mtn. 13,514' MUMMY RANGE

This is one of the few mountains in the Rockies that bears its name clearly written on its face, to be read by those who can read Greek. Ypsilon is the Greek word for the letter Y. In 1888 Frederick Chapin climbed this mountain but he recorded that his wife had christened it the year before when the two idled away a day on the banks of "the little torrent" called Wind River.

> I had been fishing a little. Later we were looking at the mountains, which from here are so beautiful in the west. One great peak with a steep wall facing the east, and a long reclining ridge leading toward the southwest, especially interested us. A large snow-field lay on the eastern face; two glittering bands of ice extended skyward to the ridge of the mountain, forming a perfect Y. My wife said to me, "Its name shall be Ypsilon Peak." So it went forth, and the name was accepted by the dwellers of the valley and by visitors to the ranches.

The name has since been accepted by the Colorado Geographic Board, by the U.S. Geological Survey, by the U.S. Forest Service, by the National Park Service, and by the U.S. Board on Geographic Names, although somewhere along the line Mrs. Chapin's Ypsilon Peak was changed to Ypsilon Mountain. No matter—the Y is still there.

SAWTOOTH

202

INDEX

NOTE: Dictionary headings are not repeated in index. Numbers in bold-face type indicate pages on which main entries occur.

Abbott, E.A. 122
Abbott, J. Dudley 18
Abbott, Louise (Mrs. E.A.) 122
Adams, Alexander and Louise 18
Adams, Alva B. 18
Adams, Alva B., Tunnel 59,171
Adams, Henry 47,94
Adams, Jay E. 18
Adams, William H. 193
Agnes, Lake 129
Alexander, J.W. 57
Alice (town) 20
Alice, Mt. 55
Allen, A.G. 90
Allen, Alonzo Nelson 21
Allen, Lon C. 46
"Alpine Vegetation in the Vicinity of Long's Peak" 199
Amache, Arapaho Indian 17
American Alpine Club 81
Ammons, Elias 5,80
Andree, W.E. 25
Andrews, Darwin M. 21,24,198
Andrews, Edwin B. 21,89,179
Andrews Glacier 74 (il.)
Andrews, Philip 21
Anne Peak 120
Apache Peak 65 (il.),87,192
Appalachian Mountain Club 39,94,95
Arapaho Glacier 75 (il.)
Arapaho Indians 22-23,92,137,138
  See also Arapahos, 1914.
Arapaho language 153
Arapaho Names and Trails 3
Arapaho National Forest 151,152,154
Arapaho, spelling of 23
Arapahos, 1914 3,16,102,159 (il.),176, 189-190,196; passim
Arbuckle, Frank P. and Emma 33
Arbuckle Reservoirs 33,146
Archangels, Lakes of the 102
Arrowhead Lake 71 (il.)
Ashton, Willard H. 100,116,168
Atkins, Ferril 57,175
Auburn (town) 86
Audubon, John James 27
Audubon, Mt. 64 (il.)
automobile in Estes, first 180-181
Azure Lake 89

Babcock, Dean 101,143,**144**,176,177, 182,200
Baker, John 28
Baker, Mt. 70 (il.)
Baker, W.B. 101
Bald Mtn. 14,137,145
Baldy, Old 49
Bancroft, Hubert Howe 49
Bangs, The 187
Barnard, George Cooper 6,53,**54**, 163 (il.),170,171,173,188,196
Barrett, Mt. 8,41
Barrows, David P. 188
Bartholf, Frank G. 87
Bartholf Park 87
Bartholomew & Baker 28
Bear Paws 183
Beattie, Irwin 147
Beaver Dam Creek 99
Beaver Meadows Entrance Station 149
Bench Creek 99
Bennay Mtn. 14-15
Bennett, James C. 198
Bennett, Joe 30
Berthoud, Edward 40
Bethel, Ellsworth 3,**10-11**,20,28,125, 136,162 (il.); passim
Bethel, Mt. 11
Bierstadt, Albert 30,55,87,135
Big Cascade Creek 169
Big Meadows 193
"Big Owl of Big Owl Hill" 30
Big Rock Lake 156
Big Trail 84,196
Billings, Jabez 33
Birch, Al 140
Bird, Isabella 7,20,34,53,78,107,116, 118,134
Bird Man (C.B. Hutchins) 102
Bissell, A.D. 188
Black Canyon 118,124
Black Coyote, Kiowa Indian 197
Black, George 177
Blanca, Sierra 52
Blaurock, Carl 119
Blue River 43
Bluebird Lake 33-34, 102, 115, 146
Bonfils, Frederick 80

Bouck, Mrs. Francis. See Vaille, Harriet.
Boulder (town) 24-25
Boulder Chamber of Commerce 198
Boulder Field 67 (il.)
Bowen, Jim 34
bows, Indian 127-128
Brackett, E.P. 188
Brady, T.A. 180
Breadline Trail 146
Bridger, Jim 88
Brinwood Mtn. 29,201
Brown, George W. 78
Bryan, Francis T. 128
Bryant, William H. (Harry) 35,132
Bryant, Mrs. William H. 35
Buchanan Creek 159
Buchanan, James 35
Buckingham, Charles 192
Buckskin. See Farrar, Henry.
Buffalo Climb 189
Bulgarians 132
Bull Pen (North Park) 6
Burbank, E.A. 197
Burlington (town) 21
Burlington railroad 180
Burnett, Lulu 123
Byerly, Frank W. 94,117,176-177
Byers, William N. 28, 34, 52, 77, 154, 183

Cabin Rock 36,108
Cairns, James 37,170
Cameron Pass 129
Cameron, Robert A. 37
Camerons Cone 37
Campbell, Richard Crawford 35,145
Campbells Point 145
Canfield, David H. 11
Caroline, Mt. 58
Carson, Kit 36,167
Cashier Mining & Milling Co. 19
Cattle Raising on the Plains of North America 155
Chambers Lake 91,109
Chapin, Frederick H. 7,34,**39**,94-96, 117,143,195,202; passim
Chapin, Mrs. Frederick H. 202
Chapin, Jennie (Mrs. Homer James) 39
Chapin, Mt. 72 (il.)
Chasm Lake 42,172
Cheesman Park Mountain Index 9
Cheley Camp 48,56,57

Cheyenne Indians 92,99
Chicago Motor Vehicle Co. 180
Chiefs Head Peak 125
Childs Trail 196
Chinese 91
Chipeta, Ute Indian 42
Chiquita, Mt. 72 (il.)
Chiquita, The Romance of a Ute Chief's Daughter 41,190
Chisel Top 101
Chivington, John M. 17
Cinder Creek 101
Circle H Brand 98
Circle, The 59
Clara Belle Mine 141-142
Clara Lake 150
Clarence King, Lake 150
Clarence King, Mt. 47-48
Cloud Peaks 9,42,101
    (Mts. Cirrus, Cumulus, Nimbus and Stratus)
Cohuila Indians 188
Cole, Harry 189
Collier, Dorothy and Robert 172
Collins Lode 173
Colonial Dames 3
Colorado Association 119
Colorado-Big Thompson Project 18, 59,89,151,153,171
Colorado Federation of Women's Clubs 119
Colorado Geographic Board **4-11**, 162 (il.),186; passim
Colorado Geographic Society 5
Colorado Mountain Club 2,9,32,106, 117,119,147,165,167,191,192; passim. Boulder group—87,146; Estes Park group—179; Nomenclature Committee—2,9,153; Outings—2,53-54,82, 158 (il.),163 (il.),173-174,188
Colorado National Forest 166
Colorado River 43; passim
    See also Grand River.
Colorado State Game and Fish Dept. 46,110
Colorow, Ute Indian 106
Colt, W.A. 193
Columbine Lake 97
Comanche Indians 125,136,138,187
Comanche Peak 4,41,125
Commodore, Mt. 35
Continental Divide 170
convict labor 80
Cook, Stephen D. 18
Cooper, Mt. (Alaska) 199

Cooper, William S. 7,19-20,47-48,122, 127,187,**199**; passim
Copeland, John B. 46-47
Copeland Lake Lodge 47
Copeland Mtn. 61 (il.),195
Copeland Park Reservoir 46
Copper King & Queen mines 131
Cornstalk Mtn. 170
Coulehan, Walter 47
Cow Creek 138,185
Crags Hotel 108
Craig (town) 49
Craig, Mt. 197
Craig, William Bayard 35,49
Craigs Point 49
Crater Lake 115
Crater, The 176
Crispin, Tom, Arapaho Indian 159 (il.),200
Crofutt, George A. 45
Cudahy, Edward A. 78
Currance, Bill 184
Curtis, Natalie 22,99

Danforth, Tad 131
Davis, William H. 46
Delaware Indians 194
Dennis, George 51
Dennison, Charles W. 129,134
Denver & Interurban railroad 119
Denver & Rio Grande railroad 131
Denver & Salt Lake railroad 89
Denver & Salt Lake Western railroad 130-131
Denver Post, The 119,120,140-141
Denver Public Library 30
Denver Tramway Co. 131
Deserted Village 56
Deux Oreilles, Les 121
Devils Canyon 51
Devils Thumb Pass 131
Diamond, The 57
Dickerson Ranch 51
Dickinson, Anna **51-53**,112,128-129, 157 (il.)
Dille, Fred 179
Dille Lake 179
Di Nio, Clara 119
Dog Trail 80,196
Dog's Lift, The 118
Dome Rock 32
Doughnut Lake 188
Douglas-fir 178
Dresden China Glacier 133
Dunning, Harold 79

Dunraven, Earl of 30,**54-56**,78,108,127, 134
Dunraven Hotel. See English Hotel.
Dutchtown 57
Dwellers of the Mountain Tops 186
Dwight Morrow Peak 120

eagle's nest 138
Eagles Nest Range 88
East Face of Longs Peak 113-115,172
East Fork of Grand River 23,35,138
East Inlet Lakes 196
Eastin, L.J. 37
Echevarría, Evilio 118,174
Echo Mtn. 170
Edmunds, Mt. 6,25,26,28
Elbert, Mt. 52
Electric Peak 190
Elkanah Valley 31,185-186
Emerald Lake 53,73 (il.),148
Emigrant's Guide to Pike's Peak 37
Emma Lake 150
Emmons, S.F. 94
Endovalley Campground 100
English Hotel 55,96,181
Ervin, William F. 120
Escalante, Father 43,93
Estes, Joel 60,77
Estes, Joel, Jr. 83
Estes, Mary L. (Fleming) (Mrs. Milton) 127
Estes, Milton 60,77,83,134,145,152
Estes National Park 2,165
Estes Park 54-55; passim
Estes Park Improvement Assn. 156
Estes Park Power Plant 109,181
Estes Park Woman's Club 50
Evangeline Road 120
Evans, Griff 47,53,54,**78**,108,127,142
Evans, Mt. 1,2
Eve, Modern. See Lowe, Agnes.
Evergreen Brook 104

Faces to the Wind 142
Fair, Fred 79,**118-119**,146,198
Fair, Isabelle 105
Fair View Hotel 29
Fairchild, Lucius 79
Fall River 100
Fall River Glacier 99
Fall River Road 80-81
Falls, The 122
Farmers Ditch Co. 116
Farrand, Livingstone 3

Farrar, Hank ("Buckskin") 36,77,78, 201
Fay, C.E. 81
Ferguson, Horace W. 29,39,95,96, 109,201,129,183
Fern Creek 195
Fern Lake Lodge 82
Ferril, Thomas Hornsby 45
Figure-Eight Trail 24
Fine, Eben 24
fires, forest 62 (il.),94,106
Fish Creek 142
Fisher, Arthur 175
Fisher, Arthur A. 172
Fisher, Mt. 175,176
Fisher, Redwood 175
Flattop Mtn. 95-96
Foote, Elizabeth 39
Forest Canyon 71 (il.)
Forest Canyon Overlook 71 (il.)
Forest Lake 116
Fort St. Vrain 168
Fremont, John Charles 43,121,168
Front Range Settlers League 1,185,186
Fry, Norman 91,109
Funston, Frederick K. 149-150

Gannett, Henry 42,154-155
Gannett Peak (Wyo.) 155
Gant, Dan 134
Garden of Pinnacles 198
Gardiner, James 52
Garetson, Katherine 31
Garrison House 18
Gaskill, L.D.C. 86
Gem Lake 166
Gemmill, Mrs. E.E. 18
Geode Mtn. 177
George, Mt. 22
George, Russell D. 5,24,86
Germans 56-57
Ghost Dance (Indian religion) 22
Ghost Dance (song) 188
Gianttrack Mtn. 8,117
Gifford, Archie E. 112
Gilpin, William 168
Glacier Basin 177-178
Glacier Gorge 73 (il.)
Glacier Gorge Lakes 93
Glacier Lake 99
Glacier Valley 185
glaciers 187
Glen Haven (town) 51
Gold Lake 40
Goodman, Bert A. 49

Gordon and McHenry road 25
Gore, Sir St. George 88
Gorge Lakes 26,53,71 (il.),89
(Arrowhead, Azure, Doughnut, Forest, Highest, Inkwell, Little Rock, Love, and Rock Lakes)
Granby (town) 89,132
Grand Ditch 29,70 (il.),170
Grand Lake 62 (il.),63 (il.),171,177
Grand Lake Yacht Club 35
Grand River 23,43,138
See also Colorado River.
Grand River Ditch 90
Grand Teton (Wyo.) 97
Grand View Hotel 125
Grandview House 18
Grant Lake 140
Grant, U.S. 38
Gravel Mtn. 14-15
Greeley (town) 37,128
Greeley, Horace 128
Green Knoll 70 (il.)
Green Mtn. 59
Green Mtn. Ranch 28,98
Green River 43
Griffith, Dan 97
Grip-sack Guide to Colorado 45
Griswold, Gun 159 (il.),182
Gunnison-Beckwith report 43

Hague, Arnold 94,154
Hague, James 94
Hagues Peak 155
Haiyaha Lake 148
Hale, Horace 104-105
Hale, Irving 104-105
Hallett Glacier 167
Hallett, Lucius; Moses; Sam 96
Hallett Peak 73 (il.),143
Hallett, William L. 39,84,95-97,116, 129,135,157 (il.),166-167,183
Hallowell, George C. 97
Hamlin, Mabel (Killie) 133
Handbook of American Indians 18, 135,136
Hanington, Charles 104,139,167,170
Hansen, Grace (Workman) (Mrs. H.C.) 89
Haquihana Valley 110
Harbison family 97-98
Harmon, Jules 29
Hart, H. Martyn 49
Hart, Stephen J. 120
Hartzell, Mr. 28
Harvey, Jim 98

206

Hawkins, David 159 (il.)
Hayden, Al 88,104,109
Hayden, Ferdinand V. 52
Hayden, Julian 27,53,88,89,**109**
Hayden, Louise (Reed) 109
Hayden Prong 98
Hayden Spire 109
Haynach Lakes 135
Head Mtn. 41
Hearst, George 134
Heeney, Georgiana 124
Heinricy, Henry 27,31
Hell Canyon 105,144
Hell Hole 198
Hell Hole, Fred Fair's 119
Helmary, Lake 98,195
Henderson, Junius **24**,79,105
Hendrie, Edna 3
Hewes, Charles Edwin 30,185,189,
  196,200
Hewes Peak 187
Hiamovi, Cheyenne Indian 22
Hickox, William 59
Hidden Treasure Mine 29
Higby, Cliff 179
High Lonesome Trail 121
Highest Peak 121
Highlands Hotel. See Ferguson,
  Horace W.
Hillyer, Granby 89
Hodge, Frederick H. 18,135,136
Hollenbeck, Michael 77
Holzwarth, John 91,98
Hondius, Eleanor (James) 20,39,100,
  189
Hondius, Pieter 32,100
Horseshoe Falls 39
Horseshoe Inn 72 (il.)
Horseshoe Park 72 (il.),97,99
Hot Sulphur Springs 177,197
Hotel de Hardscrabble 173,180
Hour Glass Lake 153
Howard, J.E. 101
Howard, Luke 101
Howard, Sour 101
Hubbell, John 142
Hudnall, Mary (Prowers) 17
Hughes, Charles R. 175
Hump, The 45
Huntington, Franklin I. 80,139
Hupps Cone 100
Husted, Shepherd 3,101,**102**,122,
  159 (il.)
Hutcheson, Henry 102
Hutchins, Charles Bowman 102

Hutchins, Emma (Moomaw) 147-148
Hutchinson, Alice 20
Hyslop Lake 49

Iceberg Lake 42
Indian names, spelling of 12
Indian Peaks (mountains between
  Longs and Arapaho Peaks) **3-4**,
  64 (il.),65 (il.),169; passim
Indians' Book, The 22,99
Indians, Canadian 146
Irene Lake 152
Island Lake 19
Isolation Lake 85
Isolation Peak 42,85
Ives, Ronald L. 120

Jackson, George A. 136
Jackson, William H. 49,55,151
Jacob, Art 106-107
Jacobs, Mr. 77
Jacobson, J.N. 81
James, Edwin 4,44,106,121
James family 39,136,164
Japanese 132
Jenkins (surveyor) 190
Jewell, Edward S. 106,107
Julian, Mt. 183

Kady 197
Kauffman, Ezra 184
Kellogg, Vernon 149
Keplinger, L.W. **110**,139
Keyhole, The 67 (il.)
Keystone Hotel 19
Killie Ranch 111,124,132
King, Clarence **47**,94,154
  See also Clarence King, Mt.
King Peak (Utah) 155
Kiowa Indians 22,111,168,169,186
Kiowa Peak 19
Kirkwood, Mary (Palmer) Hewes 20
Kirkwood Peak 187,189
Knifton, George H. 124
Knight, Harry 111,120
Koenig, Frank R. 59,83,98,153
Koenig, Hazel B. (Ramsey) 98,153

Lady of the Lake (ridge) 170
Lady Washington, Mt. 52
*Lady's Life in the Rocky Mountains,
  A* 7,107
Laguna Verde 107
Lamb, Elkanah **20**,39,95,**112-115**,129,
  130,134,185,186,198

Lamb, Ida 103
Land of Many Waters 198
Laramie River 109
Larimer, Bob 89,109
Larimer, William 121
Lark Pond 33
Lava Beds 34
Lawler, L.T. 193
Lawn Lake 153,168
Lead Mountain Mining District 116, 173
Lee, Willis T. 24,131,192
Left Hand, Arapaho Indian 137
Lefthand Creek 138
"Legend of Grand Lake, The" 91-92, 197
Lehman family 53,111,116
Levings, Louis Raymond 177
Lightning Peak 182
Lillie Mtn. 117,195
Lily Lake 33
Lily Pad Lake 140
Lincoln, Mt. 52
Lincoln, Outline of Old Abe 89
Lindbergh, Anne (Morrow) 120
Lindbergh, Charles Augustus 111,119, 120
Lindbergh Peak. See Lone Eagle Peak.
Lipton, Sir Thomas 35
Little Lumps 123
Little Rock Lake 156
Livingston, Julian 118
Locke, A.W. 118
Lone Eagle Peak 76 (il.)
Long Draw 90
Long Expedition, 1820 121,168
See also James, Edwin.
Longmont (town) 21,33,47,146
Longs Peak 30,52-53,66 (il.),68-69 (il.), 77,94,107,110,112,113-115,121,130, 139,169
Longs Peak House 112,130
Longs Peak Inn 104,130
Longs Peak, its Story and a Climbing Guide 53,57
Longs Peak Valley 185
Longworth, Alice (Roosevelt) 20
Lookout Mtn. 170
Love, Jack 122
Loveland (town) 31
Loveland & Estes Park Railroad Co. 87
Lowe, Agnes 140-141
Lowry Air Force Base 155
Lulu City 56,101,116,164 (il.)

Lulu Falls 82
Lulu Pass 123,189
Lumpy Ridge 136
Lungs, The 185
Lynes Reservoir 117
Lyons (town) 180
Lyons Reservoir 117
Lytle, George 38

McCaslin, Walter 47
McCracken, Dixie 140
McDonald, Edgar L. 124,133
McFadden, Nellie (Spalding) 107
McGinns Gulch 134
MacGregor, Alexander Quinter 32, 124,129,136
McHenry, B.F. 124-125
McLaren, Fred 120,122
McNabb, John 91,129
McQueary, Dick 80
Mack, Mt. 47
Mahana Peak 33
Maier, Cal 34
Maple, J.B. 125
Maps 6-8,16
Burlington railroad 1910—8,41, 101,122; Case, Francis 1862—6,25; Clason—101,106; Clatworthy 1913— 8,185; Colton—16; Cooper & Babcock 1911—7-8,19,36,41,48,58,101, 115,139,143,144,148,199-200; Denver Chamber of Commerce 1915— 110,143,175; George, R.D. 1913— 55,62; Hayden Survey 1877—26,117; King Survey 1876—41-44,155,156; Long Expedition 1823—6; Mills, Enos 1905—19,39,185; Nell—31,35; Pierce—16; Sprague, Abner 6,7-8, 178; Thayer—6,16,26; Township— 36,47,182; U.S. Geological Survey— 1,6-8,186,188; passim
Marshall, R.B. 1,2,105,110,143,165,175
Mather, Stephen 192
Maxwell, James P. 23
Mead, Roger 30
Medicine Bon Mtns. 128
Medicine Bow Forest Reserve 166
Medicine Bow Mtns. 137
Meeker, Mt. 52,77,121,183
Meeker, Nathan 128-129
Meeker, Ralph 51,112
Meredith, Ellis 41
Meridian Bow Range 128
Meridian Valley 185
Meteor Lake 92

Michigan Ditch 91,129
Middle Mtn. 49
Mill Creek 195
Miller, Charles D. 129
Mills, Enos 1,7,77-78,126,**129-130**,140, 156,158 (il.),195,199; passim
Mills, Ethel (Mrs. Joe) 108
Mills, Joe 36,45,**108**,146,198
Milner Pass 81
Milner, T.J. 130-131
Minnehaha Falls 18
Mize, Robert H. 102
Moffat, David 49,89,131
Monarch (town) 132-133
Monarch Gold & Copper Mining & Smelting Co. 131
Monarch Lake 23,147
Moomaw, Jack 13,82,**133**,150,189; passim
Moraine Park 177
Morris, M.O'C. 92
Morrow, Dwight 120
Mountain Boyhood, A 36
Mountain index—Cheesman Park 9; Forest Canyon Overlook 71 (il.); Toll Memorial 191
Mountain Jim. See Nugent, Mountain Jim.
Mountain Meadows Pass 112
Mountain Peaks of Colorado, The 192
Mountain Smokes 176
Mountaineering in Colorado 7,39
Mountaineering in the Rocky Mountain National Park 118, 191
Mountearl 55
Muggins Gulch 107,108,145
Mulgins Gulch 134
Mummy Range 72 (il.)
Murphy Lakes 98,175
Murray Camp 116,124,133

Nah-un-kah-rea (river) 43
Nakai, Raymond 135
Native American Religion 22
Navajo Indians 135
Navajo Peak 65 (il.)
Nawat, Arapaho Indian 137
Neeley, Rolley 33
Nelson, Aven 21
Nelson, Ruth (Ashton) 36
Nesbit, Paul 53,57,93
Nesotaieux 121
Neva, Arapaho Indian 136
Never-No-Summer Mtns. 136
Never Summer Mtns. 28,70 (il.)

Nichols, George 77,183
Niwot, Arapaho Indian 136,137-138
Niwot Mtn. 137
North Fork of Colorado River passsim; Ditch 90; Trail 196; Valley 110
North Park 6; passim
Norton, Frank 98
Norwall, Carl P. 78-79
Notchtop 163 (il.)
Nugent, Mountain Jim **107-108**,127, 134

Ochinee, Arapaho Indian 17
Odessa Lake Trail 163 (il.)
Ogalalla Horn 58
Ogalalla Peak 46,58
Old Baldy 49
"Old Men on the Blue" 45
Oldman Mtn. 58
Olive Mining & Milling Co. 141
Omaha Walking Club 106,107
Opposition Creek 90
Origin of Certain Place Names in the United States 154
Orton, Edward 142-143,144
Osborns Lake 140
Otis, Edward Osgood 95,143
Otis Gorge 38
Ouzel Falls 18
Ouzel Lake 32,33
Ouzel Lake Peak 143

Paiute Horn 192
Paiute Peak 64 (il.),192
Paradise Park 85
Park Range Forest Reserve 166
Park View 134
parks (parcs) 59-60
Parry, Charles Christopher 27-28,77, 140,183
Paternoster Lakes 89
Patterson, Thomas M. 145
Pawnee Indians 187
Pawnee Peak 192
Pear Reservoir 33,102
Peck, Allen Steele 85,106,119,120, **146-147**
peneplain 84
Pennock, Charles 147
Petite Lake 107
Pettingell, J.N. 35,147
Pettingell Lake 122
Phantom Creek 147
Phantom Valley Ranch 147,180,188
Phipps, William H. 62

pika 45
Pinchot, Gifford 156
Pine Ridge 170
Pingree Park 153
Pipe River 31
Pipit Lake 33
Pipit Rock 57
Pit Lake 34
Pomona College 188-189
Porter, Will 107
Potera's Creek 168
Potts, Merlin 13,150
Poudre Lakes Trail 196
Powder River Live Stock Co. 96
Powell, John Wesley 52,88,110,**150**
Powell, Mt. (Gore Range) 88
Prairie Club of Chicago 173
Prewitt, John T. 60
Primrose Pool 156
Proctor, Phiminster 92
Prowers County 17
Ptarmigan Lake 32

Rabbit Ear Range 137
Rainbow Lakes 104
Rams Horn Mtn. 187
Ramsey, Hugh B. 98,116,**153**
Red Gulch 142
Redburn, Lloyd 57
Reece, John 78
Reed, Sally (Mrs. Charles) 122
registers, mountain 191
Reid, Whitlaw 51
Richart, Frank 47
Richthofen, Ferdinand von 154-156
Richthofen, Manfred von 155
Richthofen, Mt. 70 (il.)
Richthofen, Walter von 155-156
Ring, Edward 155
Rist, William 129
Ritterbush, Phillip 11,42,150
Roaring Fork 131,132
Roberts, Mary Jane 127
Rocky Mountain Club 96,125,167
Rocky Mountain Jim. See Nugent, Mountain Jim.
Rocky Mountain Lumber Co. 124,131-133
Rocky Mountain National Park 1,2,6; passim. boundaries 2,165,192; dedication 158 (il.)
Rocky Mountain Railroad Co. 124, 132-133
Rocky Mountain Transportation Co. 192

Rogers, Edmund B. 156,192
Rogers, James Grafton **1**,2,5,6,**9-10**,42, 50,101,137,162 (il.),170,186,188,193
Rogerson Hotel 86
Rollins Pass 105,131,165
Roosevelt, Theodore 25,166,187
Rosa, Monte (Switzerland) 47
Round Mountain 49
Round Top 49
Routt, John L. 35,166
Routt, Mrs. John L. 49
Rowe, Israel 86,134,**166-167**
Ruxton, George Frederick 23

Sabeta, Ute Indian 42
Sage, Sherman, Arapaho Indian 102, 159 (il.),176
St. Marys Lake 127
St. Pats Cathedral 189
St. Vrain, Ceran 168
St. Vrain Glaciers 119
St. Vrain, Marcellin 168,169
Saldora Lake 122
San Rafael, Rio 43
Sanborn, B.D. 55
Sand Creek Massacre 17,137-138
Sandbeach Lake 33,102,146,200
Sarah Brook 104
Satanta, Kiowa Indian 169
Sawtooth (Nokhu Crags) 138
Sawtooth Mtn. 45
Schmoll, Hazel 105
Schnoor, Henry 98
Scott, Lester 147,180,183
Scottish Mining & Smelting Co. 19
sea serpent 40
Senator, Mt. 145
Service, Minnie March 39
Service, Sam 181
Shadow Mtn. 92
Shafroth, Morrison 117
Sharkstooth, The 76 (il.)
Sheep Mtn. 19,87,101,152
sheep, mountain 95-96; slaughter of 152-153
  See also Bighorn Flats, Ramshorn Mtn., Sheep Lakes, and Sheep Rock in text.
Shelter house, Agnes Vaille 111,172; Boulder Field 67 (il.),172; Chasm Lake 172; Lawn Lake 116
Sherman, Mrs. John D. 158 (il.)
Sherman, John King 196
Sherman, William Tecumseh 169
Shipler, Joseph L. 172-174

210

Shipler Mtn. 104
Shirt, The 151
Shoestring Lakes 196
Shoshone Peak 20
Shoshoni Indians 174
Shoshoni Peak 65 (il.)
Silent Place 7
Silver Slide, The 154
Simonds, Fred and George 56
Sioux Indians 141
Sioux Peak 105
Small, R.A. 140
Smiley, Jerome 5,10
Smith, Dudley 57
Snow, Francis Huntington 149
Snowy Range (Colo.) 127; (Wyo.) 127
Snowy Range Mining District 19
Songs of the Rockies 189
Sophia Brook 104
South America Lake 93
South Fork of Grand River 23,138
Sowers 134
Spalding, Frank 97
Specimen Mtn. 101
Specimen Mtn. Trail 196
Spectacle Lakes 72 (il.)
Spirit Lake 92
Sprague, Abner 7,29,58,96,98,115,118, 139,167,175,**177-178**,196; passim
Sprague, Alberta (Mrs. Abner) 19,178
Sprague, Fred 56,139
Sprague Mtn. 109
Squeaky Bob. See Wheeler, Robert
Squeaky Bob's Trail 162
squirrels 40-41
Stanley, Freelan O. 55,**180-182**, 158 (il.),195
Stanley, Henry Morton 54
Stanley Steamers 158 (il.),180-181
Stapleton, Patience 197
Stapps Lake Lodge 47
Statler, Milton 147
Stead, Dora (Sprague) (Mrs. J.D.) 122
Steads Ranch 177
Steele, Hugh Ribison 5,10
Steep Mtn. 201
Stewart, Lulu 123
Stidger, Helene 98
Still Lake 107
Still-water Lake 92
Stone, G.M. 167,183
Story of Estes Park, The 199
Sublette, Andrew 138
Supply Reservoir Co. 169

Swedes 91,132
Swiss Village 104

Table Top Mtn. 84,95,96
Tahosa Mtn. 195
Tahosa Valley 200
Taos Indians 125
Tawawa Peak 143
Taylor, Albert Reynolds 187
Taylor, Bayard 121
Taylor, Edward F. 43,158 (il.)
Teller City 37
Terra Tomah Lake 53
Thompson, David; Philip 31
Three Buttes 59
Thunder Lake 140
Thunder Pass 123,182
Tileston, Merrill 41,190
Timberline Lake 105
Timberline Pond 110
Toll Memorial 184
Toll, Mt. 64 (il.),89
Toll, Oliver W. 3,159 (il.),185,189, 191,196,200
Toll, Roger W. 11,54,118,167,175,176, 182,183,187,**191-193**; passim
Tonahutu 30
Trail Ridge 193,196
Trail Ridge Road 130,156
Triangulation Point 122
Trinity Lakes 196
Trowbridge, C.R. 192
Tundra Curves 196
Turck family 82,126
Tuxedo Park 182
Twin Lakes 153
Twin Sisters Peak 36,117
Two Ears, The 121
Two Guides, The 121
Tyndall Glacier 73 (il.),95
Tyndall, John 195
Tyndall, Mt. 47

Union Colony 37,128
Union Pacific surveys 98,145-146; passim
U.S. Board on Geographic Names 4, **12-15**,47-48,88,120; passim
Upper Grand Valley Peak 28
Ursula, Lake 53
Ute Horn 192
Ute Indians 17,92,106,170,177
Ute Peak 144
Ute Trail 191,193,201

Vaille, Frederick O. 3
Vaille, Harriet 2,**3**,5,7,**10**,22,94, 105,125,135,162 (il.),170,186
Velie, Jacob W. 27-28,77,183
Velies Peak 183
Volcano Creek 176

Walden (town) 91
Waltemeyer brothers 131
Wapiti Mine 59
Watanga, Arapaho Indian 197
Water Supply & Storage Co. 90
Waters, W.E. 128
Way, L.C. 140,192
Weiss, Paul 9
Welch, William A. 33,181
Welton, Carrie J. 42
Wescott, Joseph L. 18,49,92,103-104, 157 (il.),**197**
Wheeler, Alfred Truman 198
Wheeler, Herbert N. 24,123,129,156, 198
Wheeler Peak (N.M.) 155
Wheeler, Robert ("Squeaky Bob") 99,104,123,164 (il.),173,**179-180**,190
Wheeler, S.R. 198
White Bear, Kiowa Indian 169
White, Kenneth I. 19
White Owls 135
White, William Allen 149
Whitney, Josiah Dwight 154
Whitney, Mt. (Calif.) 155
Whyte, Ida (Webster) (Mrs. Theodore) 103
Whyte, Lady Maude (Ogilvy) (Mrs. Theodore) 56
Whyte, Theodore 30,54-56,85

Whytes Lake 55
Wild Basin 122,200
Wild Basin Lakes 32; passim
Will, Burns 47,48,186
Willett, Fernando C. 142
Willow Canyon 84,178
Wind River 202
Wind River Cliffs 59
Windy Gulch 196
Winston, "Winnie" 118
Wolcott, Charles 131
Wolcott, Frank H. 131
Wolf Ridge 174
Wolfe, Thomas 8
Wolverine Mine 34,86,116,172
women's names 7,13
Wooded Mtn. 170
Woodward, Brinton W. 29,189
Woolfolk, Robert 198
Worcester, Philip G. 86
Workman, Dessa 141
Workman, William J. 7,**81**,**82**,89,98, 141,193; passim
Wright, Frank 188
Wright, Frank Lloyd 72,100
Wright, Joe 108

Yard, Robert Sterling 88,103,158 (il.), 165,**175**,190,191
Young, Mary Jane (Baker) 28-29
Y.M.C.A. Conference Grounds 59,187
Youngblood, Pete 147
Ypsilon Mtn. 72 (il.),177

Zimmerman, Agnes 19
zones, life 194

212

ES PARK

CONTOUR INTERVAL 80 FEET
DATUM IS MEAN SEA LEVEL

FOREST CANYON

TRUE NORTH
MAGNETIC NORTH
14°

3000   0   3000   6000   9000   12000 FEET

1   1/2   0   1   2 MILES

CONTOUR INTERVAL 80 FEET
DATUM IS MEAN SEA LEVEL

TRUE NORTH
MAGNETIC NORTH
14°

2 MILES

12000 FEET

3 KILOMETERS

GRAND LAKE

CONTOUR INTERVAL 80 FEET
DATUM IS MEAN SEA LEVEL

TRUE NORTH
MAGNETIC NORTH
14°

INDIAN PEAKS

CONTOUR INTERVAL 40 FEET
DATUM IS MEAN SEA LEVEL

Hiamovi Mtn

Stone Lake

Copper Peak

Island Lake

Marten Peak

Canyon

Mount Irving Hale
11754

Gourd Lake

Buchanan Pass

Fox Park

Sawtooth Mtn
12304

Creek

Thunderbolt Creek

Hell

Buchanan

Cascade

Thunderbolt Peak
11938

Upper Coney Lake

Coney

Creek

Paiute Pk
13088

Mount Audubon
13223

Creek

Blue Lake

Mount Toll
12979

Pawnee Lake

ARAPAHO

Mirror Lake

Crater Lake

Pawnee Pk
12941

Pawnee Pass
12541

Mount Achonee
12649

Arapaho

Lone Eagle Peak

Peck Glacier

Triangle Lake

Shoshoni Pk
12967

Lake Isabelle

TIONAL

FOREST

Fair Glacier

Isabelle Glacier

South St. Vrain Creek

Ridge

Mt George

Apache Pk
13441

Niwot
13023

NIWOT

Navajo Peak
13409

Green Lakes

Creek

Wheeler Basin

Arikaree Pk
13150

Kiowa Peak
13276

Mount Albion
12609

Coyote Park

Satanta Peak
11979

North Arapaho Pk
13502

Triple Lakes

Caribou Pass
11851

Caribou Lake

Arapaho Glacier

Columbine Lake

South Arapaho Pk
13397

Arapaho Pass

Lake
12061

Dorothy
11906

Mount Neva
12814

LAKE GRANBY

CONTOUR INTERVAL 80 FEET
DATUM IS MEAN SEA LEVEL

TRUE NORTH
MAGNETIC NORTH
14°

MUMMY RANGE

CONTOUR INTERVAL 80 FEET
DATUM IS MEAN SEA LEVEL

TRUE NORTH
MAGNETIC NORTH
14°

NEVER
SUMMER

CONTOUR INTERVAL 80 FEET
DATUM IS MEAN SEA LEVEL

WILD BASIN

NATIONAL FOREST

ROOSEVELT

CONTOUR INTERVAL 80 FEET
DATUM IS MEAN SEA LEVEL

TRUE NORTH

MAGNETIC NORTH

14°

NEVER SUMMER

MUMMY RANGE

• Comanche Pk

• Mummy Mtn

• Mt Richthofen

Specimen Mtn
•

TRAIL

Milner Pass

RIDGE

ROAD

FOREST CANYON

• Terra Tomah Mtn

ESTES
PARK

GLACIER GORGE

Bear Lake
○

GRAND LAKE

• McHenrys Pk

Twin
Sisters

• Longs Pk

• Mt Alice

GRAND LAKE

WILD BASIN

LAKE GRANBY

LAKE GRANBY

INDIAN PEAKS

N

W ⬩ E

S

TO
GRANBY